DIRECT COSTING

DIRECT COSTING

William E. Arnstein
Frank Gilabert

amacom
A Division of the American Management Associations

BILL ARNSTEIN, as he likes to be called, retired from Main Hurdman & Cranstoun after serving as the partner in charge of a predecessor firm's management services activities. During his long career, he has designed and installed direct cost systems in diversified industries. He is an industrial engineer and an accountant.

FRANK GILABERT is currently the partner in charge of the management services activity of the New York office of Main Hurdman & Cranstoun. Prior to his work in cost accounting and other management services, he spent a number of years in auditing.

Library of Congress Cataloging in Publication Data

Arnstein, William E
Direct costing.

Bibliography: p.
Includes index.
1. Direct costing. I. Gilabert, Frank, joint author.
II. Title.
HF5686.C8A73 657'.42 79-54827
ISBN 0-8144-5512-3

Acknowledgments

WE wish to express our gratitude to the partners of Main Hurdman & Cranstoun, particularly Cecil Bybee, Leonard Prose, and Howard Zodikoff, without whose encouragement and support this book would not have been written. Special appreciation goes to Ira Bitz of Ira Bitz & Associates, Ltd. of Chevy Chase, Maryland, for his review and revisions of Chapters 18 and 19. Finally, we are grateful to Loretta Kelly and Mariela Orozco for the timely and efficient conversion of the very rough drafts to the final manuscript.

Contents

1 Introduction *1*
2 Why Companies Use Cost Systems *10*
3 Direct Costing and Other Cost Systems *17*
4 Distinguishing Variable from Fixed Costs *29*
5 Direct Costs and Product Pricing *43*
6 Inventory Valuation Under Direct Costing *60*
7 Direct Costs in Budgeting, Forecasting, and Business Modeling *72*
8 Direct Costs in Management Decisions *92*
9 Setting Standards *113*
10 Developing Variances *132*
11 Direct Costs in Cost Control *144*
12 Analysis of Marginal Contribution Variance *160*
13 Direct Costing in Marketing and Distribution *170*
14 Direct Costing in Nonmanufacturing Companies *177*
15 Special Problems *188*
16 Maintaining the Accuracy of Dollar Book Inventories *207*
17 Converting to a Direct Cost System *224*
18 Using Computers in Direct Cost Systems *236*
19 Computerizing a Direct Cost System *250*
20 A Perspective on Direct Costing *261*
Bibliography *265*
Index *269*

1

Introduction

It is safe to assume that the late Jonathan Harris had no idea of the impact that his article "What Did We Earn Last Month?" would have. In fact, at the time of its publication in January 1936 in *Management Accounting* (then called the *NACA Bulletin*), it evoked minimal interest. However, that article is now considered to mark the beginning date of direct costing, a system that has spread to a very large number of companies and has been involved in controversy, often bitter, all the way.

Neither the 1936 date nor the identification of Jonathan Harris as the originator of direct costing is completely accurate. In the first place, Harris was writing about a system that had been installed several years earlier in a company with which he was connected. Second, only about a year later G. Charter Harrison issued a series of pamphlets on the same subject as a reprint of material that had previously been privately circulated. Finally, there is some belief that at least one company, Mathieson Alkali (now part of Olin Industries), had been using an almost identical system since late in the nineteenth century.

What Direct Costing Is

Jonathan Harris, G. Charter Harrison, and their followers were recommending that only variable manufacturing costs be considered part of product costs. This necessarily means that the part of manufacturing overhead which was not likely to move up and down with changes in production levels—the part usually called "fixed overhead"—has to be considered an expense of the time period and deducted in total from the sales of the period in arriving at net profit. None of the fixed overhead was included in the cost value of finished-goods inventory or work-in-process inventory.

This concept was, of course, quite different from the normal cost accounting concepts of the time. Prior to 1936, the undisputed theory held that all manufacturing costs were costs of the product, whether or not they varied with the level of production. After all, if you didn't need it, you wouldn't have it. Similarly, it is impossible to conduct a manufacturing operation without incurring such costs as occupancy (rent or real estate taxes), depreciation, and supervision—to name just three of the costs generally regarded as fixed. Therefore, of course, these costs were considered part of product costs; the only area of disagreement concerned the proper way of allocating each of these fixed costs to departments and to products. To, in effect, ignore these costs was thought to be not only a novel concept but one that could come only from confused or irresponsible minds.

Another precursor of direct costing is "prime costing," which also had its place in pre-1936 cost accounting. Prime costing is the assignment of direct material costs and direct labor costs to products without any attempt to reflect either variable or fixed manufacturing overhead in product costs. This system (if system is the proper name for it) never had any theoretical defense, even from its users. Basically, it was a method of obtaining a very rough comparison of the costs of different products, usually for pricing purposes, without incurring the expense of maintaining a cost accounting system. It was used primarily by smaller companies whose approach to financial data was quite primitive. In addition to its clerical cost savings, it had this advantage: Because finished-goods and work-in-process inventories were stated well below true cost, annual profits were understated in years of rising inventories; thus, as a company grew, it could realize a very substantial saving in income taxes.

The Internal Revenue Service always claimed that prime costing was not acceptable for tax-reporting purposes, but in the pre-1936 era this rule was only spottily enforced, since most IRS agents lacked cost accounting knowledge and were generally uninterested in methods of inventory valuation. Prime costing was never widely accepted by accountants; but because of its similarity in certain respects to direct costing, some early opponents of direct costing attributed all the faults of prime costing to its more sophisticated cousin, direct costing. Although the figures resulting from the two systems may not be too different in some companies, the philosophy is totally different. The concept of prime costing cannot be logically defended. By contrast, proponents of direct costing claim that its logic is superior to that of absorption costing (or full costing)—the cost accounting system that does charge fixed manufacturing overhead into products. Before direct costing, this was really the only acceptable method of cost accounting (prime costing was never a serious contender). Accordingly it needed no distinctive name. Since direct costing has come along, this method of "nondirect costing" has become known as absorption costing.

Direct costing is sometimes known, particularly in England, as incremental costing or marginal costing. These are apt names, because product costs under direct costing reflect the additional or incremental expenses (or out-of-pocket costs) of producing one more piece of product. Marginal costing derives its name from the fact that the difference between the sales price of the product and the direct cost is the margin available to cover fixed costs and, it is hoped, to provide a profit.

Handling Variable Selling and Administrative Costs Under Direct Costing

In the earliest days of direct costing, all selling, general, and administrative (S.G.&A.) expenses were considered a deduction from the margin left after deducting variable manufacturing cost of sales from net sales. However, it was soon realized that much of the logic used to defend the variable concept required that any S.G.& A. found to vary with sales should be reflected in direct cost of sales. This is now generally done by companies preparing income statements and product cost sheets on a direct cost basis. Variable S.G.& A. is not included, however, in the cost value of finished-goods inventories.

Before we leave this broad definition of direct costing, the details of which will occupy much of this book, a brief comparison of income statements under absorption and direct costing may be helpful. Figure 1-1 provides such a comparison. The following points should be noted:

□ Gross sales, deductions from gross sales, and resulting net sales are the same in both approaches.

□ Under absorption costing, cost of sales includes direct materials, direct labor, and all manufacturing overhead (but no S.G.& A.). Under direct costing, direct cost of sales includes direct materials, direct labor, variable manufacturing overhead, and variable S.G.& A. (but no fixed manufacturing overhead).

□ Under a standard cost system (and Figure 1-1 is for a company using standard costs), absorption costing shows the difference between net sales and standard cost of sales as "gross profit at standard." Direct costing shows the difference between net sales and standard direct cost of sales as "marginal contribution at standard." It should be noted that some companies use the term "gross margin" or "contribution margin" rather than "marginal contribution." The three terms are synonymous. The important point is that they are quite different from "gross profit" under an absorption costing system and *must not* be equated to or compared with it.

FIGURE 1-1. Comparative income formats for internal management reporting.

ABSORPTION COSTING	
Gross Sales	$215,000
Returns & Allowances	15,000
Net Sales	$200,000
Cost of Sales at standard	$135,000
Gross profit at standard	$65,000
Variances in manufacturing costs	(5,000)
Gross profit at actual	$60,000
G.S.&A. Expenses	$41,000
Operating Profit before Income Taxes	$19,000

DIRECT COSTING	
Gross Sales	$215,000
Returns & Allowances	15,000
Net Sales	$200,000
Direct Cost of Sales at standard	
Variable Mfg. Costs at standard	$100,000
Variable S.G. & A. Costs at standard	7,000
Total at standard	$107,000
Marginal Contribution at standard	$93,000
All cost Variances	(6,000)
Marginal Contribution at actual	$87,000
Fixed Costs per Budget	
Budgeted Mfg. Fixed Costs	$35,000
Budgeted S.G.& A. Fixed Costs	33,000
Total Fixed Costs at Budget	$68,000
Operating Profit before Income Taxes	$19,000

□ Under absorption costing, manufacturing variances are applied to gross profit at standard to develop gross profit at actual; if S.G.& A. variances are developed at all, they are shown below the gross profit line along with all other S.G.&A. expenses. Under direct costing, *all* variances both in variable and fixed manufacturing costs and in variable and fixed S.G.&A. are deducted from marginal contribution at standard to develop marginal contribution at actual. Although variances must be deducted from cost of sales at standard for income statement purposes, neither direct nor absorption costing shows these variances in standard product costs.

□ Under absorption costing, operating profit is developed by deducting actual S.G.& A., with or without variances being shown separately, from gross profit at actual. Under direct costing, operating profit is developed by deducting fixed manufacturing overhead *at budget* and fixed S.G.& A. *at budget* from marginal contribution at actual. Note that the difference between budgeted and actual fixed costs has already been reflected in the difference between marginal contribution at standard and marginal contribution at actual. This reflection of fixed cost variances in marginal contribution seems to be illogical, but it has certain practical advantages which will become clear later.

Although the system shown in Figure 1-1 has certain advantages over its many variations, it must be recognized that the only basic rule applying to all direct cost income statements is that fixed manufacturing overhead is omitted from cost of sales and from finished-goods and work-in-process inventory values. All other distinctions between direct costing and absorption costing are optional; they are followed by some companies using direct costing and not by others. One interesting variation is the subtraction of variable selling expenses from net sales at the top of the income statement rather than later to indicate the contribution of the sales division to manufacturing costs.

It should be recognized that the statements shown in Figure 1-1 are for internal reporting to management. For published financial statements, the direct cost statement would be quite different. The only difference in the absorption cost statement would be the combining of the manufacturing variance figure into the cost of sales at standard and the reporting of the combined figure as cost of sales.

The use of direct costing for published financial statements has been prohibited by the accounting profession, through its spokesman, the American Institute of Certified Public Accountants (AICPA), and by the Securities and Exchange Commission (SEC). The reasons for this will be discussed in Chapter 6. Therefore, a company using direct costs must convert to absorption costing for its published financial statements. The result will then be generally the same as the statement the company would have reported had it been on absorption costing. This is done by restating finished-goods and work-in-process inventory at costs that include fixed manufacturing overhead. Specific methods of converting a direct cost statement to an absorption cost statement are also covered in Chapter 6.

Figure 1-1 assumes that finished-goods and work-in-process inventories have not changed in value during the period of the income statements. Had they done so, the operating profits would have been different in the two statements by the fixed manufacturing overhead in the change in inventory levels. The arguments as to which of the two profit figures is better and the extent of the differences are also covered in Chapter 6.

Growth of Direct Costing

It was perhaps unfortunate that Jonathan Harris chose "What Did We Earn Last Month?" as the title for his article. His belief, and that of a number of early proponents of direct costing, was that its major advantage was in its different and supposedly better measurement of net income. This not only brought down upon him the wrath of most of the accounting profession but also kept some of the other features of direct costing from the attention they so richly deserved. During the years immediately following 1936, the professional journals were full of articles on direct costing, both pro and con, and almost all focused on its effect on reporting income. Many of the articles were so vehement in tone that one professor stated that the controversy seemed to have "generated more heat than light."

Gradually, however, a number of companies began to realize that direct costing had certain advantages in guiding pricing policies (see Chapter 5) and in other types of management decisions (see Chapter 8). It also simplified income projections and forecasting (see Chapter 7) and was found to have certain advantages in cost control (see Chapters 10 and 11). Finally, it was recognized that a company which chose to maintain its books on a direct cost basis could still report its balance sheet and income statement to the public on an absorption cost basis and thus avoid controversy with the AICPA, the SEC, the Internal Revenue Service, and others who opposed direct costing for financial reporting.

To our knowledge, the first major companies to convert to direct costing were the Armstrong Cork Co., the Caterpillar Tractor Co., and the Sangamo Electric Co. All these companies publicized their systems. There may well have been, and probably were, other companies that made the move at about the same time without appearing in print.

By the 1950s and the 1960s, the trickle became a deluge. Few figures are available as to just how many of the larger manufacturing companies are today using the concepts. It should be noted, however, that in a questionnaire sent recently by Eugene A. Imhoff, Jr. of the University of Michigan (quoted in the November 1978 *Management Accounting*) to 105 randomly selected publicly held companies, well over half of the 53 respondents indicated that they used direct costing for internal reporting. The same survey showed that about two-thirds of the respondents used standard costs. Both figures may understate the application of the system to manufacturing, since the respondents included a few nonmanufacturing companies. If the medium-size companies had been included, the proportion using direct costs would undoubtedly have been smaller. However, no company is too small to benefit from direct costing. If a company is large enough to use a cost system, it is large enough to consider direct costing. In fact, some very small companies have been using the system for several years.

The percentage of service companies doing cost accounting is still quite small, though it is growing every year. Chapter 14 covers the use of cost accounting in service industries and examines which ones need absorption costing and which ones could probably benefit from direct costing.

Three Warnings

Before going further, we should issue three warnings which will affect the understanding of many subsequent parts of this book. They are relevant to all cost accounting.

Nomenclature

Certain words and phrases in cost accounting are given quite different meanings by different people. (The same holds to some extent for accounting in general and certainly for economics.) When one chemist says to another "carbon tetrachloride," both know what is meant. True, the purity may still have to be defined, but the basic chemical is clear. The same is not true when one cost accountant says to another any number of words in common use in the field. Some examples may help to illustrate this:

Indirect labor. The meaning of indirect labor is clear, but the parameters are fuzzy. Is a machine setup part of direct or indirect labor? How about the handling of material to and from the machine?

Overhead. Almost all employees of a large company read into overhead the adjective "manufacturing." These employees may be surprised to learn that in many small companies the word means the difference between direct materials plus direct labor and the selling price. "On Product X, the material costs $3, and direct labor is $2; we add 100 percent for overhead and sell it for $10." In this usage, overhead includes not only manufacturing overhead but also all S.G.& A. and presumably a profit.

Direct costing. Even the expression "direct costing" can cause trouble. Its use in this book is similar to its meaning in textbooks and professional journals. However, in government contract accounting, direct costing means the *charging* of a specific cost to a particular contract rather than to a pool for later proration to contracts. This meaning of direct costing is found in the standards issued by the Cost Accounting Standards Board and in the Department of Health, Education, and Welfare's rules on Medicare reimbursement.

These are just examples. Accordingly, cost accountants are cautioned to make sure they understand how a word is being used before they determine how an account should be handled or how an account should affect some decision they are making.

Reconciling Cost Accounting Records with the Books of Account

Almost all cost accounting systems today are part of, and tie in with, the company's general ledger. However, this was not always so, and the temptation still exists to design a freestanding cost system. One reason is that cost accounting was invented by engineers, not by accountants. Even today, there are very few CPAs who specialize in cost accounting. Also, many outstanding public accountants are quite inexperienced (and sometimes not very knowledgeable) in cost accounting.

The advantages of reconciling the cost accounting system with the books of account are not always obvious but are very real. We are familiar with several companies which, for years, undercosted (and thus underpriced) their products because they failed to pick up certain costs. This fact came to light only when outsiders were called in. One company stated: "Our product costs are absolutely accurate; we get a gross profit on each product more than high enough to cover our S.G.& A. costs; we are losing a lot of money." It was only after the absurdity of this statement was pointed out that the company found the unrecorded costs.

Even if the flaw in the system had been found much sooner, it would not have prevented executives outside the cost accounting department from losing confidence in the figures generated by the system. Such confidence, once lost, is exceedingly difficult to regain.

Limitations of a Cost System

No cost system should be designed to routinely report the answers to every question that management might legitimately ask of it. In other words, the system should report (on a daily, weekly, monthly, or annual basis) only those figures which management needs often. If the company president wants to know every other year if the company is making money on its customer repairs, the data should be obtained by making a special analysis rather than by revising the system to show the figures monthly. Unfortunately, companies do not always realize this, and some have expanded (or originally designed) their systems to a point where they become so complex that they tend to fall of their own weight.

A recent article titled "Wouldn't It Be Nice If . . .?" gave an excellent picture of this danger. The article pointed out that if a report were prepared to show every figure that someone thought "it would be nice" to have, reporting costs could skyrocket with very doubtful benefits. One of the advantages of direct costing is that it readily lends itself to special analyses. These analyses are not always easy, but they are easier under direct costing than they are under absorption costing.

Summary

From a slow and very controversial start in the late 1930s, direct costing has today achieved an importance that must be reckoned with. Any company that does not use the system is well advised to investigate its pros and cons by consulting companies now on direct costing or by studying the remainder of this book.

The fundamental difference between direct costing and absorption costing is the method of handling fixed manufacturing overhead. A less important difference, but one that is attaining constantly wider acceptance, is in the handling of variable S.G.& A. expenses.

2

Why Companies Use Cost Systems

THE value of direct costing depends largely on the needs which accounting and more particularly cost accounting are intended to meet. In many companies today accounting systems are being underutilized because some of these needs have not been recognized or because the means for meeting them has not been brought to management's attention. This may become clearer from a brief review of the growth of cost accounting.

Accounting in a primitive form was known to the ancient Babylonians and the Egyptians at the time the great Pyramids were built. Double-entry bookkeeping was developed in Italy in the 1400s. Nonetheless, the use of accounting for managing a business (as opposed to merely reflecting the results of past operations) is less than 70 years old.

Cost accounting as it is known today has developed almost entirely in these same 70 years. In the early part of the century most manufacturers doubted whether the work required by a cost accounting system was justified by the benefits gained. Many a self-made factory owner felt that he was better able to control costs by knowing his employees, his materials, and his operations than by maintaining a "fancy" bookkeeping system. As long as the operation remained small and under his personal control, the factory owner just may have been right. However, as companies grew larger, fewer and fewer were content to trust to seat-of-the-pants cost control.

Today, virtually every sizable manufacturer uses some type of cost accounting system. In fact, more and more nonmanufacturing companies are beginning to do sophisticated cost accounting. Department stores began to follow these procedures in the 1940s and banks, insurance companies, and brokerage houses began quite recently.

Both direct costing and standard costing (explained in Chapter 3) are products of the twentieth century, though the wide use of direct costing came almost 50 years after standard costing became widespread.

Possibly, the greatest change has been in the participation of financial personnel in company policy making. Not too many years ago, it was safe to assume that the head of any company had risen through the sales or production department (or occasionally design engineering), and that the head of the accounting department, under whatever title he was given, was merely the senior bookkeeper. Today, many companies are headed by financial executives, and virtually all sizable companies rely heavily on them for many purposes. It is reasonable to suppose that this change has not been accidental. If a company is to survive in today's complex economy, it needs almost daily advice from financially oriented people.

Management Accounting Versus Financial Accounting

Although it was hardly recognized 15 years ago, the distinction between management accounting and financial accounting is now generally accepted. This is perhaps best illustrated by the naming, in 1972, of the newly created top accounting policy group as the Financial Accounting Standards Board. Before 1972, similar groups had been designated as "accounting," without the modifier "financial." The adjective was added to emphasize the dedication of the accounting profession to the development of accounting standards for reporting to outsiders. It is now clear that management accounting (or managerial accounting) is the collection and use of accounting data to help a company's management operate the business—either in making decisions that will improve profits or in helping to control costs.

Financial accounting, on the other hand, is designed to measure a business's health as a guide to lenders, suppliers who grant credit, those who are considering investing in the company, and those who have already done so. Although there will always be a large overlap between the data needed for management accounting and those needed for financial accounting, it is being recognized more and more that the methods of summarizing these data should be different for management reporting than for reporting to outsiders through financial accounting. In addition, many accounting techniques are useful only in guiding management's operation of businesses. In fact, in a 1978 article in *Management Accounting* entitled "Is the Controller an Endangered Species?" William H. Hernandez proposed, giving reasons, that a company's financial responsibilities should be split. One executive would be responsible for the collection and reporting of data going into the financial statements; another executive would be responsible for the collection and reporting of data needed by management; and the two sets of reports would be unrelated.

Cost Accounting and Financial Accounting

The impact of cost accounting on financial accounting, though confined to three areas, is by no means negligible. Annual and interim profits are, of course, of great interest to lenders and investors and are affected, as are balance sheets, by the values assigned to opening and closing inventories of finished goods and work in process. Outsiders may also be interested in the relative profitability of the various product line or geographic area segments of a business, and this segregation involves cost accounting. In addition, companies doing work on a cost-plus basis need to know the cost of each contract. These contracts are usually open to review by the customer for correctness of the methods of charging costs.

The question of whether direct costing should be used for inventory valuation is discussed elsewhere in this book. Fortunately, a company keeping its books and doing its management reporting on a direct cost basis can still convert its inventory values to an absorption cost basis for financial reporting. Segment reporting is at best judgmental and can be done under direct costing with reasonable accuracy. It is, however, difficult to see how a direct cost system can be used for costing government cost-plus or negotiated-price contracts under present or foreseeable federal rules.

Cost Accounting and Management Accounting

Cost accounting is the basis of management accounting. It is used directly in many management decisions (including product pricing) and in cost control. It is used indirectly in most management activities of the financial department and in some activities of other departments. The impact of cost accounting has grown as financial people have become more and more involved in management. By the same token, financial people have become more involved in management as the uses of cost accounting have become more sophisticated and better known.

Possibly, the greatest service that cost accounting offers a company is in management decision making. The list of decisions faced by every level of management many times each week is endless. A few are listed below:

How to price each product.
Whether a particular type of labor-saving machinery should be acquired.
Whether a branch factory should be abandoned or whether a new branch should be added.
Whether a branch sales office should be discontinued or whether sales branches should be added.
Whether a product line should be added.
How many different products should be in each product line.
Whether a customer (or group of customers) is profitable.
To what extent the level of production should conform to a seasonal sales demand.
Whether overtime pays.
The best size for the industrial engineering department.
The best size for the quality assurance department.

The methods used in making some of these decisions will be discussed in later chapters. It will be seen how direct costing is the best and easiest way to assemble the figures for making the decisions and how the figures routinely derived under direct costing are applicable with the fewest adjustments.

Cost control is the earliest and still one of the most vital uses of cost accounting. Through cost accounting, it is possible to compare variations of actual costs from standards, from budgets, or from prior periods in a manner which adjusts for the effects of volume changes, price changes, or product mix changes. Today, cost accounting is so widely recognized as a necessary cost control tool that it is difficult to realize that earlier forms of cost control compared costs, often by department, from period to period without any attempt to measure the effect of production volume changes on these costs. The fallacy of this approach can be illustrated by an old vaudeville routine in which Moran told Mack that his white horses ate more than his black horses. Mack asked Moran why this was so, and Moran replied, "I don't know, unless its because I own more white horses." With the diversity of products in most companies today, a cost accounting system is necessary to enable a company to state its production volume in a common denominator. This provides management with a means of relating costs in one period with costs in another while evaluating volume changes to the extent that they can properly be expected to account for cost changes.

Cost accounting is also a part of virtually all other financial accounting activities that are designed to assist management. For example, each of the following accounting functions makes use of cost accounting data:

Budgeting.
Capital project evaluation (including lease-or-buy determinations).
Cash forecasting.
Inventory management (how much of each item to carry).
Credit granting.

In addition, the following nonaccounting functions utilize cost data:

Purchasing in make-or-buy decisions.
Personnel in staffing the production departments.
Design engineering in value analysis.
Industrial engineering in methods improvement.
The insurance buyer (risk manager) in determining the amount of casualty insurance on various types of inventory.

The functions listed above are not all-inclusive, but each is better served by a direct cost system. Some of the points will be illustrated in later chapters.

Cost accounting is the key to management's need for accounting data. A cost accounting system that will serve all these functions must meet certain basic requirements. Fortunately, a system designed to meet these requirements will also be adequate for the needs of financial reporting. The reverse is not necessarily true.

Requirements of a Cost Accounting System to Meet Management's Needs

Almost every management decision is designed to improve profits, either in the short run or in the long run. In other words, the decision maker is asking, consciously or unconsciously, "Will profits be higher if I decide this way, or will they be higher if I decide that way?" In theory, the decision maker should prepare a pro forma income statement for the whole company under the assumption that he will decide one way and compare it with a similar statement prepared on the assumption that he will decide the other way. Since the average executive makes dozens of decisions every week, many of them minor, this is obviously impracticable. Accordingly, the decision maker uses cost accounting data as a shortcut to show him how profits will be affected. A direct costing system has been shown to provide the most reliable and easy-to-use data for this purpose.

Before leaving this point, we should issue some cautions:

- Not all management decisions are profit oriented. On rare occasions a company will decide to donate to a charity for purely philanthropic reasons.
- Some decisions involve profits that are expected to occur several years in the future. In these cases, judgment based on experience may provide better answers than analysis of data. Investment in abstract research is an example.
- Many decisions involve intangible benefits. Here the analysis of data may well be a start, but again judgment (or experience) will prove to be more influential in reaching the final answer.

Another requirement of a cost accounting system for management is that it must develop costs for cost control in such a way that any variations from past experience or from standards or budgets can be analyzed to determine which variations are caused by outside factors and which are caused by the performance of supervisory management. To be effective for cost control purposes, this information must be segregated by the individual responsible.

In addition, the system must permit timely reporting. In some cases, this will be a report for the month, issued ten working days following the month end. In other cases, it may be a weekly report available a few days after the week of the report, or it may be a daily report available the next morning. On rare occasions, the system may be asked to issue an analysis of events that have not yet occurred. (See the discussion of NIFO in Chapter 5.)

A final requirement of a cost accounting system for management is that the details must be easy to summarize into a report. Often the same details will be summarized into different categories and subcategories to suit the needs of different users.

With the exception of Chapter 14, which discusses service industries and contractors, most of this book is oriented to manufacturers. This reflects in part the greater involvement of manufacturers in cost accounting in general and in direct costing in particular. However, many of the examples cited from manufacturing apply equally in service, distribution, or contracting businesses.

Summary

The involvement of financial people in management is of fairly recent origin. It has paralleled the increasing use of sophisticated cost accounting systems. Today, cost accounting affects almost every area of management, including marketing, production, and planning. We believe, as do many others, that management's needs are best served by a direct cost system. Our reasons are set forth more fully in the remainder of this book.

3

Direct Costing and Other Cost Systems

ALL cost systems can be classified as either absorption or direct. However, within this two-way classification a system may be an actual cost system or a standard cost system; in addition, it may accumulate costs by job, by process, or by operation. A full understanding of the differences between these subcategories of cost systems is necessary for determining which is most appropriate in particular circumstances. The relation of direct costing to each system is important in evaluating the benefits it may bring to a specific company. The three colums below will aid in understanding how these names relate to one another:

Absorption costing	Job costs	Actual costs
Direct costing	Process costs	Standard costs
	Operations costs	

Any company's cost system can be described by choosing one word from each column, and any mix is possible. For example, a system may be an operations-actual-direct cost system or a job-standard-absorption cost system or any other combination of one word from each column.

Furthermore, a company may use different systems for different functions or different costs. For example, some companies whose basic raw materials are subject to wide price fluctuations use actual costs for materials and standard costs for labor and overhead. These companies find the combination meets their needs better than would either an actual or a standard cost system for all their costs. Many companies use operations costing on their regular products produced for sale but use job costing on any capital assets constructed for their own use. Such assets can range from a shed in the yard for housing flammable materials to highly sophisticated machinery. This approach, too, has logic.

It is, of course, true that a person who tries to compare the merits of a system shown in one column with those of a system shown in another is merely demonstrating his confusion. Although arguments exist, for instance, as to whether standard costing is superior to direct costing, such arguments reveal only a lack of awareness that a system can be both standard and direct. In fact, a vast majority of direct cost systems are also standard cost systems.

In order to clarify how direct costing relates to each of the other cost systems, we will describe the systems below, along with their place in industry and their advantages and disadvantages.

Job Costing

Under job costing, direct materials and direct labor and some predetermined overhead percentage on direct labor (or overhead dollars per direct labor hour) are charged directly to the job. The job may be an order made to the customer's specifications, a contract, or a production order to produce a certain number of pieces of a product for finished-goods inventory. When the job has been completed, the job card or job sheet or appropriate computer record shows the total cost of the job. On the surface this appears to be the easiest system to understand, the one that requires the least paperwork, and the one that will supply the most useful information. However, many industries prefer process or operations costing, for reasons that will be discussed in connection with the advantages of process costing and operations costing.

Job costing is largely confined to industries that produce a product after the customer's order has been received. Such industries usually are supplying products made to the customer's specifications, and every order is different in at least some respects. Examples are job machine shops, job printing plants, and building contractors (including subcontractors and specialized electrical contractors, plumbing contractors, and heating, ventilating, and air-conditioning contractors). As already mentioned, a company that uses one type of costing for its products may use job costing for self-built capital equipment. In a very real sense, this function is analogous to both a specially built product for a customer—in this case the company itself—and to a contracting assignment.

Companies with government contracts frequently choose job costing because they feel the cost of each contract will be easier to audit and the system will minimize disputes with the Defense Contract Audit Agency. However, by no means do all government contractors feel this is necessary.

Some companies sell commercially on a cost-plus basis because the costs of the products they are being asked to make cannot be accurately estimated in advance. Such companies would find it difficult to operate on anything other than a job-cost/actual-cost system.

Finally, manufacturers of heavy and costly equipment with very long manufacturing cycles may use job costing in order to keep track of the cost of the item over the long time span. An item like a turbogenerator set for a public utility may take several years to build, have hundreds of parts, and be valued in the millions of dollars.

Direct costing can be used with job costing on either an actual or a standard basis. Job printing plants are an example. To our knowledge, however, it is not used by building contractors, who apparently see little advantage to direct costing in their field. This is because contracting costs that are analogous to a manufacturer's fixed overhead are generally much lower in relation to the contractor's other costs. In addition, the fixed overhead on the site of a construction job, while not related to production (for example, the number of bricks being laid per day), is directly related to the duration of the job. Thus the cost of the field superintendent, the timekeeper, and the rental of construction equipment is directly tied to the length of the job. This is not true of fixed costs in a manufacturing environment.

The chief advantage of job costing is the ease with which the final cost of a contract or a customer's order can be compared with the cost estimate made before a price is quoted or a bid submitted. This type of comparison can help cost estimators improve their estimating skills for future work. For example, a particular feature of a customer's blueprint may have slowed production compared with similar but not identical products made for other customers. Or the feature may have increased spoilage. It should be noted in this connection that job costing is most often found in companies using actual costs rather than standard costs. Under a job-cost/actual-cost system, slowed production or high spoilage will appear in the total costs of the job.

Process Costing

In process costing, all costs are charged to the process or machine as they are incurred. Thereafter, the costs of the process or machine are allocated to products according to the time each product spends going through the process or machine. For companies using standard costs, the resulting cost of the product or product lot will be no different than that obtained under job costing. For companies using actual costs, process costing employs averages; the variations from these averages will not be reflected in the cost of a particular lot, but the resulting inaccuracy is apt to be minor. In effect, process costing involves two steps: charging costs to the process and then charging the process costs to the product lot. By contrast, job costing achieves the same result in one step. The advantages of the two-step procedure will be discussed shortly.

Process costing is best illustrated by continuous-flow industries—oil refineries, some chemical processes, stone crushing, and the like. In these industries, some type of raw material is fed steadily into one end of a line of equipment, with a continuous flow of finished product or products coming out the other end. In this type of operation, there is no way of identifying a production order, since it is impossible to separate one gallon or one ton from another. Accordingly, if costs are to be accumulated in any detail, they must be charged to a piece of equipment. Thus the labor required to tend the particular piece of equipment, its power requirements, its repair parts, and, under absorption costing, its space costs and depreciation are all accumulated for the week or month. These costs are then divided by the total throughput of the piece of equipment during the time period to give the unit cost of putting the particular product through the equipment.

The data thus gathered are useful in product pricing, because in most continuous-flow industries not all products go through every piece of equipment. Frequently, intermediate chemicals are bled off before the final processes, or certain customers for crushed stone may buy coarse gravel and thus not require the final crushing stages. Some types of gravel may be oiled or dyed and others not. Accordingly, the unit cost of each stage of the process must be determined in order to price the product. Since job costing is impossible, process costing is the only way this information can be obtained. The place of process costing in industry and its advantages over job costing will be described below.

Operations Costing

Operations costing is identical in theory to process costing. Many people classify the companies using this system as process costers. These people correctly see only two possibilities: Costs are charged initially either to jobs or to processes or machines. However, other people believe that operations costing, though in concept a form of process costing, is sufficiently different from its appearance in a continuous-flow industry to warrant separate treatment.

Basically, operations costing applies in industries that use the same machine to perform operations, frequently different in nature, on many products. For example, the same lathe that was used to cut a groove near the end of three-foot shafts in the morning may be used to cut one-foot lengths of bar stock in the afternoon. The two parts worked on will have different part numbers and be on separate production orders; they may or may not end up in the same finished product, and in all probability they will require different amounts of time per unit on the lathe. This diversity of uses is most often found with machine tools. However, other types of machinery such as that used in packaging, batch processing of chemicals, heat treating, and virtually every other manufacturing process may also have a variety of uses.

Operations costing, then, is a system which initially charges costs to the process or machine and then redistributes these costs to products on the basis of the machine time required to process the specific product for the specific operation. Operations costing is a great deal more common than pure process costing simply because many more industries use multipurpose machines than use single-purpose equipment. It is also a great deal more common than job costing because of the advantages it has over that system, as described below.

Advantages of Process (Operations) Costing

The major advantage of process (operations) costing is in cost control. Clearly, efforts to reduce costs must be directed to specific processes or operations rather than to jobs. Since a specific operation will often be performed on parts that undergo other, different operations, the operation is likely to be repeated many times during a year.

By contrast, production orders that cover only parts where all operations are identical are much fewer. Therefore, it is easier to identify operations whose costs are out of line with prior experience by comparing them with previous runs of the particular operation than it is to uncover cost overruns by comparing a current job cost with previous job costs.

Furthermore, in job costing there is a tendency to look at the total of a job cost sheet and, if it is reasonable, not to bother determining whether the total has major cost overruns on some operations offset by favorable results on other operations. Under process costing, efforts will be made both to reduce the excess costs on the former and to take advantage of the saving on the latter by determining what methods changes made them possible and attempting to expand the use of such methods. Because of these advantages, most companies whose operation would permit either job or process (operations) costing have chosen the latter.

Direct costing is almost always found in connection with process (operations) costing. It is sometimes used with job costing, but the very reasons that companies use job costing are often the reasons why full or absorption costing best meets their needs. Often, such companies are working on cost-plus contracts or are attempting to compare cost results with cost estimates which have been calculated to absorb all costs.

Process or operations costing is most likely to be found in companies that are producing finished-goods inventory for sale to customers from stock. Such companies need to know, for example, what combination of price and volume will be most profitable, in what lot sizes products should be produced, and whether branch distribution warehouses pay. These and many other questions are best resolved through the data generated under a direct cost system.

Actual Costs

Actual costs, at least for direct materials and direct labor, are exactly what the name implies. If one production order uses materials which were bought at $1.00 per pound and the next uses identical materials which happened to cost the company $1.10 or $.90 per pound, the cost charged to the production order under job costing or to the operation that week under operations costing reflects this difference. Under an actual cost system, materials are always charged at actual cost. There are four ways of calculating actual cost:

1. First in, first out (FIFO).

2. Average cost in which the average following each incoming shipment is the weighted average cost of the quantity of material in inventory at the time the new shipment is received at the old average cost averaged in with the quantity in the new shipment at the new price.

3. Average cost in which the weighted average of the prices on all shipments received in the year to date is used until the next shipment is received. At this time, a new average is calculated using all receipts in the year to date, including the new shipment. This method of averaging is not recommended, since it fails to consider the inventory that has been used and accordingly will not properly account for all costs (it may result in under- or overcosting). It is typically found in companies that keep no perpetual unit inventory records.

4. Last in, first out (LIFO). This method is quite rare in cost accounting. The many companies that use LIFO for financial statements and tax reporting find that the LIFO adjustment is most easily made by groups of material and only at fiscal year end. This is because of the effect of the various layers typically found in a LIFO inventory. To try to keep track of temporary invasions of these layers on a material-by-material basis is not only difficult but may actually produce misleading costs, since subsequent purchases within the year may restore the layers to their former levels. Accordingly, companies on LIFO use either the first or second method above in calculating actual costs and make a year-end adjustment to reflect the effect of LIFO. When actual costs are used to guide pricing in an inflationary period an approach based on some aspects of LIFO can be used that involves data related to, but outside of, the cost system (see Chapter 5).

Similarly, direct labor is reported on an actual basis. If because of seniority or some other reason an employee has a higher hourly rate than would ordinarily be used on a particular operation, the job or the operation is charged the actual rate. Similarly, a learner or a slow worker who produces fewer pieces per hour will increase the cost of the job he is working on or the cost of the operation for the month when an actual cost system is used.

Although actual cost systems attempt to reflect all costs at actual, it is not possible to determine the actual overhead cost of a particular job or particular operation. Under actual cost systems, overhead is necessarily spread on a basis which at best allocates actual overhead costs each month to actual direct labor for the month, possibly by departments or cost centers. No cost system can assign overhead to jobs or operations more specifically than that. As a matter of fact, many companies on an actual cost system will estimate overhead and direct labor for the coming year and apply the resulting overhead factor throughout the year. Of course, under this system, overabsorbed or underabsorbed overhead must be reflected in the financial statements at year end and may be reflected quarterly or even monthly. Rarely is such underabsorbed or overabsorbed overhead carried through to individual product costs, though it is often reflected in the total cost value of inventories through an adjustment.

As previously mentioned, actual costing is most likely to be used in conjunction with job cost systems. Over the years, standard cost systems have increasingly superseded them in most manufacturing. However, actual costs are still used almost exclusively by building contractors and subcontractors and by small companies that have neither the manpower nor the know-how to set up a standard cost system.

Advantages of Actual Costs

In the proper circumstances, actual costs can be quite useful. These circumstances include:

1. Production of custom-made products that differ so widely from one another that no operation is performed often enough to make the setting of standards worthwhile. Certain aspects of building construction are an example.

2. Government cost-plus or negotiated-price contracts. The Cost Accounting Standards Board permits the use of standard costs but requires a large number of safeguards against overcharging the government. The complexities thus added to a normal standard cost system have caused some companies with such contracts to prefer actual costs. Generally, actual cost accumulation will reduce disputes with government auditors. Such disputes always take executive time and may result in unjustified and costly adjustments.

3. Small one-time jobs in a company otherwise using standard costs. The cost of developing standards on these jobs is often greater than the benefits gained. Such jobs include special orders, sample runs, small production runs for market testing, and construction of capital assets with in-house personnel. Although estimated standards could be used on such jobs, so many of the advantages of a standard cost system would be lost that the decision becomes a borderline one.

4. A company that has never had a cost system and needs one *right now.* This situation may arise when an unexpected loss shows up at the year-end closing in a previously profitable company and the company's executives are unable to determine what caused the change. In

such a situation, the company may even want a cost system retroactive to the beginning of the current year, which may be several weeks old. It is extremely difficult to set up an actual cost system this fast, but it is *impossible* to set up a standard cost system in so short a time.

5. As a step toward standard costs to accumulate historical data as points of reference for setting overhead standards and for uncovering major errors in material and direct labor standards arrived at by other means.

6. For costing materials whose prices fluctuate violently. In such a case, standard material costs will at times be so far from the facts that product standard costs will cease to have real meaning.

Many of the advantages of direct costing apply to actual cost systems as much as to standard cost systems. For instance, a company embarking on an actual cost system as a step toward a standard cost one could save substantial work (and suffer little disadvantage) by ignoring the allocation of fixed overhead. Also, a company that was costing materials at actual and labor and overhead at standard would get the same benefits and suffer the same disadvantages from direct costing as a company that was completely on standard costs. This is because there is no difference between direct costing and absorption costing in the treatment of direct materials (except in the few companies that apply some part of overhead directly to materials).

On the other hand, a company that uses actual costs because of government contracts will prefer absorption costing to satisfy government rules. As a matter of fact, any cost-plus contract can be fair to both parties only if absorption costing is used.

Standard Costing

A standard cost system is a method of accounting that follows specific rules and operates under a unique principle. It is much more than a system that compares costs with standards and, of course, is unrelated to the notion of standard in the sense of "generally accepted." A standard cost system charges products with predetermined amounts for all materials, direct labor, and overhead as the products flow through the various operations and departments. In using these predetermined amounts or standards, the accounting entries ignore actual costs in product costing. This means that the cost value to be shown in the accounting records of a product or a production order is known at every stage of production and finally in finished-goods inventory even before work is begun or the first materials are requisitioned. In fact, the cost values to be assigned to items that will be produced entirely in December are known the previous January unless standards are revised during the year. The various methods of setting standards are discussed in Chapter 9.

Many companies that use standard costs also use LIFO for tax reporting and financial statements. The adjustment to bring the inventories to a LIFO basis are made at year end, for the same reasons that this is done in companies using actual cost systems. Material price standards are based on the expected price of materials during the year.

Obviously, a system based on this principle must have some way of accounting for the difference between the costs actually incurred and those predicted before the production took place. In standard costing this is done through variance accounts, which accumulate the differences monthly or more often. Typically, variance accounts accumulate the spread of costs between standard and actual separately for material prices, material quantities, direct labor rates, direct labor quantities, and overhead by account. Usually, these accounts are further broken down by department and sometimes by cost center. Chapter 10 discusses variances in greater detail.

Standard costing has undergone steady growth since its introduction early in the century. Today it is used by a vast majority of large manufacturing companies, by many medium-size manufacturing companies, by a significant number of small manufacturers, and by quite a few service companies. Companies that still use an actual cost system—that is, those that charge actual costs to each operation on each lot of products—may be said to be behind the times (except, as noted earlier, for companies in those industries where actual costs are more appropriate). Of course, every company must accumulate actual costs by total account and often by department in order to compare them with standard costs and thus develop the variances.

Advantages of Standard Costs

The trend toward standard costing is neither an accident nor a fad. A standard cost system offers very real advantages in management decision making and in cost control. In addition, standard costing simplifies the work of the accounting department and accordingly reduces its cost.

In cost control, there is a great advantage to comparing actual costs with standards rather than with prior actuals. This is because previous actual costs may be higher or lower than normal. For instance, the prior lot may have been produced at an unreasonably slow rate because of defective materials, a balky machine, or a temporarily assigned inexperienced worker. Or costs may have been exceptionally low because of a bargain purchase of materials. A comparison with an objectively set, unchanging standard is much more informative. Typically, when costs are higher than prior experience, they are explained away by any number of excuses, whereas when costs show an improvement, the result is always attributed to superior performance or supervision. No one ever looks back to see whether the prior costs were high because of the very excuses used to justify increases in current costs.

Another way that standard costing aids cost control is in the delineation of cost overruns. The variance accounts separate the amount of cost overruns caused by pricing and hourly rate differences from the amount caused by differences in material quantities and production speeds. Similarly, differences in overhead are shown by overhead account.

Standard product costs are also more useful than actual costs for pricing decisions. If the cost of a particular product lot is high because of some temporary condition, the tendency in actual costing is to reflect this aberration in the price quoted for the next order. This should not happen and does not happen under a standard cost system. After all, such an aberration could have occurred on any product lot and the resulting cost should not be charged to the specific product. Under standard costing, the excess cost falls into a variance account and is spread over all products.

The same philosophy makes the determination of the profitability of a customer or group of customers more reliable on a standard cost system. When two different customers are shipped identical products from different lots, both of which were originally produced for stock, their costs should be the same for purposes of judging the profitability of the customer. Under standard product costs this will always happen, whereas under actual costs it may not happen.

It has also been found that monthly income statements can be issued earlier under standard costing than under actual costing. This is because the accounting records in standard cost systems reflect predetermined costs. Inventories can be costed out at these figures as soon as unit data are available. Variances can be calculated by comparing the costs accounted for by the production at the standard figures for whole departments with the actual material quantities at standard prices and the actual payroll. Under actual cost systems, the actual costs must be spread over the production by products.

A final advantage of standard costing is that it requires less paperwork than actual costing. Companies using actual cost systems may find this difficult to believe, but companies that have converted to standard costs have found it to be true. Again, the reason is that products are costed at predetermined amounts, so there is no need to keep track of the actual cost of each operation on each product. However, this reduction in paperwork applies only to routine bookkeeping. The cost of setting and maintaining standards may or may not offset this saving. A few companies run parallel actual cost and standard cost systems for the purpose of determining which variance amounts apply to which products. Such a parallel system obviously costs more than either system would cost alone; moreover, the data generated are generally believed to be of little value to most companies. Therefore, this approach is not recommended.

Most direct cost systems are used in conjunction with process (operations) standard cost systems. Many of the advantages of direct costing are enhanced by the use of standard product costs and standard departmental costs. This is true for product pricing and other management decisions and for cost control.

Summary

In most (but not all) industries, company managements will be aided by the use of process (operations) costing rather than job costing and by the use of standard costing rather than actual costing. Although direct costing can be used with any combination of the other cost systems, it is most often adopted in connection with process (operations) standard cost systems. When so used, direct costing offers its greatest advantages. The widespread use of direct costing in conjunction with process (operations) standard cost systems bears out the satisfactory experience of industry with this combination. The trend continues in this direction.

4

Distinguishing Variable from Fixed Costs

Although many absorption costing systems distinguish variable from fixed costs, the distinction is much more important under direct costing. The reason is that direct costing is based on the recognition of only variable costs in product costs and the nonrecognition of fixed costs. Thus the accuracy of the separation affects both the internal balance sheet and the internal income statement. This is much less true under absorption costing. Accordingly, companies using direct costing must understand completely which costs are to be considered variable and how costs with both variable and fixed characteristics are to be handled.

Definitions

In theory, a variable manufacturing cost is one that rises and falls in exact ratio to changes in levels of production. Similarly, a variable S.G.& A. cost is one that fluctuates in exact ratio to changes in sales. Thus a variable cost would rise or fall 1 percent for every 1 percent in the base to which it is related. By contrast, a fixed cost is completely unaffected by changes in production or sales and will remain at the same level month after month without regard to the level of operations.

Some companies refer to fixed costs as "period costs," since they fear that the term "fixed" will suggest to management that the level of the cost cannot be changed. This is not true. Often fixed costs can be reduced. During the depression of the 1930s many fixed supervisory costs were changed when managers at all levels were forced to accept a 10 percent cut in salaries. Fixed building depreciation costs can be cut by renting out some space to another company; real estate taxes can be reduced by tearing down an unused building. Hence many companies feel this type of cost is better described by the term "period," since, all other things being equal, it tends to be level for each period of time rather than being fixed permanently. In this book we will refer to such costs as "fixed," the more common term.

Some companies subclassify fixed costs into truly fixed costs versus programmed costs. Programmed costs are ones that do not vary with production but that, unlike such truly fixed costs as building depreciation, can be changed by management on very short notice. Examples are training, research and development, the plant newsletter, and the subsidy to the company softball team. Although from a management standpoint these costs are quite different from truly fixed costs, they are treated in exactly the same way as true fixed costs in both absorption and direct costing systems. This is because they do not vary automatically with production or sales. Even the fact that a company has decided as a policy to spend, say, 3 percent of sales on advertising does not make advertising a variable cost. The 3 percent is a management decision rather than a variable which is dependent on sales level.

Particularly important to the use of cost accounting data in pricing and other management decisions is the recognition of just how fixed costs will behave in the future. It has been said that "variable costs are variable in the short run; fixed costs are variable in the long run." Experience demonstrates that there is a great deal of truth in this statement. Typically, a company that experiences seasonal fluctuations in production will have the same monthly fixed costs in the slack season that it has in the busy season. Similarly, a company that increases its production for a few months because of a strike in a competing plant or because of a one-time large order will not show any increase in fixed costs. However, a company that adds a new product line or in some other way permanently increases its physical volume of production and sales by a substantial amount will have an increase in fixed costs in a year or two. The increase will not necessarily be proportional to the volume increase, but it will be far from negligible.

Sometimes, the rise of fixed costs with volume is hard to explain. As each cost is looked at before the volume increase, it can often be validly argued that it will not increase. The president states that his salary won't go up; that building size won't need to be increased; that present machinery can handle the new volume. The same appears to be true for each and every fixed cost. What is overlooked is the extent to which unanticipated fixed costs are added. The president finds himself so busy that he needs an "assistant to"; personnel is able to justify a plant newsletter because of the increase in the number of employees; a traffic manager can now be cost-justified. The tendency of fixed costs to rise with volume is perhaps best illustrated by the history of almost any major company over a 20- to 40-year period. Volume has increased substantially, and this in theory should cause a major increase in the profit percentage to sales. Such an increase will occur between any two years when volume rises, but somehow over the entire period the company usually ends up with about the same profit percentage to sales that it started with, despite a tripling or quadrupling of volume over the period.

The Rule of Reason

If the definitions of variable and fixed costs given earlier in this chapter were rigorously applied, it would be found that no cost absolutely meets either definition. Possibly, direct materials come closest to the definition of variable, but even here there are exceptions. If production exceeds a certain volume, quantity discounts may be available or unit freight-in costs may be lower. Fringe benefits on direct labor are usually considered variable overhead, but with annual wages subject to unemployment insurance set at a ceiling well below the average earnings of employees, obviously the percentage of the cost to wages drops as annual production increases to the point where regular employees work more hours during a year because of overtime or fewer layoffs. Occupancy expenses are possibly the purest example of fixed costs. However, a plant operating near capacity may well have to rent some outside space to take care of raw materials or finished-goods inventory.

Cost accountants recognize these facts but find that they can be ignored without undermining the value of cost accounting data for management decisions, cost control, or product costing. A useful rule of thumb is that an account which is found to be 90 percent variable is treated as if it were 100 percent variable, and an account which is found to be 90 percent fixed is treated as if it were 100 percent fixed. Also, if either a variable or a fixed account fails to meet its proper definition only in unusual and short-lived situations, this too is ignored.

Fixed costs are said to be unrelated to production. It might therefore be assumed that they would be the same in each month. This is true of some fixed costs but not of all. For example, costs of heating the building will be higher than average in the winter months; the reverse is true of lawnmowing costs. Other examples will readily come to mind. These differences are ordinarily reflected in the monthly budgets under a direct cost system.

Semivariable Costs

Unfortunately, many overhead accounts are neither 90 percent variable nor 90 percent fixed. These are referred to as either semivariable or semifixed. In some absorption cost systems, such accounts are handled by simply establishing a budget for the amount of the account at every forseeable level of production. The amounts so budgeted may be based on past experience or on management's estimate. Under direct costing, the variable and fixed elements of each such account must be determined. Some absorption cost systems also take this approach.

There are several ways of splitting semivariable accounts into their variable and fixed components:

Activity analysis. Anyone familiar with a company's operations can ordinarily determine from personal knowledge that some accounts will vary proportionately with production and other accounts will be unaffected by production. Examples of the former include fringe benefits on direct labor and perishable tools such as drill bits or milling cutters. Examples of the latter include real estate taxes, building depreciation, and senior factory supervision.

Setting up two accounts where only one existed before. A review of an account like factory supplies will reveal that every invoice can be designated as variable or fixed, according to the use of the purchase. For example, cutting oil is clearly variable and lightbulbs are just as clearly fixed. The clerk coding the invoices can be instructed on which types of purchases to charge to "factory supplies—variable" and which to charge to "factory supplies—fixed."

Account analysis. If splitting the account is not desirable, an analysis can be made for several past months. Again, from personal knowledge of the operation the analyst can determine with reasonable accuracy the dollar value of the fixed element in the account. This amount is then considered to be the fixed element for future months, and all other amounts in the account are treated as variable.

Scatter charts. The scatter chart technique is illustrated in Figure 4-1. The actual amount of expense in each of a number of past

FIGURE 4-1. Scatter chart approach to analysis of a semivariable account.

HISTORICAL DATA

Year	Month	Production in pieces (000)	Actual Machinery Maintenance Cost
1978	Mar.	85	$ 8,910
	Apr.	80	8,625
	May	75	7,900
	June	80	8,343
	July	40	10,000
	Aug.	85	8,760
	Sept.	90	9,100
	Oct.	95	9,624
	Nov.	90	9,187
	Dec.	80	8,342
1979	Jan.	75	7,920
	Feb.	70	7,711
	Mar.	80	8,428
	Apr.	80	8,392
	May	75	8,109
	June	75	7,943

(a) Step one

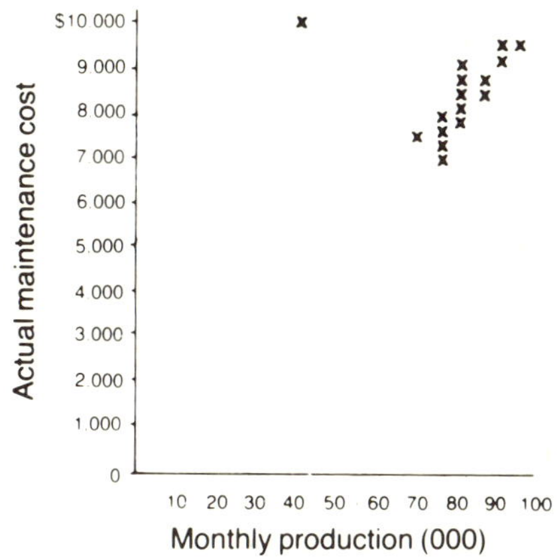

(b) Step two

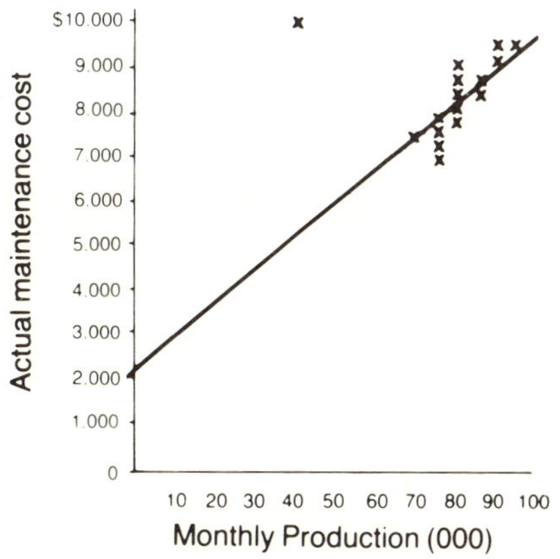

months is listed opposite the level of production in the corresponding month. To ensure a reasonable degree of accuracy, about 15 or 20 of the most recent months should be listed. These figures are then plotted with little "x"s on a piece of graph paper as in Figure 4-1(a), with production shown on the *X* axis and monthly expense on the *Y* axis. In multiproduct companies, production in pieces is frequently meaningless. In these cases, the production level shown on the *X* axis is usually measured by a common factor such as direct labor hours or direct labor dollars.

Both scales must start at 0. A ruler is then laid over the plotted points at an angle which best describes the slope on which the points lie. A line is drawn and extended to the point at which it crosses the *Y* axis, as in Figure 4-1(b). The expense indicated at 0 production (the point where the line crosses the *Y* axis) is the fixed expense component of the account. Note that the actual cost at 0 production may be much less or even zero, but the amount arrived at in Figure 4-1(b) correctly identifies the fixed element of the account when the plant is operating in its normal capacity range. The variable element can be determined from the slope of the line. In Figure 4-1(b) the variable element is:

$$\frac{\$100{,}000 - \$2{,}000}{100{,}000 \text{ pieces} - 0 \text{ pieces}} = 8¢ \text{ per piece}$$

The least-squares formula. The exact position of the line in Figure 4-1(b) depends quite a bit on the eye of the analyst. Two analysts may draw lines sufficiently different to raise questions on the validity of the result. To prove this, just ask two different people to draw the line indicated by the points in Figure 4-1(a). Fortunately, the mathematical technique called the "formula of least squares" can be used to analyze the listed figures and determine the fixed and variable cost elements of the account. Figure 4-2 applies the least-squares formula to the same data used in Figure 4-1. Note that the result is slightly different from that in Figure 4-1. This difference is a measure of the inaccuracy inherent in placing the line by eye.

The least-squares calculation shown in Figure 4-2 is usually done today by computer. Cards are punched for each set of figures in the list and the computer program, in a matter of seconds, does the rest. Companies not wishing to develop or buy a least-squares computer program for in-house use can take advantage of a time-sharing computer service. All the major time-sharing companies have least-squares programs. Or a company can process the data through its bank or auditing firm, both of which are almost sure to have access to

FIGURE 4-2. The least-squares formula applied to Figure 4-1.

Year	*Month*	*Production Pieces (000)* x	*Actual Machinery Maintenance Cost* y	x^2	xy
1978	Mar.	85	$ 8,910	7,225	$ 757,350
	Apr.	80	8,625	6,400	690,000
	May	75	7,900	5,625	592,500
	June	80	8,343	6,400	677,440
	July	40*	10,000*	—	—
	Aug.	85	8,760	7,225	744,600
	Sept.	90	9,100	8,100	819,000
	Oct.	95	9,624	9,025	914,280
	Nov.	90	9,187	8,100	826,830
	Dec.	80	8,342	6,400	667,360
1979	Jan.	75	7,920	5,625	594,000
	Feb.	70	7,711	4,900	539,770
	Mar.	80	8,428	6,400	674,240
	Apr.	80	8,392	6,400	671,360
	May	75	8,109	5,625	608,175
	June	75	7,943	5,625	595,725
	Totals (Σ)	1,215	$127,294	99,075	$10,362,630

The linear regression equation used to describe a semivariable is $y = a + bx$
where y = the dependent variable (maintenance cost)
x = the independent variable (production)
a = the fixed cost
b = the factor which, when multiplied by production, gives the variable cost.

In order to convert the data to simultaneous equations, the calculations shown on the left are made. The equations sought are:

$$\Sigma y = na + b\Sigma x$$

where n is the number of items, and

$$\Sigma xy = a\Sigma x + b\,\Sigma x^2$$

Filling in the numbers gives:

$$127{,}294 = 15a + 1{,}215b \quad (1)$$
$$10{,}310{,}630 = 1{,}215a + 99{,}075b \quad (2)$$

Multiplying equation (1) by 1,215/15 to cancel out the a factor gives:

$$10{,}310{,}814 = 1{,}215a + 98{,}415b \quad (3)$$

Subtracting equation (3) from equation (2) gives:

$$51{,}816 = 660b$$
or b = $78.5 per thousand pieces
or b = 7.85 ¢ per piece

Substituting this value for b in equation (1) gives:

$$15a = 127{,}294 - (1{,}215 \times 78.5)$$
$$15a = 127{,}294 - 95{,}377.5$$
$$a = \$2{,}127.77$$

*Not included in totals.

a time-sharing service. If the least-squares approach is used, it is wise to prepare a rough scatter chart first so that the analyst can omit from the computer input any month that is clearly an aberration. As has often been said, computers will digest any figures fed to them, however ridiculous. An example of an aberration is the company that in analyzing machinery maintenance costs included the July figures in the input. Production was shut down the first half of the month for the annual vacation, thus halving the normal production figure, but maintenance costs were higher than in any other month, since the shutdown period was used to recondition and repair machines normally in use. The full, regular maintenance crew was used along with some temporary employees. Note that the July 1978 data were omitted from the totals in Figure 4-2.

Most companies faced with the problem of splitting semivariable accounts will use more than one of the above techniques, selecting for each account the approach that appears most applicable.

Step Costs

A type of semivariable cost that is quite difficult to handle is the step cost. This can be illustrated by a plant that operates on one shift at certain times of the year, on two shifts at other times, and on three shifts for relatively brief periods. In this situation, the costs of foremen, timekeepers, and other departmental indirect labor have the characteristics of fixed costs as long as the plant is on one shift; these costs almost double when the plant goes to two shifts, stay at this level until the plant goes to three shifts, and then increase sharply again. Of course, if plant management finds that it need only put some departments on two shifts when the plant's one-shift capacity is first exceeded and then gradually add a second shift for other departments, the steps will be more gradual. In fact, almost any personnel cost is a step function as employees are added gradually to take care of increases in production requirements or dropped one at a time when production slackens.

Typically, a step cost that consists of many small increments is handled as a variable cost. A step cost that is expected to have one or two major changes is considered a fixed cost at its level during most of the year.

Supervariables and Inverse Variables

A few accounts tend to rise faster than production. Overtime premium is one such supervariable account; cost of in-plant expediters is another. Despite this tendency, the custom is to consider these accounts as variable. Cost accounting is not an exact science, and some decisions must be based on practicality.

Also, certain companies may have one or more accounts in which costs decrease as production increases. These may be termed inverse variables. Setup costs are an example in companies where increased volume means longer runs and hence fewer total setups. These costs, again based on practicality, are usually handled as fixed costs. The problem of separating variable from fixed costs requires further discussion with respect to certain accounts.

Machinery depreciation. The Cost Accounting Standards Board recommends (but does not insist) that machinery depreciation be charged on a unit-of-production basis. If a company has reason to believe that the life of its machinery varies with its use and accordingly depreciates it on a unit-of-production basis, it should consider machinery depreciation to be a variable cost. Most companies, however, consider depreciation to be time related and hence treat it as a fixed cost. The logic of viewing depreciation as time related was particularly evident shortly after World War II. A number of companies that had operated on a one-shift basis before the war found themselves operating three shifts during the war. Since the 95 percent excess profits tax was then in effect, these companies tried to reduce their taxes by charging triple machinery depreciation. This seemed logical at the time. Unfortunately, the Internal Revenue Service (which didn't get around to its audits until several years later) was often able to show that the machinery had already outlived its original estimated useful life on a one-shift basis and was still going strong. Depreciation of tools and dies, on the other hand, is ordinarily best handled as a variable cost.

Electricity. The major component of most companies' electric bill is the power used on the production machinery (and possibly the heat used for some processes). However, the bill also includes lighting, power for elevators and conveyors, and power for air conditioners and ventilating fans. Companies that have separate meters can consider the power for product processing as variable and its use for lighting and elevators as fixed. Companies without separate meters must treat this cost as semivariable and analyze it as suggested earlier in this chapter.

Fuel. Many of the same factors apply to the cost of fuel as to that of electricity when fuel is used both to heat the plant and generate process steam or to run gas-fired ovens. Again, lacking separate meters, a company must handle this as a semivariable cost.

Indirect labor. Some indirect labor is obviously variable—for example, departmental materials handlers in certain industries. Other indirect labor is just as obviously fixed—for example, a single mechanic responsible for keeping the machines in operation. Furthermore, the same type of indirect labor may be a variable cost in some departments and a fixed cost in others. Circumstances will determine the best way to handle a given type. The semivariable approach is often the most appropriate.

Direct labor. Almost every company handles direct labor as a variable cost. However, in some cases a good argument can be made for considering direct labor as a fixed cost. Often, the long-term disadvantages of laying off or reducing the hours of skilled employees outweigh the immediate cost saving that would result. These disadvantages include the possibility of being unable to rehire them, the cost of processing new employees, and the damage to the company's image in the community. Accordingly, some companies accept the cost of completely level employment regardless of the immediate need. Nevertheless, it is recommended that direct labor always be considered a variable. This encourages management to take full advantage of normal attrition to reduce costs in slack periods. It is also a constant reminder to management of the cost of its level employment policy.

A number of common manufacturing overhead accounts are listed below, along with the likelihood of their being variable, semivariable, or fixed. The list is not all-inclusive and the classification, while reasonable, will not apply in every industry. Only operating personnel in a given company can determine which accounts fall into which category.

Variations will of course occur in the behavior of a certain type of cost in different industries. For instance, design engineering may be a fixed cost in an industry producing a relatively fixed number of new products each year but a variable cost in an industry in which each customer's order is specified by unique required performance characteristics. There is also a very real problem of nomenclature. One company's quality assurance department is another company's quality control group and a third company's inspector.

Often, although separate accounts are kept for various employee grades and various expense accounts within a service department (such as industrial engineering or production scheduling), the entire cost of the department will be independent of the level of production and hence can be treated as a fixed cost. This is especially true when a service function which is ordinarily handled as a separate department is spread to production departments in a particular company without any centralized control of the function. For example, a single fork-lift truck operator on a production department payroll is clearly a fixed cost, whereas 20 fork-lift operators in a materials handling department serving 20 production departments may be a semivariable cost.

A number of functions have been listed as manufacturing overhead even though some companies do not consider them as such. Purchasing is frequently found in G.& A. Traffic may be in either selling or G.& A. as well as in manufacturing. Shipping may be in selling, and plant accounting may be in G.& A. Individual companies, for good reason, may classify other items listed as manufacturing overhead in some other category.

Despite the rather diverse nomenclature and the variegated categorization of costs, the list is a useful guide for understanding the nature of manufacturing overhead accounts and the likelihood of their being variable, semivariable, or fixed in most industries. It should be noted that any account which appears in both the variable account listing and the fixed account listing can be handled as semivariable. Indeed, frequently there is no other way to handle it. The list is given below.

Classification of Manufacturing Overhead Accounts

Accounts Usually Found to Be Variable

Fringe benefits on direct labor, including FICA taxes, unemployment insurance taxes, pensions, vacation and holiday pay, sick pay, employee welfare payments, hospital and health insurance, and workers' compensation insurance.

Fringe benefits on variable indirect labor (see list above).

Certain indirect labor. Depending on the operation, this could include materials handlers, inspectors, setup men, and others.

Power.

Process fuel, including fuel used to generate process steam, and gas, oil, or electricity for ovens, annealing furnaces, and the like.

Some factory supplies.

Perishable tools.

Depreciation on tools and dies if life is determined by usage rather than the passage of time.

Overtime premium.

Scrap.

Spoilage.

Rework.

Idle time.
Allowance for learners.
Makeup pay.
Packaging supplies if not considered direct material.
Shipping supplies.
Personal property taxes on inventory.
Casualty insurance on inventory.
Inland marine insurance on shipments.

Accounts Usually Found to Be Fixed

Supervisory salaries.
Indirect labor such as elevator operators, plant guards, groundskeepers, power plant employees, and sometimes materials handlers, expediters, inspectors, timekeepers, and departmental clerks.
Fringe benefits on fixed indirect labor and on supervision.
Whole service departments such as stock room, industrial engineering, quality assurance, production scheduling, EDP, design engineering, plant accounting, cost estimating, purchasing, research and development, traffic, receiving, and sometimes shipping.
Occupancy costs, including real estate taxes, building depreciation, building maintenance, or rent in lieu of some of these; also amortization of leasehold improvements.
Heat, light, and that part of power used to operate elevators, conveyors, air conditioning, and ventilation.
Machinery and equipment depreciation if life is determined by the passage of time.
Tool and die depreciation if life is determined by the passage of time.
Insurance on fixed assets.
Use and occupancy insurance.
Theft insurance.
Liability insurance.
Surety bonding.
Departmental supervision.
Cost of making samples.
Telephone and telegraph.
Stationery, printing, and postage.
Dues and subscriptions.
Some factory supplies.
Travel and auto expense.

Accounts Usually Found to Be Semivariable

Fringe benefits on semivariable indirect labor.
Indirect labor such as materials handling, expediting, janitorial, machinery and equipment maintenance, and setup men.
Machinery and equipment repair parts.

Some factory supplies.
Inbound trucking if done with own trucks.
Interplant trucking.

Selling, General, and Administrative Expenses

So many S.G.& A. expenses are clearly fixed that some companies do not bother to determine the variable ones and then treat them separately. However, many companies have selling expenses that are variable with sales. Each company must determine which of the following applies in its situations. Again, the list is not all-inclusive.

Salesmen's commissions.
Manufacturers' representatives' commissions.
Brokers' commissions.
Cost of cooperative advertising.
Freight out when absorbed by the seller.
Royalties for the use of a brand name.
Costs of printing coupons.

There are even fewer variable costs in G.& A. than in selling. An example is royalties paid for the use of a brand name that are charged to G.& A. rather than to selling expense. More common examples include billing costs on a manual billing operation and the cost of the keypunch operators who prepare the cards for a computerized billing operation. The cost of the invoice sets is theoretically variable but is ordinarily too insignificant to segregate from the remainder of the stationery and printing account, which is usually handled as a fixed cost.

The discussion of billing points up the extent to which cost accounting accepts inexact measures. In many situations sales volume will go up without any increase in the number of sales invoices simply because the average customer is ordering more units on each line of each order. Conversely, the number of bills may go up without any increase in sales because customers have decided to order hand to mouth. Under these circumstances, the relating of the expected cost of the billing operation to sales dollars is only an approximation. However, for cost accounting purposes, it is acceptable.

Double Counting

Occasionally, a type of cost will occur which is so clearly related to the production level of certain products that it appears logical to handle it as variable; the same type of cost may be so remotely connected with other products that its level appears fixed. For example, one company was engaged on a government defense contract in which every part had to meet close tolerances; the company was also doing commercial work with very loose tolerances. Before accepting the defense contract, the company had only two inspectors who checked the finished product on a sampling basis, and these inspectors were considered fixed manufacturing overhead. The terms of the defense contract called for 100 percent inspection following each operation and required some 20 inspectors for substantially less product value than the company's commercial business. The company therefore classed these 20 inspectors as variable direct labor. The net result was that all the inspectors on government work were charged to the defense contract and some of the cost of the inspectors on commercial work also found its way into the defense contract through the allocation of overhead. This and similar situations are referred to by the Defense Contract Audit Agency as "double counting" and are, of course, unacceptable. Much the same error can occur when a company is producing widely different product lines (even if no defense contracts are involved) and can result in inaccurate product costing.

Summary

Each type of cost has the characteristics of a variable, a semivariable, a step, or a fixed cost. There are several methods of determining the variable and fixed components of a semivariable account, and one of them is usually preferable for each specific account. Although variable costs are seldom perfectly variable with production or sales and fixed costs are rarely absolutely fixed, the purposes of cost accounting can still be served when these minor inaccuracies are ignored. Some S.G.& A. costs are variable, but they are so minor in some companies that they are not segregated or treated separately. Most companies, however, find that the segregation of variable S.G.& A. costs provides meaningful information to management.

5

Direct Costs and Product Pricing

It is generally recognized in cost accounting that direct costing makes its greatest contribution to profit improvement through the guidance it provides to the marketing division of a company. The most common problems aided by direct cost data are the selection of the most profitable price when lowering the price will increase sales volume (and vice versa) and the related problem of whether accepting a customer's order at a price well below normal will help or hurt profits.

Before the advent of direct costing, the concept that increased volume lowered unit costs was well known. Often low-price orders were accepted under the philosophy that they acted as an "overhead divisor." This may be illustrated by the hoary joke dating back at least to the days when Woolworth's was truly a 5-and-10-cent store, with nothing selling for more than a dime. The story runs like this: "They lose money on every item they sell, but their volume is so huge that they have a tremendous profit at the end of the year."

Thus the concept that volume has an effect on profits is far from new. Direct costing's contribution is that it provides specific information in readily accessible form to help marketing management arrive at optimum answers.

The Two Types of Pricing

Many companies arrive at selling prices by determining the cost of each product and adding a percentage to cover selling, general, and administrative expenses and, it is hoped, a profit. Sometimes, the selling prices thus reached are firm and not subject to deviations, but often they are "asking" prices and the actual price is negotiated with each individual customer. In the latter situation, the outcome depends on the bargaining power and negotiating skill of the parties involved. Obviously, the seller will benefit if he is able to calculate the effect on profits of every concession he is asked to make.

However, many companies have no control over their selling prices. Their product is such that it must sell for exactly the same price as that established by competitors for identical or very similar products. An increase in price by a small company will virtually wipe out its sales, and a decrease is so likely to cause competitors to follow suit that the expected volume increase will not occur.

Even here direct costing provides marketing with advantages. Companies with multiple products or even one product sold in various territories or through various channels of distribution will inevitably have different contribution margins from the various products, areas, or selling methods. When marketing knows how these contribution margins compare, it is in a position to strengthen its efforts to sell the more profitable items while decreasing its efforts on the less profitable ones. This can be done by shifting advertising appropriations, by providing incentives to salesmen slanted to certain product lines, by concentrating sales efforts on customers that ordinarily buy the more profitable lines, and even by having different credit-granting rules for such customers. In a very real sense this approach to marketing policy in a company whose selling prices are established by external forces is a backdoor type of price changing.

Significance of Marginal Contribution

The increase or decrease in marginal contribution as derived under direct costing is the key to pricing decisions or, their surrogate, marketing policy decisions. As has already been noted, marginal contribution is the difference between selling price and all variable costs. Since fixed costs are not affected by either price or volume of sales, it follows that any increase or decrease in marginal contribution brought about by changes in selling prices or volume of sales will flow through, dollar for dollar, to profits before income taxes. This fact makes it much easier to determine the profitability of any pricing decision.

Under absorption costing, the effect on profits of a change in price that causes a change in volume is much more difficult to calculate. Volume increases will reduce unit manufacturing costs because fixed costs will be spread over more units, but the amount of the reduction may have to be calculated department by department. The calculation is generally less reliable than that obtained under direct costing, where the whole accounting system is set up to differentiate between variable and fixed costs. In addition, absorption costing rarely considers the variable elements in selling, general, and administrative expenses. Ignoring this item can lead to wrong decisions in certain cases.

Price Versus Volume

In many situations, marketing management is well aware that lowering prices on a product or product line will increase volume, and that raising prices will have the reverse effect. Customers, be they consumers or industrial purchasing agents or buyers for resale, tend to shop for the lowest prices. In an industrial setting, the customer may buy the product only if it is less expensive than an entirely different product that meets the same need (a plastic part as opposed to a metal part, for example). A certain proportion of all consumers may be prepared to pay *X* dollars for a convenience item but will go without rather than pay *X* dollars plus one. The problem here is which of several prices at each one's estimated expected volume will prove most profitable. Figure 5-1 illustrates the difficulty of making this decision under absorption costing contrasted with the ease of arriving at the correct answer under direct costing. In the top half of the figure it seems obvious that, using absorption costing data, the best gross profit both in dollars and percentage terms is at the $4.00 price. This is the price that would be chosen, unless it was determined to add columns for a $4.20 price or a $4.40 price to see how these came out.

However, the bottom half of the figure, which uses direct cost data, shows the best marginal contribution percentage at the $4.00 price but the best marginal contribution dollars at the $3.60 price. Since dividends are paid out of dollars, not out of percentages, the $3.60 price will be of greatest benefit to the company.

Figure 5-1 is based on several assumptions, all of which would be

FIGURE 5-1. Rubicon Diecasting Company: Pricing a new product.

	Possible Prices			
ABSORPTION COSTING	$4.00	$3.80	$3.60	$3.40
Estimated Unit Sales	10,000	12,000	16,000	20,000
Estimated Dollar Sales	$40,000	$45,600	$57,600	$68,000
Manufacturing Cost @ $3.40 per unit	$34,000	$40,800	$54,400	$68,000
Gross Profit ($)	$6,000	$4,800	$3,200	-0-
Gross Profit (%)	15.0%	10.6%	5.5%	-0-
DIRECT COSTING				
Estimated Unit Sales	10,000	12,000	16,000	20,000
Estimated Dollar Sales	$40,000	$45,600	$57,600	$68,900
Variable Mfg. Cost @ $2.70 per unit	$27,000	$32,400	$43,200	$54,000
Variable Selling Cost @ 2% of Sales	800	912	1,152	1,360
Total Direct Costs	$27,800	$33,312	$44,352	$55,360
Marginal Contribution ($)	$12,200	$12,288	$13,448	$12,640
Marginal Contribution (%)	30.5%	26.9%	23.3%	18.6%

typically valid for a decision involving the introduction of a relatively minor new product in a large company with many products whose aggregate volume is many times that expected from the new product. These assumptions are:

- The increase in production from 10,000 units to 16,000 will not increase any fixed costs. In other words, existing plant capacity and existing supervision can take care of the added production.
- The increase in unit sales from 10,000 to 16,000 will not decrease sales of any of the company's other products.
- In the top half of the figure the increase in volume is so small compared with the company's total volume that the change in overhead rate resulting from the volume increase would be negligible and its calculation would not be worthwhile.
- Turnover is sufficiently fast that the greater investment represented by the increased units at the $3.60 price will be justified by the increase in profits before taxes of $1,248 as compared with the $4.00 price and $1,160 as compared with the $3.80 price.

Under these very reasonable assumptions, the company should definitely price the product at $3.60.

Accepting Low-Price Orders

Another common pricing decision that must be made in many companies is determining whether a customer's order that is substantially below the company's normal selling price should be accepted. Often, because of the circumstances surrounding the offer, the company's only choice is to accept the order at the customer's price or lose the sale. However, in other instances an order of this type is, in effect, an invitation to negotiate. In such a case, a good negotiator will not necessarily reach his very lowest acceptable price before allowing discussions to be broken off. He may correctly feel that it is better to lose some business than to appear totally without backbone. The stiffer attitude may pay off in the long run, as it will prevent all negotiations from ending up at prices so low that they barely cover variable costs and contribute minimally to the coverage of fixed costs.

Figure 5-2 illustrates a situation in which the marketing manager is convinced that the customer will not buy at a price higher than its offer. The only question is whether the company will be better off taking the order at that price or doing without the sale. In the figure it is assumed that the company has forecast annual sales of 100,000 units at $100 each. Each unit has variable manufacturing costs of $48 and fixed manufacturing costs of $3,700,000, or $37 per unit. The company also has variable selling costs of $2 per unit and fixed selling, general, and administrative costs of $300,000. As the first column of Figure 5-2 indicates, the anticipated profit before income taxes is $1,000,000.

FIGURE 5-2. Foursquare Wheel Co.: Problem of a very low-price sale.

	Old Business	*Antarctican Business*	*Total*
Unit Sales	100,000	40,000	140,000
Dollar Sales	$10,000,000	$2,400,000	$12,400,000
Manufacturing Costs			
Variable @ $48 per unit	$4,800,000	$1,920,000	$6,720,000
Fixed	3,700,000	-0-	3,700,000
S.G.&A. Costs			
Variable @ $2 per unit	200,000	80,000	280,000
Fixed	300,000	-0-	300,000
Total Costs	$9,000,000	$2,000,000	$11,000,000
Profit before Taxes	$1,000,000	$400,000	$1,400,000

Now assume an Antarctican customer offers to buy 40,000 units—an order that was not anticipated at all in the forecast—but only if they can be purchased for $60 each. Under absorption costing, the company's manufacturing cost appears to be the $48 variable cost plus the $37 fixed cost, or a total of $85 without even considering selling, general, and administrative expenses. Thus acceptance of the order would appear to give a disastrous negative gross profit of $25 per unit. However, as the last two columns of Figure 5-2 show, the actual result is a whopping increase of $400,000, or 40 percent in profits before taxes. Again, as in Figure 5-1, the assumption is that the increase in volume will not require any increase in fixed costs such as plant or machinery expansion or supervision. In this illustration, it is obvious that the increase in profit will give a more than adequate return on the added investment in working capital.

Return on Investment

Although the philosophy illustrated in Figures 5-1 and 5-2 is perfectly valid in most cases, it does not apply or must be applied with modifications in a number of situations. One such situation has already been mentioned in this chapter—whether the additional profit from the increased business justifies the required extra investment in working capital. In other words, does the return on investment (ROI) meet the company's ROI criteria?

This is not the place to discuss the establishment of the proper figure for ROI. However, most manufacturing companies usually think of 15 to 30 percent as an appropriate before-tax ROI. It should be noted that the "investment" element in ROI is defined differently by various users. An investor thinks of it as the market price of the stock when he buys it. A company president reporting to his directors or stockholders thinks of it as the book value of the company—its net worth. The same company president in evaluating his division managers thinks of it as the *total* assets committed to their charge. For present purposes, the most meaningful definition of investment is the working capital tied up by the increase in volume or released by any decrease in volume. Capital tied up in fixed assets is not relevant unless the decision will change this figure.

It is not easy to convert a dollar increase in profit before taxes arising from increased business to an ROI percentage. In fact, such an effort is bound to produce a pretty rough estimate, since averages and inexact data must be used. Basically, determination of the investment requires an estimate of how long the receivable represented by the sale or sales will be outstanding, how long before shipment materials must be acquired (reduced by the time between receipt of materials and the due date of the accounts payable invoice), how long before shipment direct labor and variable overhead costs will be incurred, and how long variable selling and distribution costs will be incurred before receivables are collected. Each of the variable costs of the product will be weighted by the appropriate time lapse and the total converted into an annual investment turnover figure. This turnover is then divided into the investment—that is, the variable cost of the sale—to arrive at the investment to be divided into the profit. For example, assume a sale of $300,000 with a variable cost of sales of $290,000. If the investment averages only three months—a turnover of four times per year—the $290,000 cost is divided by four. The resulting $72,500 is divided into the $10,000 marginal contribution (which is equivalent to the increase in before-tax profit) to give a before-tax ROI of 13.8 percent. This would generally be considered inadequate. On the other hand, if the average investment were only two months, the same sales price and costs would show an ROI of 20.6 percent, which could well be considered adequate.

It must be recognized that investment turnover is not calculated for every pricing decision. It is usually calculated once for the company or for each product line and then used until conditions change substantially. If a particular order is large or very unusual, a variation on the established turnover rate may be estimated. Such variations include customer-owned materials, "dating" of invoices, and progress payments.

Utilization of Capacity

Another factor that must be considered in using direct costing in pricing decisions is the extent to which unused capacity should be filled. It is, of course, obvious that a cut-price order that will require an expansion of capacity should be accepted only if the increased fixed costs will be covered by the marginal contribution. As a matter of fact, the decision to increase capacity is rarely based on one order or a group of orders. Rather, it is made on a long-term forecast, with the forecast profits converted to an ROI on a discounted-cash-flow basis. In this type of calculation, the investment considered includes both that of working capital and that of fixed assets.

Not so obvious is the fact that it may be unwise to accept orders at low prices which use up most but not all of the idle capacity. The problems are twofold: (1) the acceptance today of a low-price order may make it impossible to accept a higher-price order tomorrow because of capacity limitations and the later potential customer's delivery date requirements; and (2) a plant operating very close to 100 percent capacity loses some efficiency because it lacks flexibility in scheduling production and providing for machinery repairs.

The Robinson–Patman Act

The federal Robinson–Patman Act forbids companies to sell to different customers at different prices under certain circumstances. Although the act has been on the books since 1937, it has been so spottily enforced that many people with pricing responsibilities have never heard of it. Still, as a number of court cases indicate, a company that violates the act through ignorance or design can face severe penalties.

The act itself is complex, and the litigation supporting it has established certain hairsplitting distinctions. Any company that contemplates selling to different customers at different prices should consult legal counsel. However, certain generalities can be made:

- The basic thrust of the act is to protect small retailers of consumer goods from cut-price competition from larger retailers that buy in quantity at lower prices. However, nothing in the act exempts suppliers to industry.
- The act does not apply if two customers are clearly not in competition with each other, such as a drugstore in Alaska and one in Puerto Rico. (Note the designation of the new business in Figure 5-2 as an Antarctican customer.)
- The act permits a price cut to meet, but not exceed, an offer by a competitor of the company to the same customer. (The catch here is that the company has to prove it. A statement by the customer's purchasing agent or buyer is not considered adequate.)
- The act does not apply when the products sold are substantially different. The difference must be more than the brand label or the type of decoration.
- Economies of scale in manufacturing do not count when off-the-shelf items are involved. If Customer A ordinarily orders in 2-piece lots and Customer B ordinarily orders in 10,000-piece lots, the act considers that the manufacturing quantity was 10,002 and that each piece costs the same. Scale would be considered if each order were produced after it was received from the customer.
- Economies of scale in marketing and distribution may be used to justify price differences. For example, if Customer A receives mer-

chandise by parcel post and Customer B receives it by the truckload and the selling company absorbs outgoing freight, the selling company is permitted to reflect in its pricing the difference in the cost per unit for delivery.

□ The act does not cover discontinued products.

The Cost-Plus Trap

Many companies have some type of contracts which allow for reimbursement of their costs. The Department of Defense has thousands of cost-plus-fixed-fee (CPFF) contracts as well as thousands of negotiated-price contracts that have the same effect. In addition, some automobile manufacturers and at least one mail order and department store chain sometimes buy on a type of cost-plus basis. The acceptance of a cut-price order from a customer can spell disaster when a company has a substantial amount of cost-plus business already under way. This can be illustrated by Figure 5-3, which shows

FIGURE 5-3. Foursquare Wheel Co.: Problem of a low-price sale with a CPFF contract.

	Old Civilian Business	*Government CPFF Contract*	*Antarctican Contract*	*Total*
Unit Sales	50,000	50,000	40,000	140,000
Dollar Sales	$5,000,000	$4,427,100[d]	$2,400,000	$11,827,100
Manufacturing Costs				
Variable	$2,400,000	$2,400,000	$1,920,000	$ 6,720,000
Fixed	1,320,000[a]	1,320,000[a]	1,060,000[a]	3,700,000
S.G.&A. Costs				
Variable	100,000	100,000	80,000	280,000
Fixed	107,100[b]	107,100[b]	85,800[b]	300,000
Total Costs	$3,927,100	$3,927,100	$3,145,800	$11,000,000
Profit before Taxes	$1,072,900	$ 500,000[c]	$(745,800)	$ 827,100

[a]Fixed manufacturing costs of $3,700,000 spread in proportion to variable manufacturing costs.

[b]Fixed selling, general, and administrative costs of $300,000 spread in proportion to variable selling, general, and administrative costs. (Results would be the same if all selling, general, and administrative costs were spread in proportion to total manufacturing costs.)

[c]Fixed fee under the contract does not change.

[d]Sales figure is backed into as the total of costs plus the fixed fee.

the same offer of the Antarctican customer as in Figure 5-2, with only one different assumption: that half the original forecast of sales and costs is a government CPFF contract. The government requirement that fixed costs be spread on some logical basis to all business gives a startling result. The notes in Figure 5-3 show the derivation of the amounts. The figure assumes that, before receipt of the Antarctican order, the civilian business and the government business had identical costs and were equally profitable. However, the spreading of fixed costs to the Antarctican contract raises the profit on the old civilian business by $572,900, and with the profit on the old government business fixed by contract, this is not sufficient to offset the loss of $745,800 shown by the Antarctican business on an absorption cost basis. Net result: Under these circumstances, acceptance of the Antarctican contract would reduce profits before taxes from the $1,000,000 shown on the original forecast in Figure 5-2 to $827,100. By contrast, profits would have increased by $400,000 if all the original business had been civilian.

The Problem of "Giving Away the Store"

Critics of direct costing have claimed with some justification that it tends to cause companies to sell their product at unrealistically low prices. Such a tendency does exist and must be carefully controlled if direct costing is to improve profits rather than the reverse. It is easy to understand the temptation to sell products above their variable costs but not sufficiently above them to absorb all fixed costs.

As has already been stated, product costs under a direct cost system contain no fixed manufacturing costs. They do contain variable selling, general, and administrative costs (which absorption cost systems do not), but these are of a much lesser magnitude than the fixed manufacturing costs that are omitted. Accordingly, a product that might sell for $10 and have a cost of $8 under absorption costing—thus showing a gross profit of 20 percent—will show a cost of, perhaps, $6 under direct costing and will have a marginal contribution of 40 percent. Actually, nothing has changed except the definition of product cost. It is still necessary to obtain the $10 selling price if the company is to remain profitable.

The strength of the tendency to shave prices can best be understood by considering the way *most* salespeople think. They are trained to think first of increasing sales volume, with profits a secondary consideration. The saying "There is nothing wrong with this company that a 10 percent increase in sales won't cure" has been around for years. In fact, most salesmen believe in their hearts that the only reason they haven't set the world on fire is that the so-and-sos at the home office won't let them cut prices a trifle. When salesmen have some price discretion, as they do in some companies, the apparently lower costs are likely to be reflected in the prices they get. Of course, a company that converts to direct costing always explains the different definition of product costs to all with pricing authority and warns against this pitfall, but old habits die hard. The salesman who cuts the price and thus cuts the gross profit from 20 percent to 10 percent under absorption costing expects to have his wrist slapped. The same salesman who cuts the marginal contribution from 40 percent to 30 percent has a warm feeling that 30 percent is still higher than the figure he is accustomed to seeing for the gross profit at full price under absorption costing.

If salesmen with price discretion were the only problem, all those companies that set prices at the home office could relax. However, most sales managers, marketing vice presidents, product line managers, and others with pricing power were once salesmen themselves. Thus they often carry over into their new positions some of the same sales-type thinking, though to a much lesser degree. In fact, in two companies headed by somewhat dictatorial presidents who came out of the sales function, we recently recommended an absorption cost system because of our fear of excess price cutting, in spite of the advantages we perceived in direct costing.

The tendency to cut prices will lessen as a company adjusts to direct costing. Company personnel gradually become accustomed to the relation of product variable costs to required selling prices. High marginal contribution percentages soon cease to be an invitation to deep price cuts. However, the tendency never completely dies and it can be reinforced when people who have not previously worked in a direct cost environment join the company.

Price cutting can become unhealthy if lower prices are offered to increase volume. As has been demonstrated in Figures 5-1 and 5-2, this will increase profits. However, if competitors meet the prices, volume will soon retreat to its former status. Profits will be hurt to the extent of the price cuts without the planned offset from increased volume.

This rather bleak picture must be viewed in perspective. If there were no ways of controlling the tendency to cut costs, the many companies that use a direct cost system would have abandoned it long ago.

FIGURE 5-4. Daily marginal contribution report.

DATE____________

Customer	Amount of Invoices, $	Standard Direct Cost of Invoice $	Marginal Contribution at Standard Cost $
Totals for the day			
Previous to-date totals			
Current to-date totals			
Budget for month to date			
Favorable (unfavorable) variance	$	$	$

Methods of control vary. One relatively small company used a form similar to Figure 5-4. The company sold made-to-order products at negotiated prices. Each day it listed all accepted orders at the sales price agreed upon with the customer. It also showed the standard direct cost of the order and, by subtraction, the marginal contribution dollars. The day's orders were totaled and added to the previous day's cumulative total for the month. This figure was then compared with an allocation for that number of days of the company's budgeted fixed costs for the month to which had been added a profit target. This form proved very effective. Two other points are worth noting about this approach: (1) Control was provided sooner because it was based on orders received rather than on orders shipped, and (2) because control was based on orders received, the standard cost of the orders had to be totaled to adjust for any days in which the orders received exceeded the company's daily production capacity.

Larger companies with better-disciplined personnel find a similar control through weekly or monthly computer reports satisfactory. Usually, such companies break down the orders by the person (salesman or product line manager) responsible for pricing. Often the report is based on shipments, particularly in companies that sell off the shelf.

Updating Product Costs

When a pricing decision is to be guided by the cost of the product, the decision maker naturally should have a current cost available to him. Direct costing lends itself readily to updating product costs because the major elements in direct costs are easy to identify. In many computerized companies, a single card can be inserted into the computer to reflect in a matter of minutes a change in price of a specific material in all product costs. The same applies to a change in a specific labor rate. This is accomplished by the combination of a "where used" program with bills of materials in the one case and the combination of a "where used" program with operation (sometimes called route sheets) in the other.

Often, marketing is supplied with updated product costs for informational and pricing purposes even though standard product costs are not changed for accounting purposes. This frequent updating can be important in an inflationary period.

Purchase prices of materials in these product cost updates can be shown on a first-in, first-out basis, an average cost basis, or a last-in, first-out basis in companies using an actual cost system. Each approach is used by a number of companies. However, the best basis is next in, first out (NIFO). NIFO is never used for accounting records but has a very real advantage in pricing. If a customer's order is accepted today for an item that is presently in finished-goods inventory, it may appear that the profit is the difference between the selling price and the cost to make that specific item. However, this is not true. Assuming that the company will continue to sell the product, it must be replaced in finished-goods inventory. Thus the real profit is the difference between the product's selling price today and the cost of restoring the finished-goods inventory tomorrow to the position it would have been in had the sale not been made. It should be noted that in this context NIFO is based on the price of the next purchase order to be placed, as estimated by the purchasing agent, rather than on the price of some undelivered material already ordered. NIFO product costs can also reflect known future changes in labor rates.

Setting Targets by Product Line to Absorb Fixed Costs

Direct cost theoreticians correctly state that fixed costs are not related to specific products. Therefore, they should be viewed as a single lump of costs that have to be absorbed by all the company's products. However, assigning any part of this lump to a particular product or product line may lead to wrong decisions. (The lump includes fixed selling, general, and administrative expenses as well as fixed manufacturing overhead.) In other words, in a two-product company, it makes no difference if Product A absorbs 99 percent of the lump and Product B only 1 percent, or vice versa.

However valid this philosophy may be, it is not very helpful to the product line manager who wants to know how much marginal contribution his product line is expected to generate. Accordingly, some guidelines must be established, even though they may be ignored when it is clearly profitable to do so. (Note: This problem is not related to inventory pricing, discussed in the next chapter.)

The easiest and most common method of assigning fixed costs to product lines is to determine the marginal contribution generated by each in the prior year and adjust the amount by changes in economic conditions, differences in competitive forces, and the impact of new or discontinued products. The amount of the adjustment must, of necessity, be largely subjective, but this is a fault inherent in all goal setting. This "past history" method is acceptable, but it is not the best. The fixed costs absorbed in the prior year are calculated as the difference between the total sales of the product line and the total variable cost of sales on a direct cost basis.

A far more logical method is the "bottleneck" approach. This method can be illustrated by a company with a single machine through which all products must pass, though not necessarily at the same rate. The machine is operated to three-shift capacity at certain times of the year. Therefore, accepting an order for one product may make it necessary to reject an order for some other product because of capacity limitations. In this situation, pricing should be targeted to provide the same dollar marginal contribution per machine hour regardless of which product is being produced. In other words, the total fixed costs plus a targeted profit should be divided by the available machine hours of the bottleneck machine to give an absorption target per machine hour. Competition may not permit this goal to be realized, but the objective is clear and the company should strive to attain it as closely as possible.

The point may become clearer by considering the near disaster that occurred to an injection-molding company. Here the bottleneck was some 20 molding machines. The company had had a contract for some years to produce a product with a marginal contribution of $18 per hundred, or 27.3 percent of the selling price. The company was offered a contract to produce a different product with a marginal contribution of $12 per hundred, or 45.7 percent of selling price. It accepted the new item even though the old item had to be discontinued because of capacity limitations. Since each unit of each item took the same amount of machine time, the new product actually had an annual marginal contribution of only two-thirds that of the old ($12 compared with $18), and this was insufficient to cover fixed costs. The company was able to avoid bankruptcy only through the kindness of its friendly neighborhood loan shark.

It should be noted that pricing on the basis of capacity did not originate with direct costing, although the factors involved become clearer and can be more accurately evaluated under direct costing. Certain industries like job printing have been pricing on a press-hour basis for years.

The bottleneck concept of pricing is easy to understand in a company whose capacity is determined by the output of one machine or a group of similar machines through which all products pass at the same or different rates of speed. But how many companies are like that? Not very many. Nevertheless, the bottleneck concept can be applied to any company.

Perhaps, as rare as companies with a single-machine bottleneck are those in which capacity is limited by the availability of unskilled labor. Nevertheless, just that condition existed in two companies in small towns known to us, one in Pennsylvania and one in Texas. Other possible bottlenecks include the availability of a particular type of raw material, purchased part, or labor skill and the availability of floor space. However, all these are unusual.

Importance of Working Capital in Pricing Decisions

One bottleneck that affects almost every company is capital. The problem is not that additional capital is unavailable but rather that the investment of more capital must be justified by the resulting return on investment. Thus, just as in the case of the bottleneck machine, the company should strive to make the marginal contribution of each product and product line proportional to the working capital required. (Of course, certain machinery and even buildings may be specific to a product line, but only working capital is considered in day-to-day pricing decisions. Justification of investment in fixed assets precedes the decision to purchase such assets.) Competitive conditions may not always permit a proportioning of marginal contribution of each product line to working capital, but the logic of the goal is clear and the objective should be kept in mind.

It is not easy to determine how much working capital is being used by each product line. The usual approach is to start with the tentative assumption that working capital is proportional to the variable costs of the product. Then adjustments are made to reflect how this product or product line differs from the average company product. Points to be considered include:

- Payment habits of the industry to which the product is sold.
- Billing terms of the industries from which raw materials and purchased parts for the product are bought.
- Need to stock heavy inventories of raw materials and purchased parts going into the product because of unreliable vendor deliveries.
- Need to stock heavy inventories of finished goods because of assortment of styles or erratic customer demand.
- Need to stock heavy inventories of finished goods because of seasonal nature of sales and the desire to produce at a constant level.
- Length of manufacturing cycle, including that of subassemblies and manufactured parts.
- Proportion of materials to labor in the product. Materials usually require a longer investment than labor. Labor is generally paid for long after materials are received. An exception is certain materials for which payment may take place long after receipt.

Each of the above points requires a subjective estimate, but the result will still be an improvement over the traditional assignment of a markup percentage over total cost to arrive at a selling price.

Backward Costing

Fortunate is the cost accountant who has never been approached by someone, usually from marketing, with a request like this: “We have to sell Product A for $10.00 and it costs $9.99. It hardly seems worthwhile. But we can sell Product B for $20.00, and it costs only $11.00. Isn't there some way you can shift some costs from Product A to Product B so that both are profitable?" Since cost accounting is not an exact science, the request is not completely unreasonable. In fact, many an effort has been made to accommodate the natural desires of marketing along these lines. However, a cost accountant who does this gradually makes his product costing less and less realistic. Eventually all cost calculations become suspect and no longer properly serve the purposes for which they are made. It is far better to adhere rigidly to the figures first obtained by an analysis of cost facts without considering how they affect profits. Of course, the cost accountant can explain that there is nothing wrong with selling a product at a minimal profit or even at a loss if no other course is open to the company and if there is good reason not to discontinue the product. Such a reason might be the belief that the price squeeze is temporary or that the product is needed to satisfy customers who also buy the company's more profitable products. In view of the disadvantages of gearing costs to prices rather than vice versa, the policy should be considered a "no-no." (Joint product costing, discussed in Chapter 15, is an exception.)

Summary

The use of direct product costs to make pricing decisions can contribute meaningfully to profit improvement. The concept of maximizing dollar marginal contribution through an appropriate combination of price and volume is the key. Generally, direct costing will suggest the acceptance of low-price orders that might appear unprofitable under absorption costing. On the other hand, price concessions must be carefully reviewed by management, since the company may be hurt rather than helped by such sales, particularly if competitors react by making similar cuts.

Marketing is an art, not a science. However, the more relevant the data that accounting can supply to marketing, the better marketing people will be able to practice their art. Direct product costs are an important part of the relevant data that can be useful to marketing. The distribution of fixed costs to product lines under the bottleneck approach is another helpful tool in making appropriate pricing decisions.

6

Inventory Valuation Under Direct Costing

As previously stated, fixed manufacturing overhead is not assigned to products under direct costing. This means that the cost value for the same physical units of a manufacturer's finished-goods inventory and, to a lesser extent, its work-in-process inventory will be substantially less under direct costing than under absorption costing. Furthermore, when the ending inventory of a fiscal period is different from the beginning inventory, the amount of fixed overhead in this difference will be reflected in the net income for the period.

This effect can be illustrated by a company just starting in business. Naturally, its beginning inventory for the first fiscal period is zero. Assume that under absorption costing the cost of its ending inventory is \$100,000, but under direct costing the same physical units show a cost of only \$85,000. This, by the way, is a reasonable assumption, although the difference could be greater in some industries than in others. The percentage difference would also be affected by the proportion of the inventory represented by as yet unprocessed materials and purchased parts, which have the same value under both systems. Since cost of sales is reflected in income statements as total cost input into production less the value of ending inventory, it is obvious that the company's net income will appear to be $15,000 less under direct costing than it would be under absorption costing.

Figure 6-1 illustrates this point for three fiscal periods, showing how income is lower under direct costing when finished-goods inventories are rising but higher than under absorption costing when finished-goods inventories are decreasing. Figure 6-1 also illustrates the fact that these differences cancel out when several periods are combined and the ending inventory of the combined periods is the same as the beginning inventory. For simplicity, the figure uses a zero in-

FIGURE 6-1. Genuine Antique Manufacturing Co.: Impact of inventory changes on profits.

		1975	*1976*	*1977*
Selling price $10 per unit	Units produced	50,000	50,000	50,000
Variable Mfg. cost $5 per unit	Units sold	50,000	40,000	60,000
Fixed Mfg. cost $150,000 per year	Finished goods ending inventory in units	-0-	10,000	-0-
Fixed G.&A. cost $50,000 per year				

	1975	*1976*	*1977*	*3-Year total*
ABSORPTION COSTING				
Sales	$500,000	$400,000	$600,000	$1,500,000
Opening inventory	-0-	-0-	80,000	
Cost of production				
Variable	$250,000	$250,000	$250,000	$ 750,000
Fixed	150,000	150,000	150,000	450,000
Total	$400,000	$400,000	$480,000	$1,200,000
Less closing inventory	-0-	80,000	-0-	-0-
Cost of sales	$400,000	$320,000	$480,000	$1,200,000
Gross profit	$100,000	$ 80,000	$120,000	$ 300,000
G.&A.	50,000	50,000	50,000	150,000
Operating profit	$ 50,000	$ 30,000	$ 70,000	$ 150,000
DIRECT COSTING				
Sales	$500,000	$400,000	$600,000	$1,500,000
Opening inventory	-0-	-0-	50,000	-0-
Cost of production	$250,000	$250,000	$250,000	$ 750,000
Total	$250,000	$250,000	$300,000	$ 750,000
Less closing inventory	-0-	50,000	-0-	-0-
Cost of sales	$250,000	$200,000	$300,000	$ 750,000
Fixed costs	200,000	200,000	200,000	600,000
Operating profit	$ 50,000	$ -0-	$100,000	$ 150,000

ventory at start and finish and ignores the inventory of raw materials, which in any case would have no effect on the point being demonstrated.

It is worth mentioning again that under direct costing neither work-in-process nor finished-goods inventories reflect in their cost value the amount of variable selling, general, and administrative expenses (S.G.& A.) which are part of product costs and part of cost of sales under direct costing. Variable S.G.& A. costs are added at the time the goods are shipped. Direct cost values of finished goods, unlike absorption cost values, are lower than cost of sales values.

The Controversy

Early advocates of direct costing placed their major emphasis on the contention that the income reported under direct costing was the only true and correct income. They based their argument on the long-accepted accounting principle that profits can be recognized only when a transaction occurs with an outsider. Although they agreed that assigning a cost was not the same as reflecting a profit, they pointed out that under absorption costing the management of a company can increase reported profits by building finished-goods inventory whether sales prospects justify it or not. In a sense, they claimed, management thus had an opportunity to increase profits without the control provided through the validation of an arm's-length transaction.

This may be illustrated by a probably fictitious story going the rounds. It is said that a recently hired financial executive suggested to the president of a conglomerate that the company convert to direct costing. His reason was that division managers were manipulating their profits upward by building inventories and thus acquiring undeserved reputations for efficiency. This was particularly true of managers who were about to be promoted or retired, leaving their successors the problem of being unable to reduce inventories to more appropriate levels without hurting profits and thus their own reputations. Of course, the same action could be taken to increase bonuses based on divisional profits or to conceal a year of bad management.

The president, who had not achieved his position through stupidity, was aware of the problem, but his efforts to control it through a review of inventory levels had proved ineffective. His division managers always seemed to have some defensible reason for their action—a threatened strike, a vaguely planned sales increase, or the like. Consequently, the president was intrigued by the idea of converting to direct costing once he understood that this change would completely remove the incentive for increasing production when sales trends did not warrant it. Accordingly, he immediately authorized the change to direct costing. However, the next morning he called the financial executive into his office and said, "Does this switch to direct costing mean that I won't be able to use the technique of building finished-goods inventories to manipulate the profits I report to the company's directors and to the public?" When he was told yes, he temporarily deferred the conversion to direct costing. Ten years later, the company is still on absorption costing.

Advocates of direct costing used the fact that absorption costing had a built-in incentive to produce without regard to sales as a major argument for direct costing. They pointed out that the resulting excess finished goods increased working capital requirements, increased the needed fire insurance, risked inventory obsolescence, created a lag in improving product design, and added minor costs in stock handling, inventory counting, and in some cases space. They also pointed out that the reported profit increase would someday be offset by a corresponding profit decrease when the inventory was reduced to a proper level, but that the excess carrying costs in the interim were gone forever.

Opponents of direct costing met these arguments in many ways. Basically, they started with the premise that "costs" meant all costs and that fixed manufacturing overhead was certainly a cost because it is impossible to produce anything without it. This argument, of course, ignores the fact that absorption costing has never charged general and administrative costs into inventory, although these too are an essential cost element in manufacturing. The American Institute of Certified Public Accountants (AICPA) and the Securities and Exchange Commission (SEC) decided against direct costing on the basis of this argument and two others. They felt that comparisons of profits and balance sheets between companies, some of which were on absorption costing and others on direct costing, would cause inutterable confusion. Since, at the time, very few companies were on direct costing, they felt that in order to ensure uniformity of reporting no company should be allowed to report on a direct cost basis. An edict to this effect was issued.

The AICPA and the SEC also felt that the dividing line between manufacturing cost on the one hand and S.G.& A. expenses on the other was well understood and presented relatively few problems. However, they saw no such ease in determining which costs were variable and which were fixed. (The difficulties in making this separation have been described in Chapter 4.) Accordingly, they saw more chances for profit manipulation in this area than in the building of finished-goods inventories. Of course, both sides of the controversy recognized that there were other ways, within limits, of manipulating profits. Some of these techniques are legal and accepted in accounting theory. Deferring maintenance is one; another is accelerating shipments to customers by offering dating or return privileges. There are others.

The Internal Revenue Service also forbids direct costing. Its understandable desire to collect as much revenue as the law allows gives it every incentive to bar direct costing. As companies mature, they tend to expand. Small companies grow into large ones and large companies expand into still larger ones. Naturally, the larger a company is, the greater its physical volume of finished-goods inventory will be. During the continuing expansion, taxable profits will appear to be greater each year under absorption costing than they would under direct costing. When to this is added the inflation in costs of the same physical units that has occurred through history, and quite spectacularly in recent years, the tendency of direct costing to show lower profits is increased. Thus it may be said that the IRS simply can't afford to recognize direct costing. At this writing, IRS Regulation 1.471–11(c) requires that all fixed manufacturing overhead be included in product costs. For guidance as to just what must be included, the latest revision of that regulation should be consulted.

In the last few years, both the AICPA and the SEC have become increasingly concerned about management's propensity to shift profits backward and forward between fiscal years. Many of the recent opinions of the Accounting Principles Board and the Financial Accounting Standards Board are specifically directed at the minimization or elimination of this practice. Possibly, the time has come for both the AICPA and the SEC to recognize that direct costing as a method of public reporting would make one type of profit shifting impossible. This advantage might well be evaluated again by the AICPA and the SEC in relation to the disadvantages already mentioned. Furthermore, the number of companies that would prefer to be on direct costing has grown to the point where meaningful comparisons could be made among companies using direct costing. It would be naive to suppose that the IRS will change its stand.

It should be noted that the entire controversy focuses on the relative correctness of the balance sheet and more especially the income statement under direct costing as opposed to absorption costing.

"What Did We Earn Last Month?" was indeed an appropriate title for the article that started it all. Both sides accepted this issue as the only one worthy of discussion. From the perspective of 40-odd years later, it now appears that much of this energy was misdirected. The greatest advantage of direct costing is in the improved quality of the data available to management for all types of decisions. Its use in pricing has already been covered in the previous chapter. Its use in planning will be covered in the next chapter, and its use in other types of decisions will be discussed in Chapter 8. Direct costing also has certain advantages in cost control, as discussed in Chapters 10 and 11, and in marketing strategy other than pricing, as covered in Chapters 12 and 13.

Dual Reporting: To Management on Direct Costs—To the Public on Absorption Costs

The SEC's unwillingness to accept direct costing means that no company with securities in the hands of the general public can use it. The AICPA's failure to accept it means that no privately held company that needs certified financial statements for its bank or its vendors can use direct costing. This would, at first glance, appear to mean that only small, unimportant companies have the option to use direct costing. However, such is not the case. Many large, publicly held companies keep their records on a direct cost basis and prepare most of their reports to management with only variable costs assigned to products and with income for each fiscal period shown under direct costing. These companies, however, all report to the public (annually, quarterly, or monthly, as the case may be) as if they were using absorption costing. Their balance sheets show work-in-process and finished-goods inventories on an absorption basis. Their income statements show the costs charged to production converted to cost of sales by the change, up or down, between the beginning and ending inventory, both shown on an absorption basis. These companies prepare income statements for use within the company on a direct cost basis. However, to avoid showing one figure to management and another to the public, these internal-use-only income statements customarily show below the profit on a direct cost basis a memo figure for "change of fixed costs in inventory," followed by the resulting profit on an absorption cost basis.

The remainder of this chapter will examine the various ways of using a set of accounts maintained on a direct cost basis to prepare a set of published financial statements on an absorption cost basis. It must be recognized that the simpler methods of preparing absorption cost statements from direct cost data tend to be the least accurate, and vice versa. All include some shortcuts that will presumably give answers slightly different from the results that would have been obtained if the company had done all its recordkeeping originally on an absorption cost basis. Since these differences are indeed small and since all cost accounting uses some estimating and some averaging, the results are acceptable and accepted.

However, since the methods described below do vary in accuracy, it is important to obtain the concurrence of the company's outside auditor before a method is selected. Since the manner of collecting the original data will vary according to the method of conversion being used, concurrence should be obtained before the basic direct cost accounting system is designed and implemented (see Chapter 17).

One basic principle that applies to all the methods should be mentioned. The entire exercise of moving from direct cost data to absorption cost financial statements consists of arriving at a figure for the appropriate amount of fixed overhead to add to work-in-process and finished-goods inventories so that they can be valued as if the company were on absorption costs.

Method 1

The simplest method of converting an ending inventory on direct costs to one valued on absorption costs is shown in Figure 6-2. The method illustrated prorates the fixed overhead in the beginning inventory plus the fixed overhead incurred during the year between the direct costs in the work-in-process and finished-goods ending inventory as calculated under direct costing and the direct costs put into production during the year. In other words, the method prorates the direct cost value of the work in process and finished goods in the opening inventory plus the direct materials put into production and the direct labor and variable overhead expended in the year. These figures cannot fail to be generated by a direct cost accounting system.

This method, though simple, is also the least accurate. It has the potential of being furthest from the value that would have resulted had the company kept its books on an absorption cost basis. Whether the difference will be an overvaluation or an undervaluation is not determinable, nor is the amount of the difference. The inaccuracy arises in part from the fact that fixed overhead is being spread as if it were the same percentage in each production department. This would very rarely be true or even approximately true. Typically, the

FIGURE 6-2. Bide-a-Wee Casket Co.: Conversion of closing inventory to an absorption cost basis.

	Direct Cost Basis[a]	*Fixed Costs*	*Absorption Basis*
Opening inventory per last year's conversion	$ 85,000	$15,000	$100,000
Put into production	300,000	?	?
Incurred during the year per the totals of appropriate accounts in the general ledger		75,000	
Subtotals	$385,000	$90,000	?
Cost of goods sold per cost system	$290,000		b
Ending inventory	$ 95,000	$22,207[c]	$117,207[d]

[a] All figures in this column exclude variable S.G.&A. costs.
[b] Cost of goods sold on an absorption basis is the $290,000 on a direct cost basis plus the fixed costs of $90,000 less the fixed costs in closing inventory: $290,000 +90,000 −22,207 = $357,793.
[c] The $90,000 total of fixed costs is spread according to the proportion of direct costs in closing inventory to the direct costs put into production subtotal: $90,000 × 95,000/385,000 = $22,207.
[d] Cross-adding the direct costs and the fixed costs: $95,000 + 22,207 = $117,207.

proportion of direct labor to departmental fixed overhead varies considerably by departments because of the value of machinery being depreciated in each department, the floor space occupied by the department, and the supervision necessary.

Figure 6-2 shows fixed overhead being spread on the basis of total direct costs, which include not only direct labor but also materials and variable overhead. Since almost all absorption cost systems spread fixed overhead on direct labor, an additional inaccuracy is involved in Method 1. If, for example, the opening inventory was made up to a disproportionate extent of products with a high material content compared with their direct labor content and the reverse was true of the closing inventory, the inaccuracy could be considerable. Fortunately, such a situation is quite unusual.

Despite its drawbacks, Method 1 is so simple that the extent of the potential inaccuracies should be evaluated in light of the company's operations before it is rejected. If the company's departments have similar fixed overhead percentages and if its products have similar ratios of material content to direct labor content, it may be possible to use the approach shown in Figure 6-2.

Three variations of the method are possible.

Method 1A. Method 1A is the same as Method 1 except that the opening inventory is not included in the calculation. In this approach, the fixed costs incurred during the year (the $75,000 amount in Figure 6-2) are prorated between the direct cost of goods sold (the $290,000 amount in Figure 6-2) and the direct cost of the closing inventory (the $95,000 amount in Figure 6-2). The result is $18,500 of fixed costs assigned to the closing inventory. Although Method 1A is used occasionally, it is not as conceptually correct as Method 1 and is no easier to apply. Accordingly, it is not recommended.

Method 1B. Method 1B is the same as Method 1 except that the direct labor content that has been put into production and the direct labor content of the closing inventory are used to spread the fixed costs. This method eliminates the second disadvantage of Method 1—the spreading of fixed costs on materials and variable overhead as well as on direct labor. Under an actual cost system, the direct labor content of the opening and closing inventories is very difficult to determine, but under a standard cost system it is relatively easy. The direct labor included in the standard cost sheet for each product is summarized—not a difficult task—and the figure is used to extend the units of each product in the closing inventory. Presumably, this has already been done for the opening inventory in the calculation for the prior year.

Although Method 1B requires somewhat more work than Method 1, even under a standard cost system, its improved accuracy and clarity make it preferable to Method 1.

Method 1C. In Method 1C, a variation of Method 1B, the calculation is made department by department or even cost center by cost center. Although this method eliminates the remaining inaccuracy of Method 1, its implementation is very complex. The product cost sheets must be broken down by the direct labor in each department or cost center. The fixed overhead must be allocated to each department or cost center, and the amount of product transferred out of each department or cost center must be related to the amount of product still in the cost center. On balance, it would appear that the extra work is not justified by the accuracy gained.

It should be noted that many cost accountants strongly believe that the allocation to products of fixed costs—which would exist whether or not the products were produced—is a rather meaningless exercise. These cost accountants are quite willing to put up with considerable inaccuracy in the assignment of fixed costs to inventories. We are inclined to accept this philosophy.

Method 2

Method 2 uses time to allocate fixed costs to ending inventory. Again, Figure 6-2 shows direct costs put into production during the year were \$300,000 and direct costs in ending inventory were \$95,000. Thus it might be said that direct costs in ending inventory represented $\frac{\$95{,}000}{\$300{,}000} \times 12 = 3.8$ months of production. Under Method 2, all the fixed costs incurred in the last three months of the fiscal year (say, October, November, and December) plus eight-tenths of those incurred in the prior month (say, September) are assigned to the closing inventory. A minor variation of this approach for a company whose production fluctuates from month to month is to determine the time span working back from year end in which \$95,000 in direct costs was put into production and to use this time span to determine the fixed costs assigned to closing inventory.

One advantage of this method over Method 1 is that the actual relation of fixed costs to direct costs in the period that the closing inventory was most likely to have been produced is reflected in the assignment of fixed costs to it. This is particularly important in periods of marked inflation in labor rates, property tax rates, prices of supply items, and the like. Of course, some of the items in the closing inventory may have been produced months or even years before, and some items produced toward the end of the year may have been sold and shipped before year end. This inaccuracy is inherent in any averaging process.

Method 2 can also be applied to a direct labor base rather than to total direct costs. When the method is used in this way, it has the same advantages over its use of total direct cost for allocating fixed costs as the advantages already described of Method 1B over Method 1. It would appear that the advantages of applying Method 2 to a direct labor base, at least under a standard cost system, outweigh the small amount of extra work involved.

The choice between Method 1 and its variations and Method 2 and its variation will depend on the extent to which the company annualizes its fixed costs and accrues them monthly. For example, if real estate taxes are payable twice a year and are reflected in the cost accounting system in the month paid, Method 2 can be quite inaccurate and Method 1 is preferable. The same applies to any seasonal fixed cost such as heat, vacations, or machinery overhauls. On the other hand, if the annual amounts of these costs are estimated and are accrued at one-twelfth each month, Method 2 is preferable, since it tends to reflect changing conditions during the year.

Method 3

Method 3, which is usually found in computerized standard cost systems, consists of preparing a cost sheet for each product that shows both its direct cost and its absorption cost. The units of each product in ending inventory are extended at their direct cost for internal reports and at their absorption cost for financial statements. Computerized companies will generally find this method easier to use than either of the foregoing methods.

Method 3 is both the most accurate and the easiest to understand for arriving at an inventory on an absorption cost basis. However, the question naturally arises as to where the absorption costs on the product cost sheets come from if the company is on direct costs. Another question is whether the creation of these figures will involve the company in the sort of paperwork that companies converting to direct costing seek to avoid. There are a number of ways, varying in both accuracy and work required, that will produce standard product costs on an absorption basis without adding materially to the paperwork of a direct cost system. These techniques are described briefly below.

Method 3A. Most companies that are today initially recording their costs on a direct cost basis were once on absorption costs. At that time, each product had a standard cost on an absorption basis. This cost figure can be used for several years, adjusted by some measure of inflation—for example, the cost-of-living index, the gross national product price deflator, or an index related to the particular industry. An even better measure is the ratio of the company's own total fixed manufacturing overhead in the year to its total direct labor. The resulting factor is applied to the fixed manufacturing overhead in each product cost. It should be noted that the fixed costs assigned to a new product are determined by comparison with the most similar old product, possibly adjusted by some judgmental factor based on the difference between the two.

The overall accuracy of the fixed costs assigned to products can and should be checked each year by extending the units of each product produced plus or minus the change of units in inventory by the fixed costs assigned to each product. If the total thus obtained accounts for the fixed costs incurred, the assignments are reasonable in total. If not, they can be adjusted by a suitable factor.

Method 3B. Another way to determine the fixed manufacturing overhead to be assigned to each product cost sheet is to allocate fixed overhead to departments or cost centers, much as under absorption costing, and then to absorb these costs into products on the basis of standard direct labor of the product in the department or cost center. This method again follows the principle of absorption costing. However, when the method is applied under direct costing, considerable time and effort can be saved by using estimates and shortcuts that would not be acceptable under absorption costing. This lack of accuracy is possible because the fixed cost figures assigned to products will not be used for either management decisions or cost control. The figures will be used only in totals for reporting balance sheets and income statements to outsiders. Any inaccuracies in individual product costs may be expected to offset one another in the totals being reported.

Method 3 is generally more suitable than either Method 1 or Method 2 for converting an inventory originally valued at direct cost to its absorption cost value for financial reporting. However, the method is not practical for companies that do not use standard costs. In addition, the calculation becomes quite difficult if a company's cost accounting system is not computerized.

Summary

The controversy over the respective merits of absorption costing and direct costing for financial statements and profit reporting to outsiders has been settled by edict in favor of absorption costing. There are no signs that this edict will be withdrawn in the foreseeable future. However, the advantages of direct costing in managing a business are so great that many companies have chosen to use it for everything except the preparation of financial statements for outsiders. In order to prepare financial statements on an absorption basis from cost data collected on a direct cost basis, it is necessary to assign an appropriate amount of fixed manufacturing overhead to inventories of work in process and finished goods. A number of methods have been devised for making the necessary calculation. All require some work, but none are so burdensome as to override the saving in clerical costs that arises from using direct costing as opposed to absorption costing. The clerical saving is, of course, not the major reason for the adoption of direct costing, but it is a welcome by-product of the change.

7

Direct Costs in Budgeting, Forecasting, and Business Modeling

THE term "budget" is generally understood to apply to some predictions of the level of future financial events for purposes of measuring how actual performance conforms to the estimate. Within this broad definition, there are many different budgeting concepts, methods, and purposes. The various types of budget, broken down by descriptive categories, are listed and briefly described in the following section. It should be noted that each column in the list represents a choice; most budgets can be described by choosing only one term from each column.

Time Period	*Scope*	*Concept*	*Coverage*	*Control*
Monthly	Costs for a department, division, or company	Performance	Operating	Fixed
Quarterly	Revenues and costs for a division or company	Restrictive	Cash	Variable
Annual		Encumbrance	Capital asset acquisition	Flexible
Rolling				
Project				
Long-range				

Types of Budgets

Time Period

Monthly budgets are ordinarily prepared in advance for the coming year but show the level of each account expected in the specific month. Companies on a 13-period year or a 4-4-5-week or 5-4-4-week quarter show periods rather than calendar months.

Quarterly budgets are also ordinarily prepared in advance for the coming year but show only individual quarters.

Annual budgets show only the whole year. They are ordinarily not used for expense control but are confined to determining before the start of the year whether predicted profits will be satisfactory.

Rolling budgets are prepared each month or quarter for a specific number of future months or quarters. A common formula is to prepare, say, in November a budget for each month of the coming year. Then, on the basis of November experience, a revision is made in December for March of the coming year; on the basis of December experience, a revision is made in January for April of the coming year; and so on in each month. The advantage of this technique is that the most recent experience can be used to determine a proper goal for the next future month for which detailed planning has not yet been done and commitments have not yet been made.

Project budgets are special budgets used to measure and control the extent to which a specific project's costs are within those predicted. It can be used for the construction of a building or other capital addition that involves many separate purchases or labor operations. A project budget is inappropriate for purchases such as machine tools where the only major cost is represented by a single purchase order. However, it is often used to control research and development projects and advertising programs.

Long-range budgets are usually referred to as forecasts rather than as budgets. They are income statements prepared for three, five, or ten future years and are used for various types of planning, including product development, capital asset acquisition, upgrading of executives, and market targets.

Scope

Cost budgets are predictions of costs, usually by department, by account, and by month. In large, well-run companies they are, in effect, the details supporting the cost figures in the forecast of revenues, costs, and profits. In small companies cost budgets may be prepared independently of the forecast income statement (assuming the company has one, which is not always the case) and may cover only certain departments.

Revenue and cost budgets are forecast income statements and are more often referred to as forecasts than as budgets. However, both terms are widely used. They can, of course, be prepared for a consolidated group of companies, a single company (whether independent or a parent or a subsidiary), a division, or any department that generates revenue, even if the revenue is derived only through sales to another division of the same company. Departmental cost budgets, discussed immediately above, are used to support the cost figures on these income forecasts.

Concept

Performance budgets predict costs but expect actual costs to exactly meet the prediction only by coincidence. Variations of actual from budget are acceptable if they are not too large or are explainable by some factor outside management's control. The budgeted figures are, in effect, targets. When actual costs are lower than budget, lower-level management is praised, and vice versa. In addition, when actual costs are higher than budget, an effort is made to ensure that the same situation doesn't happen again. In industry, performance budgets are overwhelmingly preferred to restrictive budgets or encumbrance budgets.

Restrictive budgets are typically found in government agencies and nonprofit institutions. Here the amount of revenues from taxes or donations can be predicted with reasonable accuracy. However, because the demand for services is almost unlimited, it is necessary to restrict costs to the money available. Since many people are usually involved in incurring costs, each department is given an upper limit on its spending, often by individual account. In this case, the budget is referred to as a line-by-line budget.

A restrictive budget differs from a performance budget in that overruns are not permitted. Incoming purchases that represent overruns are turned back at the receiving room door. Personnel may be laid off and programs cut back. This type of budget is rarely found in industry but is sometimes used to control research and development, training, advertising, and other departments which, like government and charitable institutions, are characterized by unlimited demand.

Encumbrance budgets represent an attempt to improve the effectiveness of restrictive budgets. The encumbrance technique consists of setting up the total amount available for the department or the account for the period and deducting from it each commitment as it is made. Thus purchases are deducted when the purchase order is placed or even before that when it becomes apparent that the purchase must be made. The charge is made against the balance available for the month in which the purchase is expected. Minor adjustments are made for differences in incoming freight at the time the goods are received. Similarly, monthly salary and wage costs are charged against the funds available for each month of the entire year at the time personnel are hired or at the beginning of the year for existing personnel. Care must be taken to think of every possible expense. One nonprofit hospital working under a federal research grant ran into serious trouble because it failed to consider separation pay due employees at termination of the contract.

Encumbrance budgeting requires a completely separate set of encumbrance records in addition to the normal payroll and accounts payable bookkeeping. The two sets of records tie together but are used for different purposes. Encumbrance budgeting is rare in industry. Occasionally, it is used as a tool to make restrictive budgeting work in departments where costs are particularly difficult to control and major cost control problems have been common. Typically, department heads in the very departments where restrictive budgeting applies are by temperament least likely to adhere to a budget. Encumbrance budgeting is used to force them to do so.

Coverage

Operating budgets predict amounts for revenues and costs (or costs alone) for the normal operations of a business. When the word "budget" is used without any modifying adjective, this is usually what is meant.

Cash budgets, also called cash forecasts, are predictions of the cash that will be on hand at any future time. Generally, they are prepared on a monthly basis and are important in that they highlight the projected peaks and valleys in the cash account. In modern cash management these budgets are very useful for improving profits—through minimizing borrowings, on the one hand, or maximizing income from short-term investments, on the other. The higher the going interest rate, the greater the value to be gained from good cash forecasting.

There are two basic methods of cash budgeting. One starts with the profit shown by the operating budget and adjusts the figure upward by noncash costs such as depreciation, leasehold improvement amortization, and deferred income taxes; in addition, the operating profit is adjusted downward by anticipated capital expenditures, repayment of borrowings, and the like. Many companies stop here. Others make adjustments up or down for anticipated changes in other balance sheet accounts such as inventories, accounts receivable, accounts payable, and accrued income taxes. These further adjustments will approximate the results obtained by the method described below.

The second method of cash forecasting involves predicting each balance sheet account. Anticipated sales and collections are used to forecast the value of future accounts receivable; anticipated materials usage and purchases are used to forecast raw material inventory; anticipated production and shipments are used to forecast finished-goods inventory; and so on. This method is more accurate than the approach described above, even when the latter is carried to the point of adjusting profits by the changes in balance sheet accounts. In addition, the second method allows operating management determine which account or accounts caused any difference between the forecast cash balance and the amount actually on hand when the period ends. This knowledge frequently leads to corrective action. For example, if raw material inventories are higher than forecast, purchasing can be slowed down. If accounts receivable are higher than forecast, collection effort can be stepped up. The company's past ratios or industry ratios can be used to monitor and control each of the major balance sheet accounts.

Good cash forecasting enables a company to arrange for borrowings well in advance. When a bank is told that a company will need to borrow in the fiture, it has time to analyze the company's creditworthiness. This will often result in a lower interest rate than when a company borrows to meet an immediate crisis. Also, lacking reasonable notice, a bank may take so much time to make up its mind that the company is unable to meet its accounts payable on time. This hurts the company's reputation with vendors. The other side of the picture is that good cash forecasting may enable a company to make short-term investments for longer periods than it could if its future cash position were known less accurately. Generally, the longer the period for which an investment is committed, the higher the interest rate available.

One important point should be emphasized. Most cash forecasting uses predicted month-end balances. The last day of the month is by no means always the day when cash reaches its lowest point. Some companies prepare forecasts showing the predicted cash on hand for each day of the month or at least each week. Other companies minimize the daily peaks and valleys by consolidating all payments to vendors on two or four days of each month. This technique has been found to work well in certain industries.

Capital asset acquisition budgets, like project budgets for capital assets (already discussed), are sometimes referred to as capital budgets. The two should not be confused. A capital acquisition budget is a technique for spreading the planned capital acquisitions for the year over the whole year so that the impact on cash in any one month will be acceptable. This type of budget is used in large, divisionalized companies. Each division manager puts in an annual request for capital additions for his division. Since the total almost always adds to more than top management cares to spend in the coming year, a number of items are deferred until the following year. When these items again appear in the request for that year, they are likely to be authorized. Since the division managers look on this authorization as already a year late, unless the authorization has been spread by months managers will tend to order everything for immediate delivery.

Control

Fixed budgets recognize only the forecast level of sales and the forecast level of production. If the predicted levels turn out to be accurate, the forecast costs can properly be compared with actual costs. However, if either sales or production differs materially from the forecasts, there is no way under fixed budgeting to determine whether the difference between actual costs and forecast costs is a result of the change in operations or whether it reflects management's performance.

A fixed budget is entirely satisfactory for a company that is able to forecast sales accurately. A fixed budget may also be used for the prediction and control of fixed costs—those that are not expected to vary with changes in the level of sales or production. In fact, in most cost accounting systems the control of fixed manufacturing overhead involves a budgeting technique of the fixed budget type. Many companies use variable budgets (discussed below) for manufacturing costs but fixed budgets for S.G.& A. expenses because so few of these expenses are variable.

Variable budgets are sometimes called flexible budgets, and vice versa. However, the two types are distinct and will be referred to separately throughout this book. A variable budget is one that predicts a dollar amount for each fixed cost and a unit amount per piece produced for each variable cost. In most companies, units are meaningless because of the variety of products; thus the unit amounts are usually related to direct labor hours or direct labor dollars. In other companies, the unit amounts may be related to sales dollars or to standard cost of production.

The forecast for a month or year is identical to a fixed budget. The unit amounts are extended by the predicted sales or production to give the forecast. However, when the month is over, actual costs are compared against a budget that reflects the amount of budgeted variable costs as the unit costs times the actual production in the month. Thus the variance reflects management's performance purified of any influence arising from changes in production level from the production forecast.

Under an absorption cost system, which recognizes only the two cost categories of variable and fixed and splits semivariable costs between these categories, the preparation of a variable budget is relatively easy. Preparation is equally easy under direct costing. In addition, there is no need to reconcile the actual profit reported to the forecast profit by the overabsorbed or underabsorbed fixed costs arising from the change in production level. This makes the result substantially easier to understand.

Flexible budgets predict manufacturing overhead without splitting variable from fixed costs. A schedule is prepared similar to Figure 7-1, in which each overhead account (whether variable, semivariable, or fixed) is predicted for each level of production within the likely range. Each account is looked at separately and, on the basis of historical data and the judgment of operating management, is assigned a cost amount at each level of production. As Figure 7-1 indicates, the following accounts meet the definitions:

Variable—factory supplies.

Semivariable (a fixed component and a constant variable component)—floorboys and janitors.

FIGURE 7-1. Monthly flexible overhead budget (all figures in thousands).

Direct labor hours at standard (A)	15	20	25	30	35	40
Percent of normal capacity	60%	80%	100%	120%	140%	160%
Factory superintendent	2.0	2.0	2.0	2.0	2.0	2.0
Foremen	6.0	6.0	6.0	6.0	6.0	6.0
Assistant foreman	3.8	3.8	5.0	5.0	6.2	7.4
Mechanics	10.6	11.8	13.0	14.2	16.4	18.0
Floorboys and janitors	9.6	11.8	14.0	16.2	18.4	20.6
Factory supplies	1.5	2.0	2.5	3.0	3.5	4.0
Heat, light, and power	1.9	1.9	2.0	2.1	2.1	2.2
Rent	5.0	5.0	5.0	5.0	5.0	5.3
Telephone and telegraph	.5	.5	.5	.5	.5	.5
Depreciation	6.0	6.0	6.0	6.0	6.0	6.0
Total budgeted overhead	$46.9	$50.8	$56.0	$60.0	$66.1	$72.0
Standard overhead per standard direct labor hour (B)			$2.24			
Total standard overhead (A) × (B)	$33.6	$44.8	$56.0	$67.2	$78.4	$89.6
Volume variance	($13.3)	($6.0)	$0.0	$7.2	$12.3	$17.6

Irregular semivariable—assistant foremen; mechanics; heat, light, and power; rent.

Fixed—factory superintendent, foremen, telephone and telegraph, depreciation.

The totals then indicate the amount of overhead that is proper at each level on the schedule and, by interpolation, at any intermediate level.

Although flexible budgeting is not used in direct cost accounting, its advantages should not be overlooked. It is the only way to properly reflect step costs in a control system (other than by footnotes on a departmental cost report), and it properly takes into account any expected failure of a variable cost to be truly variable at all production levels and of a fixed cost to be truly fixed. It also allows for the reflection of supervariables and inverse variables. Even more important, a flexible budget is the type of report that a relatively uneducated, shirtsleeves foreman can understand at first glance.

Cost Accounting and Budgeting

In many manufacturing companies and many service companies, cost accounting and budgeting are closely related. Although in some companies the chief cost accountant and the budget director go their separate ways, there is no justification for this. Cost accounting's handling of fixed costs, both manufacturing and S.G.&A., is identical with the way they are budgeted, and the figures should be the same in both functions. For a fixed budget, the budgeted amount for variable costs should be determined by multiplying cost accounting's unit cost figures by the sales or production forecast. Cost accounting's unit cost figures should be used in the same way for a variable budget. Budget revisions arising out of changes from the original forecast in anticipated sales or production levels need the same unit cost data. It is easier to prepare or revise any one of these budgets under direct costing than under absorption costing, and there is less chance of error.

The relationship between cost accounting and cash budgeting is just as real but not quite so obvious. It is best understood by examining the mechanics of forecasting purchasing and payroll levels. Typically, an operating forecast starts with a prediction of sales by months, preferably by product or product group. The procedure may involve a study of the economy or trends in the industry, evaluation of competition, extrapolation of the company's own sales trends by products, or a grassroots evaluation of the prospects of sales to each and every customer.

The next step is to determine the level of finished-goods inventory required at the beginning of each month to meet the forecast sales. Many companies think in terms of a certain number of days' supply of each product (say, 30 days'), but modern inventory management takes a different approach. Today, it is customary for manufacturers producing for "the shelf," as most do, to produce in an economic lot size (ELS). This means that slower-moving products will ordinarily average larger stocks in terms of days' supply than faster-moving products. Also, products with relatively high total setup costs will have larger stocks than others. In contrast, products with high total costs per piece will be carried in lesser unit quantities than those with lower costs per piece. In addition, many manufacturers with seasonal sales peaks will choose to build inventory in the slow sales season in order to reduce fluctuations in production levels. This policy, too, must be reflected in the desired inventory of finished goods at the end of each month.

Next, the production of each product required in the month is calculated by subtracting beginning inventory from sales plus desired ending inventory. Then, through an explosion of the bill of materials for each product scheduled to be produced (i.e., multiplying the scheduled production in pieces by the amount of material in each piece), the required level of raw materials is obtained. The bill of materials may have originally been an estimate, but it has been updated and revised through the cost accounting system. Under the economic order quantity (EOQ) formula, materials are often purchased in quantities larger than immediate needs. This factor must be considered in determining the cash needed for purchasing direct materials.

Similarly, direct labor can be forecast from the scheduled production in the month by exploding the operation (route) sheets by the number of units scheduled to be produced. Finally, overhead fixed cost payments come from the fixed cost budgets and variable overhead costs come from the unit costs related to the scheduled production. Thus cost accounting data can be used to prepare a meaningful cash forecast. Again, direct costing can more readily serve this purpose than absorption costing.

Use of Budgets in Cost Control

The primary use of budgets, but by no means their only use, is in cost control. The budget shows what costs are reasonably expected to be by department, by account within the department, and by month or other period. Actual costs for the time period are compared with the budget, and any excess of actual costs over the budget is investigated. If possible, corrective action is taken to bring future costs into line with the budget. In a manufacturing company, particularly one on standard costs, the cost control function is primarily part of the cost accounting system rather than the budgeting system. However, as previously stated, the control of fixed manufacturing costs is a budgeting technique. Also, many companies use budgeting rather than cost accounting techniques to monitor S.G.& A. costs and often those of other departments such as research and development.

Many of the techniques of analyzing variances from standard costs also apply to analyzing variances from budget. These techniques are described in Chapter 10 and will not be repeated here. However, a few points that are more applicable to budgets than to cost accounting should be mentioned.

For cost control purposes, it is essential that the people whose costs are to be controlled participate directly in setting the budget. If financial people establish the targets, operating people will not feel any real responsibility for staying within the budgeted figures. If costs exceed the budget, operating managers will merely shrug their shoulders and say the budget was wrong in the first place. Since it is likely that certain factors were involved that were not known to the financial people, this attitude is understandable. On the other hand, financial people should review the budget figures prepared by operating people to make sure that no unreasonable cushions are included.

As indicated in Chapter 9 in relation to the setting of standards, budget figures should be attainable. If a budget is so tight that it is unlikely to be met, it will mislead management about the prospects of profit. In addition, it will have a poor psychological effect on operating personnel, who are likely to feel that they are up against a stacked deck. Their motivation will be substantially less than if they are able to operate within budget at most times.

Breakeven Calculations and Charts

Figure 7-2 shows one method of drawing a breakeven chart, sometimes referred to as a profit-volume chart. On the chart, line *ab* represents all fixed costs, S.G.& A. as well as manufacturing. The line *ab* is intended to be valid only in the anticipated production range, although it has been drawn as if fixed costs remained level even at zero production. Obviously, if a strike or other catastrophe shuts down a plant for an extended period, many fixed costs drop out. Line *cd* represents variable costs and rises from zero at a constant rate, reflecting the concept that variable costs rise in proportion to sales. Line *ae* represents total costs and is drawn parallel to line *cd* from the point where the fixed cost line, *ab,* crosses the *Y* axis. The sales line is *cf.* Sales in dollars is, of course, a variable in terms of sales in physical units.

The sales line, *cf,* intersects the total cost line, *ae,* at point *g,* which represents the breakeven point. The intersection of this point with the X axis gives the breakeven point in units, point *j,* and its intersection with the *Y* axis gives the breakeven point in dollars, point *k.* The distance between the forecast sales level, *h,* and any lower breakeven sales level is referred to as the margin of safety. Sales could fall this far without causing the company to go into the red.

The breakeven formula uses the marginal contribution concept of direct costing. The breakeven point is that point at which the average marginal contribution per sales dollar times the actual sales dollars

FIGURE 7-2. Breakeven chart and formula.

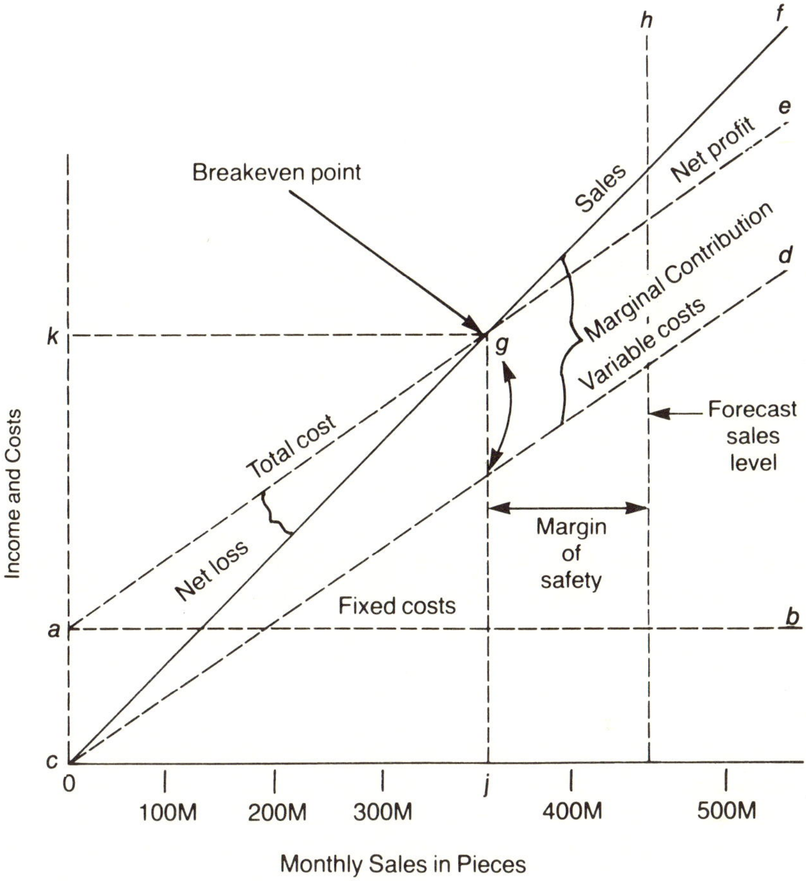

Unit marginal contribution = Unit sale price − Variable cost of unit sale
Breakeven is reached when Unit marginal contribution × Units sold = Total fixed costs

equals the company's total fixed costs. In this formula, the marginal contribution is, as already stated, the difference between the average sales dollar and the average variable costs of the sale.

In addition to indicating the breakeven point and the margin of safety, breakeven charts help management visualize the relationship between fixed costs and total costs at various operating levels. They also show graphically the profit improvement that can be expected from volume changes.

Breakeven charts can be prepared for the company as a whole or for a division, a product line, or any department that generates revenue. When charts are prepared for anything less than the whole company, the question arises as to what should properly be shown as fixed costs. Under absorption costing, fixed costs are usually allocated to divisions, product lines, and departments. These costs include charges from the corporate office, charges for building and machinery depreciation specific to the segment that has been committed and cannot readily be changed (often called sunk costs), and charges for fixed salaries and items like heat that are specific to the segment but that can be changed. A good argument can be made for omitting all three of these categories, thus converting the breakeven chart to a mere graph of marginal contributions. In practice, most companies on absorption costing show all three types of fixed costs, although they recognize that segment operations below the breakeven point developed on this basis may still be contributing to corporate costs and the sunk costs of the segment.

Most breakeven charts are constructed from data in the cost accounting system. Last year's sales or this year's forecast sales of each product in units is extended by the average sales price to give the sales line, and by the variable cost as shown on the product standard cost sheets to give the variable cost line. The fixed costs are taken from the appropriate general ledger accounts. This can be done under a direct cost system or under an absorption cost system that splits variable from fixed costs.

Another approach is to list actual sales and actual profits for a number of past periods in order to develop the cost of sales and S.G.& A. for each period. The total cost line can then be determined by using a scatter chart or the least-squares formula (described for another purpose in Chapter 4). This method is accurate under a direct cost system, but it may be inaccurate under an absorption cost system, since cost of sales is affected by changes in the level of finished-goods inventory. The use of production costs related to production is also inaccurate under an absorption cost system because it fails to recognize S.G.& A. costs that vary with sales rather than with production.

It must be remembered that a breakeven chart is valid only as long as sales prices remain constant and product mix does not change. In one case, a company was able to sell more in dollars than it had originally forecast despite an industrywide price war. However, the loss of profits through price cutting more than offset the increase in sales. In another case, a company was having difficulty at midyear in meeting its sales forecast. In order to correct the situation, the company began to promote aggressively a product line with a low marginal contribution percentage. By year end its total sales had returned to the level of the annual sales forecast, but profits in the second half of the year were even worse than those in the first half. An analysis showed that some of the sales of the low-margin product line had been generated by a reduction in sales of the company's more profitable product lines, and the net result was a disaster.

A final point on breakevens. It is not unusual to hear an executive reject a low-price order with the statement, "If we had only reached our breakeven point, I would take this order, because it would add to profits. However, since we are still below our breakeven, I just can't afford to do so." Such a statement shows a basic misunderstanding of the profit-volume relationship. If accepting an order after the breakeven point has been reached will add X dollars to profit, then accepting the order below the breakeven point will reduce losses by X dollars. The question of the merits of accepting or rejecting low-price orders has been discussed in detail in Chapter 5. The only matter that should be considered is whether the sale has dollars above its variable costs which can be used to help cover fixed costs.

Business Modeling

Business modeling, sometimes referred to as simulation or as profit planning, is a technique for thinking up imaginative changes in policies and operations and then calculating on paper the effect of the changes on future profits. When the phrase "profit planning" came into use some 15 years ago to describe this technique, it became confused with the idea of budgeting. Some public relations type discovered that the word "budget" carried unfortunate connotations to many people. A budget is what you put your family on and they hate you for it. Also, many people are first introduced to budgeting through a restrictive budget, which is indeed hard to live with. Accordingly, without being aware that a technique called profit planning existed, the public relations man suggested that his company henceforth refer to its budget as its profit plan. The idea caught on, and many companies today use this term. The resulting confusion set profit planning, as it will be described below, back about ten years. Actually, some degree of profit planning goes into the preparation of many budgets, particularly when the first draft shows an unsatisfactory profit. However, there are real differences between this type of budget revision and the technique described below. These differences will be covered after profit planning has been more fully explained.

Figure 7-3 shows a simplified example of profit planning (business modeling). The exercise starts with the preparation of the preliminary profit plan, shown in the first column. This column reflects nothing more and nothing less than would be shown in an annual budget. Basically, the figures are prepared from the prior year's income statement, adjusted for the annualization of known changes that occurred during the year. For example, if an across-the-board wage increase of 4 percent occurred at midyear as the start of a two-year contract, it may be assumed that average wages in the coming year will be approximately 2 percent higher than last year's average wages. The first column also reflects known changes that will occur in the coming year. If a piece of labor-saving machinery is on order for delivery at the end of the first quarter, the figures should reflect both the labor saving and the depreciation increase for three quarters of the year. Sales and cost trends will also be used in estimating the figures. None of this differs from ordinary methods of preparing an annual forecast or budget.

The next step usually involves a meeting of the company's top executives. Each is asked to make suggestions on what might be done to improve profits. For example, after reviewing the first column in Figure 7-3, the sales manager may observe, "I always knew Product B had a higher margin than Product A, but I never realized how much higher it was. Perhaps we could shift some of the sales effort now going into Product A to Product B. No, on second thought, that won't work, because we would probably lose $200,000 in sales of Product A to get $150,000 additional Product B sales. You know, increased sales are harder to get than renewals."

Such a manager may also have in mind the fact that if he ever wants to change jobs, an overall sales decrease won't look too good on his résumé. The president, however, wants to see how such a shift in sales would affect profits. The second column shows this first revision of the profit plan, tracing the effect of the decrease in Product A sales and the increase in Product B sales through every account that would be affected. The result is a near tripling of profit, despite the decrease in total sales.

At this point, the advertising manager suggests an increase of $25,000 in the advertising budget, all to be directed to Product B. The sales manager feels that this would add $100,000 to Product B sales. The president finds it difficult to justify costs of advertising alone

FIGURE 7-3. Working of the annual profit plan.

	Preliminary Profit Plan	*First Revised Profit Plan*[a]	*Second Revised Profit Plan*[b]	*Third Revised Profit Plan*[c]
Net Sales				
Product A	$1,000,000	$ 800,000	$ 800,000	$ 696,000
Product B	1,000,000	1,150,000	1,250,000	1,600,000
Total	$2,000,000	$1,950,000	$2,050,000	$2,296,000
Variable Cost of Sales at Standard				
Product A	$ 600,000	$ 480,000	$ 480,000	$ 360,000
Product B	400,000	460,000	500,000	800,000
Subtotal	1,000,000	940,000	980,000	1,160,000
Other Variable Costs				
Estimated Variances[d]	90,000	84,600	88,200	104,400
S.G.&A. Expenses[e]	100,000	97,500	102,500	114,800
Total Variable Costs	1,190,000	1,122,100	1,170,000	1,379,200
Marginal Contribution	$ 810,000	$ 827,900	$ 879,300	$ 916,800
Fixed Costs				
Manufacturing Expenses	$ 400,000	$ 400,000	$ 400,000	$ 410,000
Advertising	150,000	150,000	175,000	200,000
Other S.G.&A. Expenses	250,000	250,000	250,000	250,000
Total Fixed Costs	800,000	800,000	825,000	860,000
Net Profit before Taxes	$ 10,000	$ 27,900	$ 54,300	$ 56,800

[a] The first revision reflects the statement of the sales manager that he can persuade certain customers to buy $150,000 in Product B, but in doing so he will lose $200,000 in Product A sales.

[b] The second revision reflects the statement of the advertising manager that a $25,000 additional advertising expense for Product B will produce $100,000 in additional sales volume.

[c] The third revision reflects the president's opinion that a 16% price increase on Product A would result in a 25% decrease in physical unit sales; a 20% price decrease on Product B together with a $25,000 increase in Product B advertising would result in a 60% increase in sales of Product B; and the added production would necessitate an increase of $10,000 in fixed manufacturing overhead.

[d] Estimated at 9% of cost of sales at standard.

[e] Estimated as 5% of sales.

which run to 25 percent of the sales resulting from it, but he asks to see how the figures would come out. As indicated in the third column of Figure 7-3, the profit resulting from this second revision is almost double that of the previous revision.

Finally, the president suggests a change in prices to bring the percentage margins on the two products closer together, along with an additional increase in advertising. The details of the proposed changes are given in note *c* of Figure 7-3, and the estimated resulting income statement is presented in the last column of the figure. The profit increase from the prior revision is only $2,500. The group may well decide that this increase is too small to justify the risks inherent in changing prices, particularly since it is often difficult to change prices back again if expected results don't occur. Also, the third revision requires substantial extra working capital, since total costs have increased more than $240,000 over the prior calculation. This obviously raises an ROI question that was not worth considering in the first two revisions.

Figure 7-3 is limited to three suggestions for illustrative purposes. In practice, a dozen or more suggestions would probably be considered, and each one might be tried at several levels. For example, the advertising on Product B could be increased by $10,000 increments to $150,000 as variations of the second revision. Furthermore, the three changes in the third revision could be tried out separately and in each of the three possible combinations of two suggestions. These, too, could be tested at various levels. With 12 suggestions tried out at, say, six levels, it would be possible to create tens of thousands of trial income statements. Since few companies have as short a product line as that illustrated in Figure 7-3, the task of doing a thorough profit-planning job on a manual basis becomes mind-boggling. In fact, when the technique was introduced in the early 1960s, most companies limited themselves to testing half a dozen basic suggestions, usually at one level, without trying all possible combinations.

In the late 1960s and early 1970s, computers came into the field in a big way. Usually, the computerized technique is called simulation or business modeling rather than profit planning. Today, many companies have their own computer programs for carrying out business modeling. Others, even many with large computers, prefer to use time-sharing computer service bureaus. The time-sharing bureau supplies instructions to the company so that it can quickly feed the facts into the bureau's program, which will create the basic rules on which changes in which accounts will affect other accounts and, if so, how they will be affected. Thus, once the preliminary income statement is in storage in the computer along with the set of rules, the insertion of a single card altering one or more of the figures in the income statement will generate a whole new statement. Generally, in order to save computer or terminal printer time, only the net profit figures for the various trials are printed until the results are of sufficient interest to warrant a detailed printout for analysis and review. Only since business modeling has been put on the computer has it begun to approach its full potential.

Some of the computer programs developed for business modeling can also be used to prepare projected balance sheets and pro forma source and application of funds statements. Thus the added profits can be viewed in the light of total investment and cash flow. Obviously, some suggestions that appear to make sense from a profit viewpoint will prove unworkable for various reasons (for example, because of loan agreements that require certain current ratios). In addition, the same computer program can often be used to prepare monthly financial statements, including year-to-date information and comparisons with the prior year or the forecast or both.

Currently, very few companies are using either probability theory or sensitivity analysis in business modeling, although a number use both in evaluating major capital projects. Briefly, probability theory assigns a probability percentage to each level of the dependent variable. The percentages assigned must add to 100. Thus, in the second revision of Figure 7-3, the sales manager might say that the addition of $25,000 in advertising has a 20 percent chance of increasing sales by $150,000, a 45 percent chance of increasing them by $100,000, and a 35 percent chance of increasing them by only $50,000. Each possibility is then run through to the net profit line. The net profit at the $150,000 sales increase is multiplied by .20, the net profit at $100,000 by .45, and the net profit at $50,000 by .35. The total of the three figures is a more accurate measure of adding the advertising than is the single figure at the most likely sales increase of $100,000.

Sensitivity analysis is probability theory applied to an area not directly subject to the change being considered. Thus, using sensitivity analysis, the president might ask what would happen to profits if the $25,000 increase in advertising did indeed produce $100,000 in additional sales but if, entirely independent of the advertising increase, the price of the raw material in Product B went up $.10, $.20, $.30, or $.40 per pound. Obviously, the $25,000 advertising cost would not change. However, assuming the selling price could not be raised, the expected profit from the increased sales would drop, thus raising the question of whether the advertising was justified. Each raw material price would be assigned a probability percentage, and the profits before and after the $25,000 advertising cost would be tested at each price at the appropriate probability percentage. The two totals would then be compared. For most companies, both probability theory and sensitivity analysis require the use of a computer because of the many interlocking variables involved and the number of calculations required.

As noted at the beginning of this section, even if a company is not consciously doing profit planning, it will probably attempt to improve the results shown in the first draft of the annual forecast income statement by doing some constructive thinking. Such an attempt, though worthwhile and potentially quite effective, is different from true profit planning in two important ways. The first difference consists of the extent of the work. In business modeling, many more ideas are tried out, including some that at first blush seem rather silly. The second and much more important difference is that the profit-planning approach is interfunctional.

In traditional budget reviews, each executive usually looks at his own function. The sales manager tries to think up ways to increase sales and gross profit margins; the production executive considers cost-cutting possibilities; and each subdepartment manager looks at the revenue and cost figures of his own department. Under profit planning, the discussion among top executives goes a long way toward ensuring that ideas which can benefit the company as a whole are considered, even if they appear to hurt the showing of one department. Thus the additional advertising expenditures in the second revision shown in Figure 7-3 will increase, not decrease, the costs under the advertising manager's control. Under the traditional budget review approach, the advertising manager might well restrict his thinking to ways of decreasing advertising costs while maintaining the company's share of the market. As demonstrated above, the broader approach pays off. Similarly, the manufacturing vice president might propose to add costs in his quality control department for the purpose of reducing sales returns.

Whether profit planning is done manually or by computer, the basic tool is the recognition that variable costs vary with volume and fixed costs do not. In other words, whether a company uses direct costing or absorption costing, for purposes of trial income statements it must separate variable costs from fixed. Company executives will generally find the application of business modeling easier and less confusing if they are oriented in terms of direct costs.

Summary

Budgeting is a very important part of management, and in a manufacturing business it is closely related to cost accounting. Breakeven analysis and breakeven charts are useful management tools and are also related to cost accounting. Profit planning (business modeling) has opened up a whole new vista to management and has given financial management in particular added responsibilities and opportunities. Business modeling is a perfect example of the type of management decision discussed in Chapter 2—one in which the net results for the company of making the decision one way are compared with the results of making it the other way. Finally, in all three areas discussed in this chapter—budgeting, breakeven analysis, and business modeling—direct costing appears to have substantial advantages over absorption costing.

8

Direct Costs in Management Decisions

THERE are many types of management decisions, ranging from the decision to purchase a company as large as the company itself to the problem of working half a dozen people overtime one evening to complete an order for a customer who has asked for shipment the next day as a special favor. Although in theory each of these decisions should be made through the preparation of alternative pro forma income statements, there are many times when much simpler approaches are satisfactory. Intangibles play a major part in many decisions, but these can be weighed more accurately if the basic effect on immediate net profit is known. This effect can often be calculated from a comparison of very limited cost data. As the examples in this chapter demonstrate, direct costing provides the most useful data for such evaluations.

Case Studies of Management Decisions

Most of the case studies below are disguised and simplified real-life problems that have come to our attention. It must be emphasized that the chances of exactly similar problems arising in any other company are slim. The cases have been selected to illustrate an approach that can be applied to almost any problem in any company, no matter how unusual the situation may be.

Case Study 1: Make-or-Buy

Figure 8-1 shows a wrong and a right calculation of whether to continue making a part for one of the company's end products or whether to purchase it from an outside source. Under the company's absorption costing system the part had a manufacturing cost of $4.00, as shown in the first column. The outside vendor was prepared to sell the part to the company for $3.50, for an apparent cost saving of $.50. Since the company used several hundred thousand of these parts each year, the saving appeared to be considerable.

The correct calculation is shown in the second column, using direct costing. Since that part of the 150 percent overhead on direct labor represented by the allocation of fixed costs ($1.05 in this illustration) would not be saved but would merely have to be allocated to other parts or assemblies, the cost saving of not manufacturing the part would be only $2.95. In other words, the total out-of-pocket cost of manufacturing the part is $2.95. Since this is $.55 less than the cost from the outside vendor, the company should continue to make the part. Of course, an analysis of the cost under an absorption cost system would result in the same answer, but the danger is that such an analysis would not be made and that the part cost of $4.00 as shown in the various reports would be compared with the vendor's price of $3.50.

Alert management might well question the decision to continue manufacturing the part without further study. Possibly the space and supervision presently used for the part could be more profitably em-

FIGURE 8-1. Wheel Reinventors, Inc.: Make-or-buy decision.

	Wrong	*Right*
Materials	$1.00	$1.00
Direct labor	1.20	1.20
Overhead at 150% of direct labor	1.80	
Variable overhead		.75
Total	$4.00	$2.95
Outside offer	3.50	3.50
Gain (loss) from outside purchase	$ .50	($ .55)

ployed in making some other part that is currently being bought outside because of space limitations. Certainly, if capacity is being so fully utilized that expansion is being considered, management might do well to see if the expansion, with its concomitant increase in fixed costs, could be postponed by buying this and possibly some other parts outside. Manufacturing management might also wonder whether the outside vendor has developed some production methods that enable it to sell a part, presumably at a profit, at less than the company's cost. However, the vendor's costs may be low because he is operating in his garage or because he is using his family as his labor force, or for some other reason equally unsuitable to the company.

Case Study 2: Product Line Profitability

Figure 8-2 shows the gross profit on an absorption basis of the three product lines that make up the sales of a company. After analyzing the data in the top half of the figure, management decided to promote bureaus at the expense of chairs and succeeded in shifting $2,000 in sales from chairs to bureaus without changing the total sales of $30,000. Management expected a nice profit improvement and was surprised when profits dropped. As the bottom half of Figure 8-2 shows, profits could be expected to drop by 6.2 percent of the sales

FIGURE 8-2. Product line profitability, annual forecast.

	Total Company	*Chairs*	*Tables*	*Bureaus*
ABSORPTION COSTING				
Net Sales	$30,000	$12,000	$10,000	$8,000
Cost of Sales	21,200	9,000	7,000	5,200
Gross Profit ($)	$ 8,800	$ 3,000	$ 3,000	$2,800
Gross Profit (%)	29.3%	25%	30%	35%
S.G.& A. Costs	7,500			
Operating Profit	$ 1,300			
DIRECT COSTING				
Net Sales	$30,000	$12,000	$10,000	$8,000
Variable Costs				
Manufacturing Costs	15,800	6,000	5,300	4,500
S.G.& A. Expenses	1,500	600	500	400
Total Variable Costs	$17,300	$ 6,600	$ 5,800	$4,900
Marginal Contribution ($)	$12,700	$ 5,400	$ 4,200	$3,100
Marginal Contribution (%)	42.4%	45.0%	42.0%	38.8%
Fixed Costs	11,400			
Operating Profit	$ 1,300			

shifted, or $124. Thus management should have looked at the marginal contribution percentages and then shifted as much sales from bureaus to chairs as circumstances permitted.

The fact that the relation of the marginal contributions of the product lines is exactly the reverse of the relation of their gross profits is, of course, caused by the higher fixed costs required to manufacture chairs as compared with those required for bureaus. Management might well consider that the recovery of these fixed costs is essential and therefore chairs are not really more profitable than bureaus. However, fixed costs by definition are related to time rather than production, so a management decision to promote chairs would be a valid one.

Case Study 3: Use of Overtime

Figure 8-3 represents a rather unique problem. The company had a market well beyond its single-shift production capacity for its prod-

FIGURE 8-3. Use of overtime.

	Normal Workweek Without Overtime	*Saturday Shift*
INCORRECT APPROACH		
Selling Price per Unit	$ 10.00	$10.00
Costs		
Materials	$ 4.00	$ 4.00
Direct Labor	3.00	4.50
Overhead, S.G.& A.	2.90	2.90
Total Costs	$ 9.90	$11.40
Profit (Loss)	$ .10	$(1.40)
CORRECT APPROACH		
Selling Price per Unit	$ 10.00	$10.00
Direct Costs		
Materials	$ 4.00	$ 4.00
Direct Labor	3.00	4.50
Variable Overhead, S.G.& A.	.80	1.20
Total Direct Costs	$ 7.80	$ 9.70
Contribution to Fixed Costs and Profits	$ 2.20	$ .30
Units Possible per Week/Saturday	1,000	200
Total Contribution	2,200.00	$60.00
Fixed Costs Excluding Interest	2,100.00	-0-
Profit (loss) Excluding Interest	$100.00	$60.00
Interest Expense	$130.00	-0-
Net Profit (loss)	$(30.00)	$60.00
Total Net Profit with Saturday Shift	$30.00	

uct at $10 but, because of a special situation, no market at all above that price. Furthermore, the company was located in a small town with such a limited labor supply that second-shift operation was impossible, as was any complex plan of operating seven days a week with 40-hour employees by staggering workweeks. At the time, the company was producing 1,000 units per week at an operating profit of $.10 each, or $100. However, interest costs of $130 were shown below operating profit, so that the net each week was a $30 loss.

The company was aware that its employees would have been glad to work Saturdays at time and a half, but it had determined, as shown in the top half of Figure 8-3, that Saturday production would show a substantial operating loss. This appeared to be true even though unit overhead had not been increased to reflect any extra overhead required by the higher labor cost.

Because the company had been showing a loss for a number of months and saw no way to improve the situation, an outside consultant was called in. He quickly analyzed the manufacturing overhead and the S.G.& A. accounts into their fixed and variable components. The results are shown in the lower half of Figure 8-3. For conservatism, variable overhead in this calculation is shown as rising in proportion to the labor increase, including the overtime premium. This will not occur with every part of overhead ordinarily considered variable. For example, medical insurance costs are usually based on number of employees rather than on amounts paid to them. There is a strong possibility that neither holiday nor vacation pay would reflect overtime premiums and might even be based on a five-day week. As a result of this analysis, Saturday work was instituted. The following month, the company was in the black for the first time in many months and continued to be so.

This management decision illustrates an interesting point about overtime. Assume a worker is paid $6.00 per hour for time within the 40-hour week. It appears that any work over 40 hours will cost $3.00 per hour more because of the 50 percent overtime premium. However, most workers today receive fringe benefits of 20 to 30 percent of base pay. These benefits include FICA, unemployment insurance, pensions, medical insurance, holiday pay, vacations, and sick pay. For purposes of illustration, assume a company's fringe benefit package is 25 percent of base pay. In this case, the worker is costing the company $7.50 for every $6.00 he earns. However, when he works overtime many of these benefits don't go up. FICA will apply to his extra earnings, but medical insurance and probably unemployment insurance will not. Depending on the union contract or, in the case of nonunion companies, the company policy, holiday pay and vacation pay may reflect average earnings. But by no means is this always true. The pension cost may be based on total earnings or merely guarantee a certain annual payment.

Under these circumstances, the fringe benefit on the $9.00 overtime pay is more likely to be 10 percent than 25 percent and may be lower. Assuming it is 10 percent, total pay for an overtime hour is $9.00 plus 10 percent, or $9.90. Thus the increase over a straight-time hour costing $7.50 is not $3.00 per hour but only $2.40 per hour *and* this includes a major portion of variable overhead.

Case Study 4: Two-Man Setups

Figure 8-4 shows the calculation used to arrive at the conclusion that the company involved would be well advised to use two workers to set up its bottleneck machines—in this instance, a machine called a boltmaker. Although this company was in an entirely different industry and section of the country than the company in Case Study 3, it faced the same situation in that it could market in excess of capacity but could not raise prices. However, in this case, the company was operating on three shifts and was in a position to hire more labor if needed.

A suggestion was made that two workers might be able to set up a machine twice as fast as one because certain parts of the setup operation were very clumsy for one worker to handle. A number of setups

FIGURE 8-4. Hypothetical analysis of profitability of using two workers on setups.

Assume that one worker can do a boltmaker setup in two hours.

—He is paid $3 per hour and fringes are 20%, for a total of $3.60 per hour or $7.20 for the job.

—It is found that one worker with a helper can do the same setup in 1½ hours. To keep it simple, assume that the helper is also paid $3 per hour. The setup now costs 3 man-hours at $3.60, or one man-hour more than with one worker. In other words, the extra cost is $3.60.

The machine, however, is back in service a half-hour earlier than it would have been with a one-worker setup. Assume that in this half-hour it produces an average of 1,500 pieces of a part; this part has an overall selling price of $15 per thousand. Thus, with two workers the company can sell $22.50 more than it otherwise would. This is not to say that the one machine alone does this, but we are assuming that boltmakers are the bottleneck operation.

If the company has a gross margin of 20% on the average, it has increased profits by $4.50 by spending $3.60.

---

were timed using one worker and then using two. Unfortunately, the idea that two workers could halve the time turned out to be a very bad guess. Only a quarter of the time was saved. Accordingly, production management reported that costs would be increased by one man-hour (or $3.60) if the idea was implemented and recommended against the change.

However, further analysis revealed that the time taken to make the setups was reducing productive capacity, which in this company resulted in an equivalent reduction in sales. The amount of sales added by the use of the second worker was conservatively estimated at $22.50 per setup. Since the company's product had a marginal contribution of 20 percent, the gain in profit was $4.50 compared with a cost increase of $3.60 or a net gain of $.90 per setup. This saving looks small, but since the company had over 100 setups per day, the annual total came to well over $20,000 for this minor change.

This case relates to the use of the marginal contribution percentage in direct costing. Had the gross profit percentage under absorption costing been used, the company would almost certainly have rejected the two-worker concept and failed to realize the $20,000 profit increase.

Case Study 5: Standby Workers

The company described in Case Study 4 faced another problem: absenteeism among that group of workers which alone, under union rules, was permitted to operate the boltmakers and headers. (A header has the same function as a boltmaker but performs only one of the operations required to make a bolt; a boltmaker performs virtually all of them.) A study of the amount of absenteeism was made, and the results are shown in Figure 8-5. The question raised was whether it would increase company profits to staff each shift with 23, 24, or more employees in this union category to avoid the loss in sales that occurred when one of the 22 machines was idle because of absenteeism. The calculations shown in Figure 8-5 led to the conclusion that one extra operator would be profitable whereas two would not. Note that the approach involves not only the marginal contribution concept (as in Case Study 4) but also probability theory, a concept that is not likely to be well understood outside the financial department of the average company.

An interesting footnote to this case study is that the production manager was intrigued by the result but pointed out that absenteeism tended to be higher on the evening and night shifts than on the day shift. The personnel records were reanalyzed by individual shifts and a separate calculation was made for each. With this refinement, the

FIGURE 8-5. Hypothetical analysis of profitability of having standby production workers.

—Assume that the crew needed to man the boltmakers and headers on any one shift is 22.
—Assume that a check of attendance records shows that:
There are no absences 30% of the time
There is one absence 35% of the time
There are 2 or more absences 35% of the time
—Assume that an idle machine causes the company to lose sales figured at 3,000 pieces per hour for 5 hours out of the 8. These 15,000 pieces, at a selling price of $15 per thousand, are worth $225 in sales dollars. If gross margin is 20%, this is $45 in profit.

If an extra worker were brought in at $3.60 per hour for 8 hours, the cost would be $28.80. This would be wasted 30% of the time for a loss of $8.64, against a gain of 70% of $45, or $31.50.

A second extra worker would be wasted 65% of the time, for a loss of $18.70. He would add to profits 35% of $45, or $15.75. Unless the wasted time could be used in some way, the addition would not be worthwhile.

---

company found that one standby operator was still justified for the day shift but two each were justified for the evening and graveyard shifts.

Case Study 6: Projection of a Very New Product Line

The top half of Figure 8-6 shows the projection into 1978 made by the controller of a company's baby carriage product line, which it had begun early in 1977. The projection was made very late in 1977 when results for the full year could be accurately estimated. The company had been manufacturing machine guns for the Army and Air Force for some years and expected to continue to do so but had branched out into a civilian product in a probably unwarranted fear of peace. Historical data indicated that costs of machine guns fluctuated violently with sales volume. In fact, the doubling of unit sales between 1976 and 1977 had turned a $350,000 loss into a $400,000 profit.

In making the projection for baby carriages, the controller noted that unit overhead costs of machine guns had dropped by one-third when production doubled, as had unit S.G.& A. expenses. The controller had reviewed the sales forecast on baby carriages and was satisfied with the 1978 figure of 20,000 units, compared with first-year sales in 1977 of only 5,000 units. In order to be conservative, he applied the same one-third drop in unit costs the company had experienced when machine gun sales doubled to the projected quadrupling of baby carriage sales. This turned the 1977 loss on baby carriages of $35,000 into a respectable profit of $80,000.

FIGURE 8-6. The Highly Diversified Co., Inc.: Profit projection.

	Machine Guns		Baby Carriages	
	Actual		*Actual*	*Projection*
	1976	*1977*	*1977*	*1978*
Sales in Units	1,000	2,000	5,000	20,000
Incorrect Approach				
Sales	$2,000,000	$4,000,000	$250,000	$1,000,000
Material	300,000	600,000	90,000	360,000
Labor	400,000	800,000	30,000	120,000
Overhead	900,000	1,200,000	90,000	240,000
Overhead per unit	$900	$600	$18	$12
Percentage Decrease in Overhead per unit		33.3%		33.3%
Total Cost of Sales	1,600,000	2,600,000	210,000	720,000
Gross Profit	400,000	1,400,000	40,000	280,000
S.G.& A.	750,000	1,000,000	75,000	200,000
S.G.& A. per unit	$750	$500	$15	$10
Percentage Decrease in S.G.& A. per unit		33.3%		33.3%
Net Profit	$ (350,000)	$ 400,000	$ (35,000)	$ 80,000
Correct Approach				
Sales	$2,000,000	$4,000,000	$ 250,000	$1,000,000
Material	300,000	600,000	90,000	360,000
Labor	400,000	800,000	30,000	120,000
Variable Overhead	300,000	600,000	75,000	300,000
Fixed Overhead	600,000	600,000	15,000	15,000
Total Cost of Sales	1,600,000	2,600,000	210,000	795,000
Gross Profit	400,000	1,400,000	40,000	205,000
Variable S.G.& A. Expenses	250,000	500,000	45,000	180,000
Fixed S.G.& A. Expenses	500,000	500,000	30,000	30,000
Total S.G.& A.	750,000	1,000,000	75,000	210,000
Profit (Loss) before Taxes	$(350,000)	$ 400,000	$(35,000)	$ (5,000)

One evening the controller laid the forecast shown in the top half of Figure 8-6 on the president's desk. That night he began to have some doubts, so the next morning he asked his cost accountant to review the figures. Although the company was using absorption costing, the cost accountant was aware of the contribution direct costing could make to problems of this type. Accordingly, he split both overhead and S.G.& A. into their fixed and variable components on the basis of his knowledge and prepared the projection shown in the bottom half of Figure 8-6. As a result, the controller's original projection of a 1978 profit of $80,000 from baby carriages became a loss of $5,000.

This result came about because of differences in production between machine guns and baby carriages. Machine guns were being produced on heavy machinery in an owned plant. Furthermore, production required heavy staffing of design engineers, inspectors, plant security, and production scheduling personnel. Selling expense consisted of trips by the company president to the Pentagon once or twice a year. By contrast, baby carriages were basically an assembly operation of purchased parts in rented quarters. Labor was unskilled and required a strawboss for every few added workers. The proposed increase in sales would require the rental of additional space. Baby carriage sales were on commission. When these differences were taken into account, it became apparent that the cost accountant's figures were quite accurate.

To emphasize the problem, the cost accountant prepared the breakeven charts shown in Figure 8-7. The baby carriage chart indi-

FIGURE 8-7. Breakeven diagrams; The Highly Diversified Co., Inc.

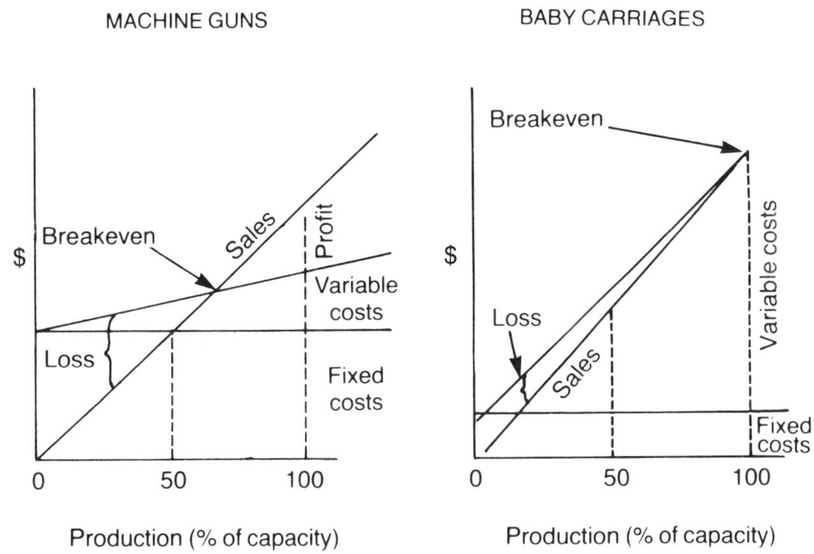

cated that profits would be minimal even if sales expanded well beyond the 20,000 units in later years. The president's first reaction was to abandon baby carriages altogether. However, the cost accountant pointed out that the chart also showed that volume was unimportant in the baby carriage business, whereas it was very important in the machine gun operation. Accordingly, the president asked the sales manager how volume would be affected by a price increase and possibly a reduction in consumer advertising. It turned out that a lower volume of baby carriages at a higher unit price could be quite profitable.

Case Study 7: Credit Policy

Figure 8-8 illustrates a credit-granting problem posed to a number of credit managers. Most said that orders from Groups 1 and 2 should be accepted and possibly some from Group 3. Many indicated that it

FIGURE 8-8. Hypothetical analysis of a credit-granting problem.

Assume that a company receives $1 million in orders in one month.
The companies from which these orders came break down into 5 groups:

Group 1	$900,000	Negligible credit risk
Group 2	25,000	Good credit history but borderline D&B rating
Group 3	25,000	Borderline credit history with the company and poor D&B rating
Group 4	25,000	Not paid for last shipment, poor D&B rating
Group 5	25,000	Not paid for last two shipments

The credit department estimates that:

Group 1 will result in .1% bad debts
Group 2 (if accepted) in 5% bad debts
Group 3 (if accepted) in 15% bad debts
Group 4 (if accepted) in 40% bad debts
Group 5 (if accepted) in 55% bad debts

Resulting bad-debt percentages for the company will be:

If only Group 1 is accepted (900/900,000), then .10%
If Groups 1 and 2 are accepted (2,150/925,000), then .23%
If Groups 1, 2, and 3 are accepted (5,900/950,000), then .62%
If Groups 1, 2, 3, and 4 are accepted (15,900/975,000), then 1.63%
If Groups 1, 2, 3, 4, and 5 are accepted (29,650/1,000,000), then almost 3.00%

The new credit manager looks at prior history and finds that his predecessor showed .5% bad debts for several years. Which orders should he accept?

was very difficult to calculate the odds on a particular customer being able to pay.

The same problem was presented to a group of cost accountants. They also voted for accepting orders from Groups 1 and 2 and some of the orders from Group 3. However, they were puzzled as to how this problem was relevant to cost accounting.

Granting that the problem noted by the credit managers in calculating odds on a particular customer is a very real one, if this can be done the correct answer depends on the company's marginal contribution percentage. If the company's marginal contribution is over 55 percent, all orders should be accepted. If the percentage is less than 55 percent but over 40 percent, orders from Groups 1 through 4 should be accepted. If the contribution margin is less than 40 percent but over 15 percent, orders from Groups 1 through 3 should be accepted. It is extremely unlikely that any company's marginal contribution would be under 15 percent on a direct cost basis.

Of course, this change in credit-granting policy will drive up bad debts in both dollars and percentages. However, it will also increase profits. For example, assume an order has a marginal contribution of 45 percent. This means that the cost to the company of accepting the order is the complement of 45 percent, or $55 on a $100 order. If, on the average, bad debts are only 40 percent in Group 4, then for every $100 sold to Group 4 customers $60 will be collected, or a clear addition to profits of $5 per $100 of orders accepted from Group 4 customers. Similarly a company with a marginal contribution percentage of 60 percent should accept the orders in Group 5.

The credit manager who makes such a change in policy should, of course, clear it with his superiors all the way up to the company president to avoid being blamed for any resulting increase in bad debts. To make the new policy effective, the credit manager should ask the cost accountant to supply him with the marginal contribution percentage on each product line. This is sufficiently unusual to have caused the foregoing reaction of the accountants. The credit manager will then be in a position to decide on borderline situations on the basis of the product being ordered.

A few words of caution. An order from a poor credit risk should never be accepted if it is likely to force the later rejection of an order from a top-credit customer because of production capacity limitations. Usually poor credit risks, if they pay at all, will delay payment. If such a delay will put the company in a cash bind, this fact must be considered. Possibly the $5 average profit in the example will not provide a sufficient return on investment to justify taking the orders.

Finally, it should be emphasized that nothing discussed here is relevant to collection efforts. Once an order has been shipped, the gain from collecting the receivable is the amount of the receivable and is unrelated to the cost of the shipment.

Case Study 8: Product Line Abandonment

Figure 8-9 shows the breakdown of a company's income statement into the income derived from each of its two product lines. The top part of the figure indicates that under absorption costing Product Line B is losing $65,000, thus reducing the $80,000 profit of Product Line A to a combined profit for the whole company of $15,000. It would appear that abandoning Product Line B would raise the company's profit to the $80,000 derived from Product Line A.

However, the same data under direct costing (the lower half of Figure 8-9) show a marginal contribution from Product Line B of $97,000, indicating that its abandonment would convert the company's profit of $15,000 to an $82,000 loss. This answer, too, is wrong. A special analysis shows certain facts not ordinarily reported under a direct cost system. These facts are that some fixed costs would disappear if Product Line B were abandoned, although they would not change with minor changes in the production or sales levels of Product Line B. Such costs include machinery used only on Product Line B, supervision in departments working only on Product Line B, specialty salesmen and advertising for Product Line B, and accounting personnel that would be surplus if only one product line were produced. These costs add to $80,000, reducing the real contribution of Product Line B to $17,000.

The profit figure of $17,000 may or may not be sufficient to justify continuance of Product Line B. The decision would depend on a number of factors, including whether another, more profitable product line could be brought in to replace Product Line B; whether the working capital that would turn into cash upon abandonment of the line could be used to reduce the stockholders' investment; and whether working capital invested in new machinery for Product Line A could improve Product Line A profits. Many companies feel that retaining a product line with such a small contribution perpetuates the unhealthy condition. Accordingly, they will abandon the line to, in effect, bring pressure on executives to make some worthwhile moves toward developing new products.

This case study, like all those preceding, illustrates the advantages of a direct cost approach over an absorption cost approach. It should be recognized that the same results can be obtained from an analysis of costs originally gathered in an absorption cost system, particularly

FIGURE 8-9. Product elimination decision.

	Total	*Product Line A*	*Product Line B*
INCORRECT APPROACH			
Sales	$900,000	$600,000	$300,000
Material	180,000	100,000	80,000
Labor	160,000	90,000	70,000
Overhead[a]	320,000	180,000	140,000
Subtotal	660,000	370,000	290,000
Gross Profit	$240,000	$230,000	$ 10,000
Selling Expenses[b]	75,000	50,000	25,000
G.&A. Expenses[b]	150,000	100,000	50,000
Subtotal	225,000	150,000	75,000
Net Profit	$ 15,000	$ 80,000	$(65,000)
CORRECT APPROACH			
Sales	$900,000	$600,000	$300,000
Variable Expenses			
Material	$180,000	$100,000	$ 80,000
Labor	160,000	90,000	70,000
Manufacturing Overhead	80,000	45,000	35,000
Selling Expenses	24,000	16,000	8,000
G.&A. Expenses	30,000	20,000	10,000
Subtotal	474,000	271,000	203,000
Marginal Contribution	$426,000	$329,000	$ 97,000
Fixed Expenses related to specific product lines[c]			
Manufacturing Overhead	$100,000	$ 50,000	$ 50,000
Selling Expenses	50,000	35,000	15,000
G.&A. Expenses	75,000	60,000	15,000
Subtotal	225,000	145,000	80,000
Profit before Company Expenses	$201,000	$184,000	$ 17,000
Company Fixed Expenses			
Manufacturing Overhead	$130,000		
Selling Expenses	11,000		
G.&A. Expenses	45,000		
Subtotal	186,000		
Net Profit	$ 15,000		

[a]The company's ratio of manufacturing overhead to direct labor is 200%. This ratio to actual direct labor charged to products has been used in allocating overhead to products.

[b]The company's ratios of S.G.&A. expenses to sales are 8.33% for selling and 16.67% for general and administrative expenses. These ratios have been used in allocating the S.G.&A. expenses to products.

[c]These expenses relate to machinery, floor space, executive personnel, and the like, which are used exclusively on one product or the other, but not both. They do not vary with production. The elimination of a product line may or may not eliminate its related fixed expenses.

one that segregates variable from fixed manufacturing overhead costs. However, as previously stated, direct costing has two advantages over an analysis of absorption cost figures. First, direct product costs include variable S.G.& A. expenses. Second, executives tend to think in terms of the total costs of product as shown by the system in use. Only under direct costing will the total product cost reflect variable product costs and exclude any allocation of fixed costs to products.

Case Study 8, in deducting certain fixed costs from the marginal contribution of Product Line B, is essentially a simplified example of relevant costing in an analysis to determine if a product line should be abandoned. Relevant costing is not a system of cost accounting but rather an approach to using costs in management decisions. It recognizes that the only costs that are *relevant* to a decision are those which will be different depending on which way the decision is made. Frequently, fixed costs will change as well as variable costs, but the important point is that only some fixed costs will change. Absorption costing is based on the assumption that all fixed costs will change, which is never true. It has been found that it is much easier to add the relevant fixed costs to data developed under a direct cost system than to subtract the nonrelevant costs from data prepared under an absorption cost system. A similar problem in relevant costing with a few more complications is presented below.

Case Study 9: Product Line Abandonment II

Figure 8-10 shows the income statement of Product Line X in a company with a number of product lines. Initially, a direct cost approach showed a respectable marginal contribution of $175,000 on $500,000 in sales. However, this product line was so different from the company's other products that it required special machinery for almost all processes and was produced primarily in production departments that did nothing else. This fact was recognized by segregating the fixed costs that applied only to Product Line X, as shown in the lower part of the first column of Figure 8-10. It then appeared that rather than contributing $175,000 to company fixed expenses, the product line was actually costing the company $20,000, even before any joint expenses were allocated to it.

However, the second column in Figure 8-10 shows a somewhat different picture resulting from a more careful study. As the notes to the figure indicate, certain costs that are related only to Product Line X will nevertheless remain after it is abandoned. Because of this, the negative contribution will actually be $32,000 greater if the line is abandoned than if it is retained.

FIGURE 8-10. Special analysis of product elimination decision.

	Product X	*Expenses Remaining If Product X Is Dropped*
Sales	$500,000	
Variable Expenses		
Materials	$120,000	-0-
Labor	120,000	-0-
Manufacturing Overhead	60,000	-0-
Selling Expenses	10,000	-0-
G.&A. Expenses	15,000	-0-
Subtotal	325,000	-0-
Marginal Contribution	$175,000	
Fixed Expenses Related to Specific Product Line		
Foreman (age 60)	$ 10,000	$ 5,000[a]
Assistant Foreman	20,000	-0-
Other Indirect Labor	40,000	2,500[b]
Depreciation Tools and Dies	15,000	15,000[c]
Depreciation Plating Tanks	15,000	15,000[d]
Depreciation Electric Trucks	15,000	-0-
Personal Property Taxes on Equipment	30,000	-0-
Assistant Sales Manager (age 55)	15,000	5,000[e]
Sales Office Personnel	15,000	-0-
Credit Manager (age 30)	10,000	-0-
Repair and Clerks	10,000	10,000[f]
Subtotal	$195,000	$ 52,500
Profit before Company Fixed Expenses	$(20,000)	$(52,500)

[a]The foreman would have to be pensioned at half salary.
[b]One worker is considered too old to retrain for other work. He will have to be pensioned at $2,500 per year.
[c]The tools and dies have several more years of life but would have to be scrapped if the product were discontinued. The annual charge is shown here for convenience.
[d]The plating tanks cannot be moved or used for other work. Therefore they are treated in the same way as tools and dies.
[e]The assistant sales manager will have to be pensioned.
[f]The company will require the services of two clerks for several years to handle repairs on Product X now in the hands of customers. This is a loss operation and has always been charged to Product X rather than to the company as a whole.

In this example, even more than in Case Study 8, the company will presumably make every effort to find a more profitable product to absorb the fixed costs now related to Product Line X. In fact, it may well abandon the line anyway rather than buy new tools and dies when the current ones wear out. The same applies to the plating tanks. It should be kept in mind that under the income tax law a company will always get a substantial percentage of the undepreciated book value of scrapped fixed assets.

Case Study 10: Substitute Materials

Figure 8-11 shows a comparison of the costs associated with two different materials from which a part could be made when the choice of materials also affects the operations required. The top half of the figure is an analysis under absorption costing, the bottom half is an analysis of relevant costs.

Note that the relevant costs do include some fixed costs. The sheet

FIGURE 8-11. The Worm Can Opener Co.: Substitute materials.

	Unit Costs If Castings Are Used	*Unit Costs If Sheet Metal Is Used*
ABSORPTION COSTING		
Materials		
Castings	$3.00	
Sheets		$2.50
Regular screws	.40	
Self-tapping screws		.30
Direct labor		
Drilling	.30	
Countersinking	.20	
Tapping	.50	
Stamping		.50
Overhead at 200% of direct labor	2.00	1.00
Total Cost	$6.40	$4.30
RELEVANT COSTING		
Materials (as above)	$3.40	
Direct labor (as above)	1.00	.50
Overhead		
Fringe benefits, at 40% of direct labor	.40	.20
Perishable tools	.15	
Depreciation		
Stamping press		.60
Stamping die		.80
Inspector		.30
Total relevant costs	$4.95	$5.20

metal operation will require an inspector as well as an additional stamping press. Drills and taps (perishable tools) are used on the castings. In contrast, the stamping die on the sheet metal has a short life, and its depreciation is considered a variable cost. Power consumption, machine repairs, factory supplies, and all other fixed costs are considered to be equal.

The absorption cost analysis shows an advantage to using sheet metal, but the correct analysis, based on relevant costs, is just as clearly in favor of using castings.

Inventory Management

Inventory management is a complex subject and is generally beyond the scope of this book. However, the economic lot size (ELS) and economic order quantity (EOQ) formulas (both mentioned in the discussion of budgeting in the previous chapter) involve four important terms for our present purposes:

Unit cost of the product.
Cost of placing a purchase order.
Cost of placing a production order, including the cost of setups.
Cost of storage.

All four of these factors should be given their values under direct cost concepts. To include in any of these factors costs that will not change regardless of the size or frequency of the production or purchase orders will give misleading answers. Thus, the full profit potential available through the ELS and EOQ formulas will not be realized.

Personal Investment Decisions

The discussions in Chapters 5, 6, and 7 all lead to the conclusion that an increase in sales has a greater effect on the profits of a company with a high proportion of fixed to variable costs than it does on a company with a low proportion of fixed to variable costs. Similarly, a decrease in sales has a greater negative impact on the profits of a company with high fixed costs than on one with low fixed costs. It might then be assumed that knowledgeable investors would switch their common stock holdings into high-fixed-cost companies in times of economic expansion and reverse the process when economic forecasts were gloomy. In order to follow such a policy, of course, investors would have to be able to identify the high-fixed-cost companies from their published income statements. This is rarely possible, although some conclusions can be drawn from the nature of the industry. Also, rough breakeven charts can be prepared from quarterly reports through the use of scatter charts and the least-squares formula (see Chapters 3 and 7).

Unfortunately, any conclusions drawn in this way may be misleading. Often the last-quarter statement of a company contains year-end adjustments which make the figure noncomparable to the interim quarters. More important, in most companies profits are influenced more by special factors than by the proportion of fixed to variable costs. These factors include acceptance by the market of new products, success of foreign operations, contract awards, changes in executive personnel, lawsuits (including antitrust suits), industry price wars, and labor union negotiations. Nevertheless, the proportion of fixed to variable costs is one factor to be considered along with many others in investment decisions. Certainly, a backlog of orders in those industries where orders precede shipment by a substantial period is a factor to weigh with the others, particularly in companies with high fixed costs.

Income Statements Based on Orders Received

Figure 5-4 in Chapter 5 showed a form used by one company to guard against improper price cutting. The concept behind this form —a marginal contribution statement based on orders received—has a much broader application in informing management of the health of the company month by month.

Under standard direct costing, it is perfectly possible to forecast profits accurately for as many months ahead as are contained in the sales order backlog. In industries that typically ship from stock already in finished-goods inventory, such an approach is meaningless; but in industries that have relatively long manufacturing cycles and that produce basically to the customer's order, the pro forma income statement based on orders received can provide much useful information to management. Direct standard costing is an important part of any such calculation.

Who Makes the Management Decisions?

Each of the ten management decisions presented in this chapter involves a thorough knowledge of the company's accounting system, including the exact meaning of each account title and the types of transactions which affect the account. In addition, the solutions require an ability to analyze figures with somewhat complex interrelationships. Accounting executives are much more likely to have this knowledge and ability than other company executives. Accordingly, any company that fails to obtain the thinking of, say, its controller in selecting an approach to the types of problems illustrated here may well be letting some potential profits slip away. In most cases, the analysis and advice of the controller will merely confirm the judgment of the executive most closely involved, in effect providing insurance against a wrong decision. In other instances, the analysis will cause the executive in charge to change his mind. It should be emphasized that the final decision is never the controller's.

The involvement of financial personnel in management decisions is growing. However, the degree of involvement varies widely from company to company and may even depend on chance—such as who is having lunch with whom on the particular day the problem arises. It is by no means easy for accounting personnel to participate in the decisions of other divisions, particularly when the custom has not yet been firmly established. Often accounting people do not even hear of the problem until long after the decision is made. In fact, they may never know that a choice existed. Certainly, a controller who demonstrates to an executive how wrong, not to say stupid, a contemplated decision is will be resented. Nobody enjoys being made to look like a fool. Executives tend to guard their prerogatives closely.

How, then, can financial people make sure they are consulted on management decisions that would benefit from their advice? A short answer is that they can't. However, they can use a number of techniques to ensure that they will be consulted more often. The choice of techniques depends to a large extent on the personalities of people both inside and outside the financial department, as well as on the personal relationships of those involved. Here are several possible approaches:

□ Have a social lunch with the marketing VP and, apropos of nothing, describe a successful analysis of a problem in the production area. Or have lunch with the manufacturing VP and describe a successful solution to a marketing problem.

□ Make an appointment with the marketing VP to review the revised standard product costs for the coming year. Comment on the implications of the fixed and variable elements.

□ Drop in on the purchasing agent to show him the revised standard product costs of parts and bring up their use in make-or-buy decisions.

□ Prepare an analysis of the savings resulting from a methods change recently instituted by the industrial engineer. Offer him a copy for submission to his superior.

Often, financial people come up with clever approaches of their own. In one company that had just installed its first computer, the controller ran off a list of last year's sales by customer in descending order of the volume of the company's sales to each. He then calculated the cumulative percentage of the company's sales on each line. The analysis was sent, without comment, to the sales manager. He took one look and came up with an idea of his own. As it happened, this was the very idea that the controller had been contemplating when he prepared the analysis, but he didn't say so. The analysis showed that the last 423 customers on the list accounted for the difference between 99 percent of total sales and 100 percent of total sales. The sales manager came to the conclusion that the profits derived from these 423 customers couldn't possibly cover the costs of servicing them. He then asked the controller to determine the gross margin and cost to service the next lowest group, consisting of 311 customers that together accounted for an additional 3 percent of sales.

Clearly, an interesting and successful analysis of one problem will lead to requests for assistance on subsequent problems. A controller who just happens to be in another executive's office when a phone call comes in on which he is able to offer sound advice will often be asked to advise on the next problem. When a problem is raised in an executive meeting and obviously requires advice from financial personnel, it may suggest other problems that would profit from the same type of analysis.

Summary

The range of management decisions that can benefit from consideration of their profit implications is virtually endless. In a manufacturing company, most of these profit implications relate to cost accounting. Many of the decisions can be based on the normal output of a direct cost system; others require analysis of data not regularly reported in any cost system. These problems can be more easily analyzed if the company is on a direct cost accounting system.

9

Setting Standards

A standard cost system uses predetermined standards for its accounting entries, as more fully described in Chapter 3. It is important not only that these standards be accurate but also that they include appropriate related costs in order to provide management with the most information. The fact that a company's system is a standard *direct* cost system does not change these requirements. In fact, the only difference in setting standards under absorption costing as opposed to direct costing is that the standards for fixed costs under absorption systems are allocated to departments and products.

This chapter will examine several methods for determining standards and the costs that are ordinarily included in each. The methods and rules described are common in industry and will offer certain advantages for most companies. However, there are many variations that also provide satisfactory results and that may be preferable in particular industries.

Types of Standards

Textbooks refer to three types of standards: ideal, base period, and attainable. Only attainable standards are in wide use today. We know of no company operating on ideal standards and only one company operating on base period standards. This company later converted to attainable standards. Because the philosophy of ideal standards occasionally creeps into a company's thinking on attainable standards, we will define ideal standards below. It should be emphasized, however, that their use in the early days of standard costing clearly demonstrated that the system was a poor one.

Ideal standards were set on the assumption of perfection or near perfection. Only the fastest operator's output was considered, and only at his most efficient time of day. Materials were assumed to be flawless and machines were considered to be operating perfectly. Under such a system, the comparison of actual costs with standard costs always showed unfavorable variances. They were likely to be quite large. A standard product cost was always much less than the real cost of producing the product. Although this system has been completely discredited, it is not unusual to hear an executive criticize a particular standard set on the "attainable" philosophy by pointing out that it is higher than the cost shown by a very good worker under favorable conditions. "If he can do it, everyone else should be able to. The standard should be reduced." If the suggestion is followed, the standard is no longer attainable.

The one company we know of that used base period standards also had a parallel set of attainable standards for certain purposes. The base standards had been set as attainable standards some 20 years earlier and were never changed. The fact that they were not changed over a very long period distinguishes this system from others. The manufacturing vice president used the old standards to determine whether the cost reductions achieved through improved methods were sufficient to offset the cost increases resulting from inflation in material costs and labor rates.

A good definition of an attainable standard is "that figure which will show as many favorable variances as unfavorable ones when considered in relation to the smallest unit being measured." The smallest unit being measured may be the production of one worker on a short job or on one day of a long job; the amount of material used on a job; or the level of an overhead account for the month. Even under such a definition, however, total variances are almost always unfavorable. This is because unfavorable variances tend to be larger in amount than favorable ones. Assume a standard of 100 pieces per hour. Under normal conditions a fast worker might be able to produce 120 pieces and a slower worker 80 pieces. However, the rate of 120 pieces per hour is the maximum. Any special problem such as faulty material, an erratic machine, or a Monday morning hangover could reduce either worker's production to 50 or 60 pieces. Thus, when a number of variances are combined, the total is almost sure to be unfavorable but probably by a relatively small amount.

Attainable standards have psychological as well as accounting advantages. The fact that many favorable variances are generated under attainable standards suggests to both workers and supervisors that the standards are fair. Workers do not become discouraged, feeling that they are up against an impossible target and that there is no sense trying to reach the standard. If praise is given for favorable variances, any criticism for unfavorable ones will be taken much more seriously. From a management and accounting view, attainable standards produce realistic standard product costs. Also, any sizable unfavorable variance is worth looking into, as it indicates a departure from realistic expectations.

Standards can also be classified as engineered (scientific) or historical. Engineered standards are set by an experienced and knowledgeable person, very often an industrial engineer, who determines the amount of material and the amount of labor each operation should take, with due allowance for normal waste and normal time losses.

Historical standards are set merely by assuming that the average cost of each part of the standard for some past periods is what is to be expected in the future. This approach has the merit of making the setting of standards fast and easy. In addition, no specially trained industrial engineers are required. However, these advantages are generally outweighed by the fact that such standards have built into them all the abnormalities, good and bad, of prior periods and are therefore a poor basis for determining whether current operations are being carried out at a reasonable cost. Historical standards may be justified in certain special cases—for example, when a company on standard costs acquires a company on actual costs and wishes to integrate it into the parent's standard cost system without taking the time to set engineered standards.

Today, a very high proportion of all companies on standard costs use engineered standards for direct materials and direct labor and a few overhead items such as perishable tools, machinery repairs, and setup costs. However, most overhead standards are set on a historical basis because there is no other way.

Occasionally, it is necessary to estimate standards. An estimated standard is merely an educated guess. It may be used on new products before there is an opportunity to make the study necessary to set a proper standard. An estimated standard may also be used when a product is made so infrequently and in such small quantities that the cost of a study is not justified and any inaccuracy will be so small in dollars that it can be ignored.

Cost is an important consideration in determining the time to be devoted to making a standard accurate. Accuracy should be greatest when the cost of the material or labor operation is expected to be highest annually. Two industrial engineers met one year after their college graduation. One had been doing time studies in a job shop in which the average operation was performed by one worker for half a day per year. Thus, the cost covered by each standard was very low. He reported having set 1,200 standards in the year. The other engineer had initially been assigned to an operation involving 25 workers throughout the year, a very heavy cost. He was still working on his first standard. Both men were applying the proper perspective to their very different situations.

Material Price Standards

Material price standards reflect average expected invoice prices of materials and generally include any incoming freight paid by the purchaser. In theory, they should also include an allocation of purchasing department costs, receiving department costs, and incoming inspection and handling costs; however, they rarely do, since the work involved is not justified by the accuracy obtained. Invoice costs are the usual source for these standards, although an average of sources may be used. Quantity discounts are always deducted on the basis of normal quantities purchased. Cash discounts should also be deducted, despite the desire of many financial people to consider cash discounts as financial income rather than a reduction in purchase price. Generally, any realization from expected sale of scrap is not considered. An exception is an item like X-ray film where the silver recovery realization is substantial compared with the cost of the film.

When materials that are usually bought from producers are bought from distributors in emergencies, the cost from the usual source of supply is used. For example, if steel is ordinarily purchased from the mill, the difference in cost when a steel service center is used should be considered a variance. On the other hand, if some types of steel are used in small quantities and are normally purchased from a service center, the center's price is used.

Sometimes a company is able to pick up distress material at a favorable price once or twice a year. Such a purchase would not be averaged into the standard but rather would create a favorable purchase price variance when it occurs. However, if distress material is available quite regularly, it should be reflected in the standard.

Slightly defective or off-standard material may also be available at a very favorable price. Such material frequently creates an unfavorable material quantity variance when it reaches production and will probably create an unfavorable direct labor quantity variance as well. In order to prevent production people from assaulting purchasing people, these related variances should be fully footnoted on the respective performance reports. In addition, some companies prepare a special report to show how net profits were affected by the unusual purchase. This type of report ordinarily requires data from production on the material quantity and labor quantity variances created by the lot of materials.

The most difficult problem in setting material price standards is determining the proper way to reflect price changes that are expected to occur in the upcoming year. This problem will be discussed later in the chapter in the section on changing standards. However, no matter how often material price standards are changed, the question remains as to whether the standard should reflect the price at the beginning of the year or quarter, or the estimated average price throughout the period. Both approaches are widely used. In an inflationary era, the former method virtually ensures a sizable unfavorable variance for the period. The latter method will ordinarily produce favorable variances during the first half of the period, probably offset by unfavorable variances in the second half of the period. The favorable variances in the first half of the period should be credited for internal reporting purposes to a reserve for future cost increases rather than to the income in the months in which they occur.

Material Quantity Standards

The material quantity standard reflects the amount of material needed to make the part or the product and includes normal waste. For example, if circular parts are to be stamped from rectangular metal sheets and it is possible to obtain ten 11¾″ circles from a 12″ × 120″ sheet, the standard is one-tenth the weight of the sheet, thus including not only the difference between the shape of the circle and the shape of the square but also the narrow side strip and the somewhat wider piece on the end that is wasted.

Figure 9-1 demonstrates a related problem. In this instance, the standard for material quantity for the 13½″ squares was set at 200 square inches (converted to pounds and then to dollars) because the

FIGURE 9-1. Use of sheet metal.

Standard size:
28″ x 100″
Standard output:
14 squares, 13½″ x 13½″
Square in. per square:
2,800 ÷ 14 = 200 sq. in.

Actual size:
36″ x 120″
Actual output:
16 squares, 13½″ x 13½″
Square in. per square:
4,320 ÷ 16 = 270 sq. in.

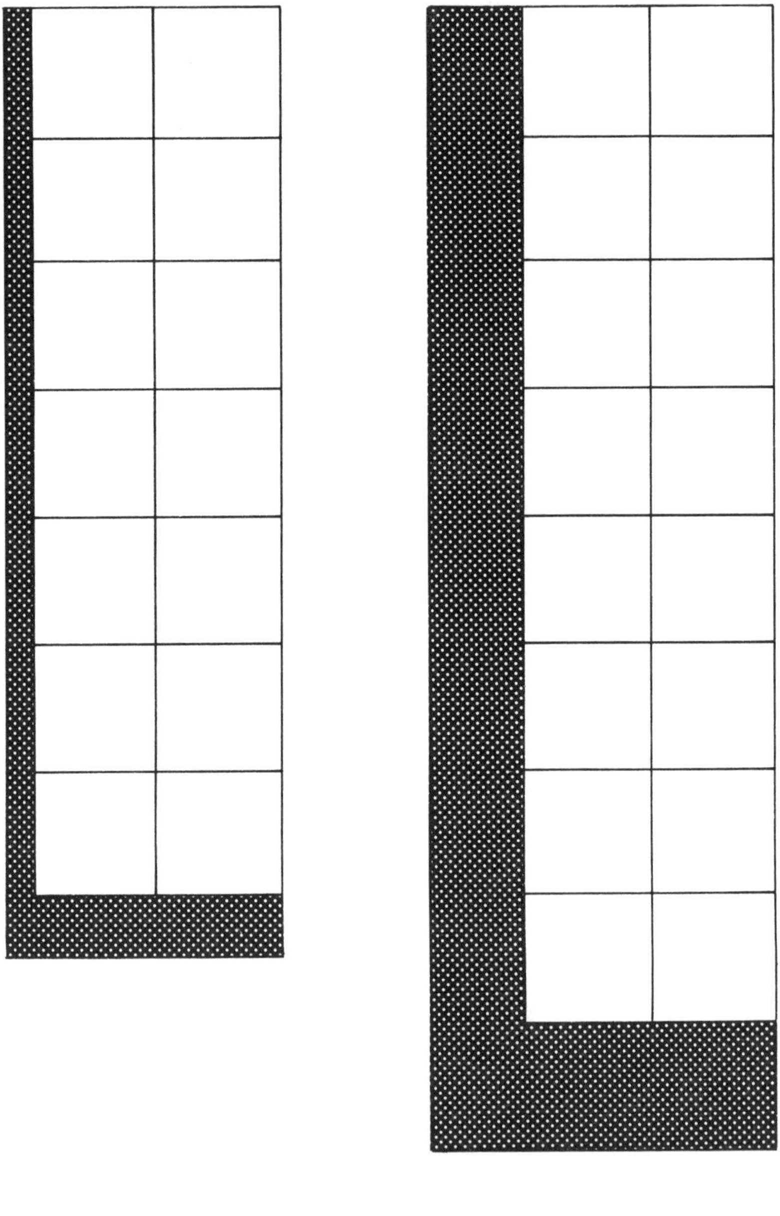

required material was available from the vendor in 28″ × 100″ sheets. However, when the part was run, the stockroom had only 36″ × 120″ sheets; these created much more waste, to the point where actual usage was 270 square inches. Furthermore, inventory control personnel indicated that, because of space limitations and the tieing up of capital, it would be impractical to stock all sizes of every gauge and specification that happened to cut most efficiently for some part. This might well be a wise decision, depending on the number of 13½″ squares required per year. In such a case, the proper standard would be 270 square inches. Still, every effort should be made to find other parts that could be cut from the 28″ × 100″ sheets in order to justify stocking them.

In addition, if the nature of the blanking die or the process is such that an average of 5 percent of the pieces are ruined, this waste should be included in the material quantity standard. If the waste pieces can be used to make some other part, the material price standard can be credited at the scrap value or the purchase price of material suitable for making the other part less the inefficiency involved in using single pieces rather than strips of new material. Generally, a material quantity standard includes only the scrap generated on the operation at which material enters the process. Scrap or spoilage on subsequent operations that the material may go through, even if it is considered normal for such operations, is generally charged to an overhead account labeled "scrap" or "spoiled work." Such an account is part of variable overhead. The part using the leftovers should not be charged with a combined material and labor figure higher than it would have to pay an outsider.

Material quantity standards are almost meaningless for control purposes when purchased parts are simply assembled into a product and when it is rare to get fewer than 100 products from every 100 parts. Material quantity standards have somewhat greater value when standardized material such as metal sheets are used to make standardized parts. They have their greatest value when nonstandard materials such as hides are used to make leather garment parts of many shapes and sizes, when textile fibers sold by weight are used to make yarn that will be used by the yard, and in similar situations.

It should be noted that some materials shrink in storage. Gasoline will show some loss through evaporation. Textile fibers and other hygroscopic materials may lose weight in a dry atmosphere. Since they are bought by the pound and requisitioned by the pound, any such loss will have to be included in the standard. Most powders and liquids delivered in containers have "cling losses"—that is, some material clings to the inside of the container and cannot be recovered. This too should be reflected in the material standard for the product.

This type of loss can be handled in several ways. It can be reflected in the price standard so that production can fairly compare pounds requisitioned with pounds allowed; it can be reflected in the quantity standard so that purchasing can compare prices paid with prices allowed; or it can be charged to an inventory reserve account shown separately on the product cost sheets. All three methods are in use, and the choice depends on management's objectives in measuring performance.

Direct Labor Rate Standards

The first rule of labor rate standards—the standard hourly pay rates assigned to particular types of direct labor—is that they are related to the job, not the worker. In other words, if a worker on a particular operation is paid a higher than normal rate because of seniority or some other reason, the average rate for those qualified to perform the job is used. Shift premiums are ordinarily added in, based on a weighted average of the number of workers on each shift.

A number of companies use an "inclusive" or "expanded" labor rate. Such a rate includes all fringe benefits and costs that are a percentage of payroll dollars (for example, social security taxes, pensions, unemployment taxes, vacation and holiday pay, health insurance, and workers' compensation insurance). Any company that finds recordkeeping easier under this approach should use it. Companies using an inclusive labor rate feel that it helps management see the total cost of direct labor more clearly and that elimination of the fringe costs from overhead makes it easier to observe fluctuations in the other overhead accounts. However, companies that do not use this approach seem to have no difficulty in viewing each overhead account individually. Accordingly, from either a control or management decision point of view, there are really no advantages to this approach compared with putting these fringes into variable overhead accounts.

Many companies feel that labor rate variances are likely to be small and that the ones that do occur are almost certainly outside the control of departmental management. Therefore, they combine them with labor quantity variances. Of course, companies that include overtime premium in the direct labor rate may find substantial variations in the labor rate, depending on the amount of overtime work incurred. However, the best control of overtime is through a separate overhead account for overtime premiums with a standard of its own.

If the variances are to be combined, there is no need to show separate standards on the product cost sheets, although setting the combined direct labor standard inevitably requires separate consideration of the hourly rate and the time required to perform the operation on each piece or on each 100 pieces. The question of whether the standard rate should reflect the rate at the beginning of the period to which it will be applied or the estimated average rate for the period has been discussed in reference to material price standards. The two methods will have the same effect when applied to labor rates as when applied to material prices.

Direct Labor Quantity Standards

The direct labor quantity standard is the number of pieces per hour converted to a direct labor cost per piece. This standard, whether stated alone or combined with the labor rate standard, generally receives more attention from management at all levels than any other. Here, especially, it is important to bear in mind that attainable standards are those which permit an average worker to perform above the standard (that is, at lower cost) at least half the time.

In companies that pay labor piece rates, the piece rate is the standard. Unions have largely eliminated piece rates in heavy industry. However, many companies in the garment industry and other light manufacturing pay their workers piece rates with the enthusiastic support of unions. When a company pays its workers on piece rates, it generally guarantees an hourly wage at some level below what a worker is expected to earn on piece work. If circumstances arise such that a worker actually earns less on a piece-work basis than the guarantee, he is nevertheless paid the guaranteed rate. The difference, referred to as "makeup pay," is ordinarily charged to a variable overhead account.

The setting of standards has much in common with the setting of piece rates and the setting of production bases for certain types of incentive payment plans related to piece rates. However, because piece rates and incentive plans directly affect the pay of workers, more care is ordinarily taken on them. Basically, the methods include stopwatch time studies, standard data systems, and work sampling.

Most stopwatch time studies record the time taken by each element of each operation. A time that is clearly out of line with other times recorded for a given element is ignored when the times are averaged. This provides a more normal total time for the operation than if only abnormal times for the whole operation were eliminated from the average. It also helps the time study man determine if a worker is deliberately lengthening the operation during the study. However, such a determination is very difficult to make, and time study men must subjectively figure in an adjustment factor. This is called leveling. Frequently, films of workers doing jobs at normal speeds are used to sharpen the observer's judgment on the proper leveling factor to use. Nevertheless, the accuracy of the leveling factor depends on the skill of the time study man.

Today, this problem is being avoided to a large extent by the use of standard data systems. These systems use a catalog which shows the normal time allowance for each motion required in any operation. The motions are subdivided by length of carry, weight of part, use of one hand or both, need to move feet, and the like. In effect, these systems use a tape measure rather than a stopwatch to establish the standard. The system requires considerable training as well as standard data to be effective. Two well-known systems are MTM (Method-Time-Measurement) and WOFAC (Work Factor). Generally, unions find standard data systems more satisfactory than stopwatch time studies.

A third approach, called work sampling (sometimes referred to as ratio delay), is used almost entirely for diversified operations performed by the same individuals, such as maintenance or clerical workers. Here the analyst observes what an individual is doing at different times of day, as determined by a table of random numbers. One analyst will often observe several workers at once. At each observation the analyst notes what the individual is doing. A standard time is then calculated from the analyst's observations. For example, if at the end of four weeks the number of observations of a maintenance worker changing a faucet washer is 20 percent of the total observations, it is concluded that 20 percent of the 160 hours in the period were used in changing faucet washers. These 32 hours are then divided by the number of faucet washers changed in the four weeks to determine the standard time for the job. Thus, if the number of faucet washers changed in any subsequent period is known, an allowed time can be calculated. This standard is, of course, a historical one, but it is likely to be the only way of establishing a standard for diversified operations.

All labor quantity standards set by stopwatch or standard data make allowances for personal time and fatigue. Generally, they do not allow for lack of experience. Under this concept, any unfavorable variances caused by learners or inexperienced workers are charged to a variable overhead account. However, some companies set standards for learners (based on a learning curve) in order to measure their progress. The difference between the regular standard and the learning standard goes into an overhead account; the difference between the learner's actual performance and the learning standard goes into the direct labor variance account. Thus the department's performance can be measured against the standards for workers after considering what can be expected of them on the basis of their length of employment.

Labor quantity standards include setups, cleanups, and materials handling when these tasks are performed by the worker. Obviously, for setups and in some industries cleanup, the cost per piece produced will depend on the length of the run. If runs tend to be of roughly equal lengths, there is no problem. If runs vary in length, separate standards may be set for these operations, but they must still be integrated into the product cost standard sheet by the assumption of some average length of run.

In many companies, labor quantity standards that are set by industrial engineers and time study men must be approved by departmental foremen before they are put into use. Often the approval of a union representative is also required.

Variable Overhead Standards

In most companies, a large part of variable overhead is represented by fringe benefits on direct labor and variable indirect labor. Of course, in companies that use an expanded labor rate, fringe benefits are not part of overhead. Since fringe benefits tend to be on formulas, arriving at a standard is relatively easy. History will ordinarily indicate how employee turnover affects the ceiling on unemployment insurance and how short weeks on the one hand and overtime on the other affect the per-hour costs of fringes such as health insurance plans related to calendar months.

With certain types of indirect labor, the entire function is considered variable, or the function is considered semivariable and only the variable component is included in variable overhead. Both of these represent sizable portions of the total variable overhead. For the former, the standard will be based on history and, for the latter, on history combined with one of the techniques discussed in Chapter 4 for splitting semivariable accounts.

Standards for power, process fuel, perishable tools, and overtime premiums can be set by engineers or, more often, from history.

With variable overhead accounts that represent temporary assignments of employees ordinarily on direct labor—for example, idle time, rework, cleanup, materials handling, machine repair, and setup —standards are set partly from history and partly from the judgment of operating personnel as to reasonable allowances for these items.

Some variable overhead accounts by their nature represent charges that are ordinarily made directly to individual departments. These include the various charges for the time of direct labor personnel transferred to overhead accounts, certain indirect labor functions, overtime premiums, factory supplies, and perishable tools. Other accounts by their nature are billed to the plant as a whole and must be allocated to departments on some basis. These include power (unless departments are separately metered), process fuel, insurance on work in process, and certain indirect labor such as interdepartmental materials handling.

In some companies, certain overhead accounts are charged directly to departments; in other companies they are recorded on a plantwide basis and then allocated to departments. Fringe benefits and insurance on inventory are examples.

When a variable cost originally recorded on a plantwide basis must be allocated to departments, the method of allocation should be the same as that used to allocate the cost to products within departments. (An exception is cost of power, which is frequently allocated to departments on the basis of connected load.) Since the latter allocation is the key one, the choice of allocation bases should consider the logic of allocation to products first. Almost every company on direct costs uses one of two bases: Either it allocates variable overhead as so many dollars per standard direct labor hour or it allocates variable overhead as a percentage of standard direct labor dollars. Although certain theoretical advantages can be claimed for each of these systems, the advantages are so minor and the results of the two methods so similar that most companies base their choice on the relative convenience of the recordkeeping required. Depending on other aspects of the company's payroll recording and summarization, one method or the other may entail less bookkeeping, and that is the method to choose.

Many companies on absorption costing use one of the above two methods, but a number of other absorption cost companies use machine hours. When fixed costs such as machinery depreciation and space costs must be allocated, as in absorption costing, it may well be found that the most expensive machines use relatively the least direct labor. Thus machine hours, often on an individual cost center basis, can make more sense than direct labor hours or dollars. (A cost center is a machine or a group of very similar machines for which cost data are accumulated within a department.)

Certain variable overhead items such as power, depreciation of tools and dies, and perishable tools are more closely identifiable with machine hours than with direct labor. However, generally it has not been found worthwhile to use machine hours as a base in direct cost companies, since these costs are relatively unimportant compared with the costs that are more clearly identifiable with direct labor rather than with machine hours. In fact, some companies using direct costs find that a plantwide variable overhead rate is quite accurate. This would rarely be true for companies using absorption costs, because of the very different fixed costs of departments.

A few companies create a separate overhead pool for those overhead costs that are more clearly identifiable with materials than with either labor or machines. These items might include purchasing department costs, receiving costs, stockroom costs, insurance on inventories, materials handling costs, and shipping department costs. Such costs are allocated on the value of material put into production. Although accuracy is improved thereby, it must be recognized that the *value* of materials is still a very rough approximation. Obviously, in most of these overhead functions it takes more time to process $1,000 worth of sand than it does to process $1,000 worth of diamonds. A very small part of the overhead functions identifiable with materials are variable. These include incoming inspection, materials handling, and certain storage costs. Accordingly, companies on direct costs are unlikely to use materials as a base to absorb any variable overhead. The absorption of these variable costs on a labor base will not create inaccuracies in product costs beyond the acceptable limits of inaccuracy caused by averaging in any cost accounting system.

It should be noted that the total costs of most service departments tend to be fixed rather than variable. Accordingly, under direct costing, they are not allocated at all. However, in certain firms, service departments such as machinery maintenance and materials handling may have enough of the characteristics of variable expenses to be allocated to production departments and thus to product costs.

The question then arises as to whether a service department that serves one or more other service departments as well as production departments should have any of its costs allocated to other service departments. In the early days of cost accounting, such allocation was quite common and much time was spent discussing the best method of taking care of the many situations when two service departments served each other. Today, however, under both direct and absorption costing, almost all companies use as the denominator in the allocation formula the total direct labor dollars or hours of only the production departments. Although this labor-saving shortcut may be unsound in theory, it yields results that are close enough to the theoretical approach to be acceptable. This is certainly true in a direct cost system, where the only service department costs to be allocated—the variable costs—are minimal in any event.

Variable S.G.& A. Standards

Standards for certain variable selling, general, and administrative expenses can be set by formula. For example, commissions to salesmen, manufacturers' representatives, and brokers are a certain percentage of the product selling price. If the commission percentage varies by product, so must the standard. The weight of the product and the average distance shipped by the usual method will determine the freight-out cost when the company absorbs outgoing freight. Royalties too are a percentage of selling price. Although a formula is also applied with cooperative advertising, it must be modified by the historical percentage of customers using this privilege. Cost of invoicing (whether on a typewriter, bookkeeping machine, or keypunch machine) can be determined in much the same way as direct labor rate and quantity standards.

The absorption base for S.G.& A. variable expenses is either the number of units shipped or the sales value of each product to which standard variable S.G.& A. expenses have been assigned. In the case of invoicing costs, the assignment to products is frequently based on sales value. Although this reflects neither the number of units per invoice nor the number of units per invoice line, the cost is relatively minor and no other method is practicable.

Fixed Overhead Standards

Under direct costing, the assignment of a standard to fixed overhead accounts is a budgeting process. The level of each account is estimated for each month, based on history and any known or expected changes. As previously stated, these amounts can vary with the seasons or with other logical factors. Comparison of the actual amount of the cost with the budgeted or standard amount generates a variance that is reflected as a current cost on the company's income statement. Under direct costing, this is all that needs to be done with fixed manufacturing overhead accounts. There is no need to charge them directly to departments or to allocate them to departments from a plantwide account. Furthermore, no attempt is made to charge them to products, so no bases for allocation to products need be established.

However, when a company on direct costs converts its financial statements to an absorption basis (using Method 3 described in Chapter 6), it must be able to approximate the fixed costs in each product in finished-goods ending inventory. For this purpose, fixed manufacturing overhead must be analyzed and assigned to departments and then to products, not as part of the accounting system but as a special analysis. Because these allocations are outside the accounting system, more shortcuts are acceptable than would be tolerated under absorption costing.

For example, companies on absorption costing are likely to use half a dozen or more bases for allocating plantwide fixed costs (of which there are many) to departments. Occupancy expenses will be allocated on square feet; superintendent's salary and salaries for the personnel department and certain other staff on number of people; fringe benefits on labor considered a fixed cost on dollar labor payroll of the fixed labor; power on connected load; elevator operators on area served; machinery depreciation on value and useful life of machinery in operation. It is common to use cost centers within departments to absorb these costs and machine hours as a means of assigning costs to products. An overhead percentage applied to materials is not uncommon.

The special analysis required for converting product direct costs to absorption costs usually follows simpler rules. Three bases for allocation to departments are generally satisfactory. Square feet is used for occupancy costs (including power in many cases); either number of people or payroll dollars (but not both) is used for plant supervision, staff, and payroll fringes; and machinery value with or without consideration of useful life is used for machinery depreciation. Cost centers within departments are rarely used. This means that machine hours within a department become no more meaningful than direct labor in assigning departmental overhead to products. The absorption of overhead on the basis of materials used is rarely found. Furthermore, the need to reconcile monthly is avoided. Thus the work required is considerably less under direct costing.

S.G.& A. Fixed Cost Standards

As in the case of manufacturing fixed overhead, the setting of selling, general, and administrative fixed cost standards is a budgeting process. The budgeted or standard amount is compared with the actual each month and the variance is calculated. This is all that has to be done. Since no S.G.& A. expenses are charged to inventory under either direct or absorption costing, fixed S.G.& A. expenses are never allocated to products and do not present a problem in converting a direct cost company's finished-goods inventory to absorption costs for financial statements.

Who Sets the Standards?

Generally, standards are set by the person or department most likely to have specialized knowledge in the area. Although many types of standards are set outside the accounting department, the rules of the game are determined by financial people, especially the cost accountant, along with advice from others. For example, financial people have the final say on whether incoming freight should be part of the material price standards; whether depreciation of tools and dies should be in variable overhead; whether scrap sales should be credited to materials; and whether spoilage should be considered a material quantity variance or an overhead expense.

Since purchasing is knowledgeable in current and future costs of materials and purchased parts, it has the primary responsibility for setting material price standards. Purchasing usually keeps a set of records of past prices on each item purchased, but if a record is missing accounting is expected to supply the data. Accounting may also provide purchasing with data on freight-in and cash discount terms. Because the performance of purchasing will be judged in part on its ability to meet the standards, financial people will frequently review the standards to make sure they are not set with unreasonable cushions. Such cushions can make a mockery of the use of variances for cost control. They can also produce unrealistic product costs and result in poor management decisions on pricing and other policies.

Material quantity standards may be set by design engineering or industrial engineering, depending on the company's method of operation. Labor rate standards are set by the department foreman or by the personnel department, or by the two working together. Labor quantity standards are almost always set by industrial engineering, with the concurrence of the departmental foreman.

Variable overhead standards are generally set by the accounting department—specifically, by the cost accounting section. It is accounting that keeps the historical records which are so important to this process. Advice of specialists is often needed, however. Plant engineering may have a clearer picture of a proper standard for machine repair costs than that revealed by past records. Certainly, any allocation of power costs to departments on the basis of connected load can use help from plant engineering. Personnel may have data on upcoming changes in fringe benefit costs which have not yet appeared in the accounting records. In some companies, other accounts will need review by those outside the accounting department.

In addition, the conversion of total anticipated variable overhead in an account to a variable overhead rate per direct labor hour or per direct labor dollar requires an estimate of the amount of direct labor to be used in each department in the fiture. This estimate is best derived from the sales and production plan for the coming year. The plan is usually prepared by the accounting department, in consultation with many people, including the company president, marketing and sales executives, and production personnel.

The standards for fixed costs, both manufacturing and S.G.&A., are usually set by accounting personnel on the basis of past experience, again in consultation with others. For example, future real estate taxes may be known quite accurately by the company's tax expert and may be substantially different from last year. Often the setting of standards for fixed costs is assigned to the budget director.

When Should Standards Be Changed?

In the average company, certain changes occur daily or even more frequently that would justify revising one or more of the company's product cost standards. These include changes in method, in product design, in labor rates, and in material prices. However, a change in standards requires that an inventory be taken (physically, or from the records) of all unshipped products produced under the old standard, including that part of work in process which has already gone through the pertinent operation. Then an adjustment must be made in the costs already booked so that shipments at the new standard will clear the company's books of all the standard costs charged to the shipped products and no more than these costs. To do this on a daily basis is clearly impracticable.

Accordingly, in the days before double-digit inflation (say, through 1970) most companies changed their standards once annually, at the beginning of their fiscal year. A number of companies allowed two changes per year, one at the start of the year and one at whatever time of year a labor rate increase occurred, in accordance with the company's union contract. This, of course, was appropriate only when the majority of a company's employees belonged to one or more unions with the same contract years. It could not be used when employees were represented by several different unions with different contract years or by nonunion employees who received raises at different times of the year.

Freezing standards for half a year or more obviously gives rise to many problems. One is the problem of using standard product costs that are no longer realistic as a guide to pricing. This difficulty has already been discussed in Chapter 5, along with a generally acceptable solution. However, the reporting of the actual to standard cost comparison for cost control purposes requires a different solution.

A good many companies just shrug their shoulders and accept as unavoidable the variances that result from comparing actual costs with a standard that no longer reflects the current method in use or the current product design. Often reports showing such a variance are footnoted with the explanation that "X dollars of this variance arose from a change in method." Of course, the variance may be favorable or unfavorable. It is likely to be favorable if the change in method or product design was made to reduce costs but unfavorable if the change was forced on the company because the quality of products made under the former method or design was unacceptable.

Today, many companies have solved this problem by using new standards that properly reflect current methods and product design to prepare performance reports while using the old standards to value finished-goods inventory and cost of sales. This can be done by making an adjusting entry to the cost of each lot of products as it passes from the last operation in work in process to finished-goods inventory. The balancing amount in the entry is to a change-in-standard variance account. The entry looks like this:

Debit Finished-goods inventory at the old standard	XXXX	
Credit Work in process at the new standard		XXXX
Debit or *Credit* Change-in-standard variance account for the difference	XX or	XX
To transfer XXX whammits from production to finished-goods inventory.		

It should be understood that however many changes are made to the standard product cost of the product during the year, each new change merely updates the net difference between the old standard cost and the new standard cost. Thus there is no need to calculate the separate effects of the many changes in the standards for a single product.

Often, a change will affect more than one product. For example, a change in the method of making a part used in several end products will affect the standard cost of each end product, as will a change in the materials going into that part. A change in the labor rate of a particular skill category may affect the standard cost of every product the company makes, though possibly to varying extents. In a computerized company, a "where used" computer program can readily update the product cost records, with or without a complete printout of the new data.

Despite the effectiveness of the foregoing methods, a number of companies, unhappy with once-a-year changes in standards in the face of double-digit inflation, now revise their standards quarterly. Since standards are more likely to be revised upward than downward because of the effect of inflation, it is useful to consider the accounting aspects of a standards revision. At issue here is a revision to the standards used for accounting purposes and for finished-goods inventory—in other words, the "old" standards discussed just a few paragraphs above, not the "new" standards used for performance reporting. The need for the revision is signaled by a buildup of the amount in a variance account. If the buildup is caused by inflation, it will be a large unfavorable variance, and the standard will have to be revised upward. When finished-goods inventory is restated at the new standard, costs will be added to it; this is, of course, a debit entry. The offsetting credit, made to the variance account, reduces its balance. When this type of revision is made at year end, the offsetting credit will sometimes reduce the variance account to an immaterial amount. This avoids the need to prorate the account between cost of sales and ending inventory, as discussed in more detail in the next chapter.

Summary

Methods of setting standards vary considerably from company to company. The various components of a product standard also differ from company to company. However, certain fundamentals apply in all companies. The first is that the standard-setting process is of major importance in both cost control and management decisions. The second is that the distinction between variable manufacturing overhead and fixed manufacturing overhead is of particular importance in companies using direct costing. The third is that accounting or cost accounting sets the rules but is responsible for setting standards only in certain overhead accounts. The fourth is that accounting must help those actually setting the standards by providing historical information in suitable form. The fifth is that in setting certain standards, accounting can often benefit from the advice of operating personnel.

Finally, the question of when to revise standards deserves a thorough analysis. Because acceptable and usable standards are so important to the successful operation of a direct standard cost system and because a good cost system is so important to a company, the value of setting appropriate standards cannot be overemphasized.

10

Developing Variances

UNDER a standard cost system, a variance is the difference between the actual costs incurred and the standard costs of the product produced. Actual material costs are compared with the standard material required by the number of pieces produced; actual direct labor costs for a period are compared with the standard labor for the pieces going through each operation in the period; actual variable overhead is compared with the variable overhead absorbed at standard; and actual fixed overhead is compared with budgeted fixed overhead for the period.

Many accounting systems use the variance account as a clearing account and make the original entries to it. In these systems the total appropriate actual costs are debited to the variance account and the standard cost of the pieces produced is credited in total to the same variance account. At the end of the accounting period any debit balance remaining in the account is an unfavorable variance and any credit balance is a favorable variance. It should be noted that some companies show unfavorable balances on their reporting forms in parentheses; other companies show favorable variances in parentheses. As long as a consistent policy is followed and the company's executives are properly interpreting the parentheses, either system is acceptable. In this book parentheses will be used to denote unfavorable variances.

Variances are used chiefly in the control of costs. They indicate not only the extent to which actual costs are out of line with those that can be reasonably expected but also whether the overrun is due to material prices, material quantities used, labor rates, direct labor quantities used, or the spending on individual overhead accounts. Proper design of the variance section of a chart of accounts can give a wealth of information on cost performance and in certain cases can pinpoint the individual responsible for favorable or unfavorable results. Variance accounts are also used to tell management whether standard product cost sheets are accurate when originally prepared and whether they continue to reflect product costs realistically as conditions change during the year.

Basic Variance Accounts

Here is a list of the basic variance accounts under a direct cost system:

Purchase price variance.
Material quantity variance.
Direct labor rate variance.
Direct labor quantity variance.
Variable overhead spending variance.
Variable overhead efficiency variance.

Variable selling expense variance.
Variable G.& A. expense variance.

Fixed overhead spending variance.
Fixed selling expense spending variance.
Fixed G.& A. expense spending variance.

Marginal contribution variance due to selling price variations.
Marginal contribution variance due to variations in physical volume of sales.
Marginal contribution variance due to variations in product mix.

The major difference between this list and the variance accounts under an absorption cost system is the absence of an overhead volume variance account. In addition, most absorption cost systems have not developed standards for S.G.& A. though they may have budgets from which variances are calculated. The results of variances from budgets are very similar to the results of developing variances from standards in the S.G.& A. accounts; however, budget variances are rarely part of the basic accounting system of a company on absorption costing.

The three marginal contribution variances under direct costing are discussed fully in Chapter 12. An absorption cost company could develop a gross profit variance and divide it into the same three parts, but this is much less useful than the marginal contribution variances under a direct cost system.

The direct cost presentation of variances has one rather important advantage over the absorption cost approach. Under direct costing, the volume variance cost appears as a marginal contribution variance and therefore appears to relate to the performance of the marketing and sales function. Under absorption costing, the overhead volume variance is a manufacturing variance and seems to be the responsibility of the production function. It is true that some companies are able to sell all they can produce, and therefore a drop in sales volume is indeed the responsibility of production people. However, such companies are the exception. Most companies can produce more at any time than the marketing and sales functions are able to sell. In these companies, showing the volume variance on the manufacturing performance reports simply confuses lower-level manufacturing management. The foreman sees his departmental report with, say, a large unfavorable volume variance. He knows he produced all the product he was told to make. Nevertheless, he feels he is subject to criticism for having costs substantially higher than the standard. In this case, the cost variance is entirely outside of his control.

Certain of the accounts listed above deserve special comment. There are two accepted methods for recording purchase price variances. The most common method is to record the purchase price variance at the time the materials are received or when the vendor's invoice is posted to accounts payable, whichever is more convenient. Under this method all raw materials and purchased parts enter the company's inventory account at the standard price. The other method is to inventory raw materials and purchased parts at actual cost and record the variance when the materials are issued to production. The first method has two advantages. To begin with, the bookkeeping is much simpler. The invoice is at hand when the entry is made and there is no need to determine actual costs of the material at requisitioning time by the FIFO or average cost methods. Also, there will be fewer conversions from actual to standard, since incoming shipments are ordinarily much larger than individual requisitions. A second advantage is that the variance is recognized earlier and its effect on profits can be seen sooner. In a very real sense, the profit or loss is realized at least as soon as the material is received. In fact, it could be claimed that the profit or loss is realized as soon as the vendor accepts a priced purchase order. However, tradition is opposed to this approach, and to the best of our knowledge purchase price variances are never picked up until the material or invoice is in the house.

Although direct labor rate variances and direct labor usage variances are listed separately above, they are frequently combined into a single direct labor cost variance. In fact, this must be done in companies that have not established separate standards for labor rates and labor quantities for each product.

The distinction between variable overhead spending variance and variable overhead efficiency variance requires some explanation. Variable overhead standards are established as an amount per direct labor hour or a percentage of direct labor dollars. Clearly, the variable overhead accounts can be expected to vary according to actual direct labor, but the cost system absorbs them on the basis of the standard direct labor required to make the product. Thus the variable overhead spending variance is the difference between the actual cost of the particular variable overhead account and the amount accounted for by the formula for the standard applied to actual direct labor. This variance is a measure of the accountability of the person responsible for the account. When actual direct labor exceeds the standard, the standard amount of variable overhead applied to the excess direct labor is a loss that lies at the door of the person responsible for the excess direct labor (usually the department foreman). Such a loss must be added to the cost of the direct labor itself to arrive at the true loss resulting from the excess direct labor.

This principle is illustrated in Figure 10-1. The shaded area in the upper right corner is not accounted for by either formula and, in theory, should give rise to a third variance account. In practice, most companies calculate the spending variance first, recording whatever is left of the total variance as an efficiency variance. Of course, for some variable overhead accounts, the spending variance is also the responsibility of the department foremen. Variable factory supplies and perishable tools are good examples of such accounts. In fact, almost every variable overhead account whose charges originate in the department

FIGURE 10-1. The three variable overhead variances.

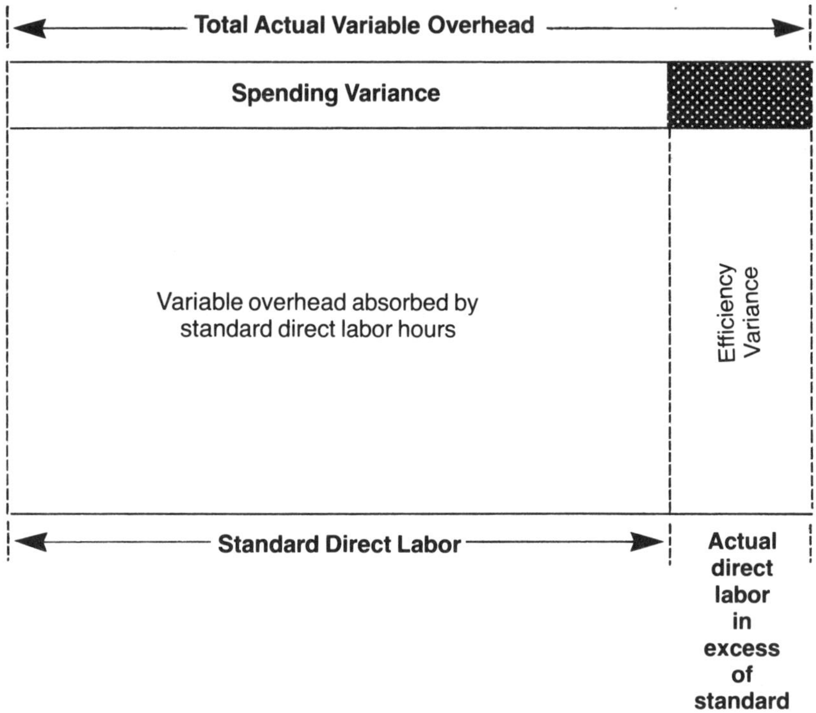

are the foreman's responsibility. These include indirect labor, overtime premium, and direct labor temporarily charged to such overhead accounts as rework, spoilage, and scrap.

In many companies, certain types of machinery repairs are performed by a separate department, called maintenance or plant engineering. Some of these firms have developed standards for every common repair job, from changing a bushing to rewinding an armature. In these companies, the maintenance department is responsible for keeping the costs of repair jobs requested by the production department within the standards for those jobs. On the other hand, the production department is responsible for keeping its requests at standard cost within the standard allowed for the amount of product produced. This is another example of a spending variance being the responsibility of one person—the maintenance chief—and the efficiency variance being the responsibility of another—the production department foreman.

Similarly, some companies set a standard for each type of machine setup. The difference between the actual cost of the setup and the standard cost is a spending variance. The fact that the production run using the setup is shorter or longer than contemplated in the standard is an efficiency variance. In most companies, efficiency variances in setups are the responsibility not of the production department foremen but rather of the production scheduling department personnel.

Departmentalizing Variances

Most companies have separate variance accounts for each department where the nature of the variance indicates the cost is within the control of the department. This is ordinarily true of the material usage variance, the direct labor variance (both rate and usage, if shown separately), all variable overhead efficiency variances, some variable overhead spending variances, and some fixed overhead spending variances. The types of variable overhead spending variances within the production department foreman's control have already been described. The fixed overhead spending variances within his control include fixed departmental indirect labor and the fringe benefits on such labor. If a department is large and has two or more quite different types of operations, breakdowns by subdepartment or cost center may be useful. To the extent that variances can be broken down by areas of responsibility, cost control is improved.

In purchasing, for example, purchase price variances can be broken down by the specific assistant purchasing agent in charge of a group of materials. Or they can be broken down by groups of materials within the area of responsibility of one assistant purchasing agent to help him monitor price trends. The general and administrative expense spending variances can be broken down by the particular individual in charge of the area. Generally, the president, the treasurer, the controller, the EDP manager, the purchasing agent, the personnel director, and others are considered to have separate areas of responsibility in monitoring actual costs against standard. Each company must determine how far it wishes to expand its chart of accounts in order to improve its knowledge of just where costs are out of line and who is responsible. Obviously, companies that do their cost accumulation on a computer will find that more detail is acceptable in making the cost-benefit test than companies using manual systems.

Special Variance Accounts

Every industry, even every company, is different and will have special areas where costs tend to get out of hand. Frequently, the normal chart of accounts is too summarized to reveal all the information required about a problem. Here a company has a choice. It can revise its chart of accounts, making corresponding revisions to its standard product cost sheets, or it can keep subsidiary records tied to the total of the account on the books until costs have improved to the point that such tight control is no longer needed. Either way, the accumulation and coding of actual cost data become more burdensome, as does the calculation of the variances. A computerized company will find the calculation of variances relatively easy, but the other steps would be roughly as burdensome as on a manual system.

An example of how special variance accounts can help resolve a problem may be useful here. One company had an operation on a product that could be performed on an automatic machine or on a manually controlled machine. In visits to the shop floor, top management noticed that the hand machines were being used during many hours when the automatic machine was idle, despite the potential cost saving of the automatic operation. Management suspected that the department foreman was reluctant to use his own time to set up the automatic machine and had not trained anyone else to do it. Rather than issuing general orders to the foreman which might be inapplicable under certain circumstances, top management asked him to keep a separate record of the idle time of the automatic machine and the time in use of the hand-controlled machines. The resulting variance motivated the foreman to make greater use of the automatic machine.

Ordinarily, variances are not accumulated by specific product type. In direct labor, for example, the variance account (if it is used as a clearing account) or "direct labor—actual" is charged with the actual direct labor per the clock cards for the day or week. The variance account or "direct labor—standard" is credited with the unit standard direct labor cost extended by the production of every operation on every product going through the department in the same period. The balance in the variance account or the difference between "direct labor—actual" and "direct labor—standard" measures the performance of the *department* but tells nothing about which operation on which product contributed how much to the net favorable or unfavorable variance. In 99 cases out of 100, there is no need to identify specific operations or products through the accounting records. Identification can be made by the foreman, by a review of each worker's production, or by informal tally records. In the exceptional case, a collection of variance data by operation and product may pay off.

One further point should be noted here. The fact that a particular product generates 50 percent scrap one day is not necessarily something that should affect that product's cost. It may well be that it was just the bad luck of the product to be produced at a time when a machine was defective or when a worker was drunk. If this is the case, the loss is not related to the product and should be spread over all products, as is done automatically when variances are picked up in total rather than by products.

However, if a certain product appears to generate large variances because of its nature or design—most commonly, because of high spoilage or slowed production rates to avoid high spoilage—it may be worthwhile to inform marketing so that an attempt can be made to reflect the situation in the pricing of the product. Care should be taken here to avoid "double counting"—that is, informing marketing of the cost of spoilage on the particular product and letting this cost figure be added to the previously determined standard product cost, which already contains the departmental average spoilage allowance.

Change-of-Standard Variance

As described in Chapter 9, most companies have a real need for a change-of-standard variance account. Such an account makes it possible to report standard costs based on updated standards to operating management for cost control purposes while retaining the standards set at the beginning of the year for accounting purposes. The account should be used to reflect changes in methods of operation—for example, substitution of a progressive stamping operation on a single die for the three prior operations of blank, form, and trim on three separate dies. The account should also reflect changes in product design—for example, substitution of a plastic part for a metal part or elimination of an identifying coat-of-arms.

The change-of-standard account should not be used for temporary changes, such as doing an operation manually because the automatic machine reflected in the standard is in use on another product or is down for repairs. Nor should it reflect the use of a higher-priced material because the normal material is temporarily out of stock. The extra cost may, of course, be fully justified by the need to ship to customers on time. Nevertheless, the cost properly belongs in the direct labor variance account or in the purchase price variance account, since there is at least an implication of inadequate planning when such a cost must be incurred.

As noted in Chapter 4, step costs are fixed costs that assume an entirely different level when the volume of production reaches a certain point (for example, the need to go to a two-shift operation). Since fixed costs are not part of product costs under direct costing, there is no need to revise the standard when this occurs or to utilize the change-of-standard variance account. A simple and entirely satisfactory method of handling step costs under direct costing is to calculate the spending variance just as if the change to a two-shift operation had not occurred. The performance report is then footnoted to explain what part of the variance arose from the change.

Using Variances to Revise Standards

If a direct labor usage standard consistently generates unfavorable variances, it is a sure bet that someone will suggest that the standard be raised. If the standard *is* raised on the basis of this evidence alone, an engineered standard is in effect transformed into a historical standard. In such a case, all the advantages of engineered standards are lost. On the other hand, consistent unfavorable variances certainly raise a doubt about the accuracy of the standard. The proper course to follow is to restudy the standard. If the new study validates the existing standard, it should not be changed. In fact, any contemplated change should be based on the new study, not on the amount of the unfavorable variances. This restudy requirement applies not only to direct labor quantity standards—the most common area of dispute—but to any engineered standard (a material quantity standard, certain variable overhead standards, and so on) that is challenged on the basis of unfavorable variances.

When the reverse of this situation arises—when an engineered standard consistently generates favorable variances—in theory, a restudy should also be made. However, lowering a cost standard without a related change in method of operation can have poor psychological effects on both the worker and the supervisor. Both worker and supervisor feel that they are being penalized for their superior performance when they should be rewarded. Unless failure to make a change will cause standard product costs to be significantly inaccurate, it is usually preferable to continue the old standard.

When standards are set initially on the basis of history, as is the case with many overhead standards, any consistent pattern of variances (good or bad) should be used to revise the standard. Here the only question is how soon. Generally, such revisions are held off until the end of the year and are simply reflected as part of the annual updating of standards before the start of the next fiscal year. This applies both to the standards being used for accounting purposes and to those being used for performance reporting.

Reflecting Variances in Inventory

In most industries, standard costing has been shown to be far superior to actual costing for management purposes. However, for reporting to outsiders, standard costing is considered acceptable only if the resulting balance sheet and income statement are close to what would have been shown had the company been on actual costs. The discrepancy between standard costs and actual costs is, of course, measured by the variance accounts. For this purpose, the fact that variances have been written off monthly to cost of sales must be ignored. It is the cumulative amount of the variances for the year that is pertinent to any adjustment that must be made.

Under absorption costing, the largest variance is very often the volume variance on fixed overhead. Although a volume variance account does not exist under direct costing, the assignment of fixed costs to ending inventory under Method 1 or 2 in Chapter 6 automatically takes care of the amounts that might have appeared as volume variances under absorption costing. If Method 3 is used, it is necessary to determine the amount of fixed costs absorbed at standard by production in the period and to compare this figure with budgeted fixed costs. Any difference must be handled like any other variance account, as described below.

However, under both direct and absorption costing, many other variances must be considered when a determination is made as to whether the standard cost results are close enough to those that would have been shown under actual costing so that the difference can be ignored. If not, an adjustment to the inventory being reported on the financial statements must be made. The standards are, however, not changed. When this determination is made, the variance accounts are looked at in total, with those showing favorable amounts being offset against those showing unfavorable amounts. The total is then compared with the total standard costs in cost of sales, adjusted by the change in beginning and ending inventory values at standard costs, to determine whether the percentage variance is material to the inventory value on the balance sheet. It is also necessary to determine whether the dollar variance when spread between cost of sales and ending inventory is material to the company's net profits.

It should be noted that an unfavorable variance which is spread in part to ending inventory will have the effect of increasing profits for the period. A favorable variance will have the reverse effect. Any company that fails to spread an unfavorable variance to ending inventory on the grounds that the amount is immaterial should ask itself if an IRS agent will take the same view, given the fact that more income taxes could be collected if the variance were allocated in part to the company's ending inventory. It is, of course, extremely unlikely that an IRS auditor will insist on the company picking up a net favorable variance.

The company's outside auditor, on the other hand, is much more interested in favorable variances. A favorable variance, after all, says that actual costs were less than the standard costs at which the inventory is being valued. There is a long-established and highly regarded accounting principle which holds that inventories must be valued at "cost or market, whichever is lower." Valuing an inventory at standard cost when a net favorable variance exists would appear to be a clear violation of this rule. Materiality also affects this determination, but on balance it would appear that the criteria for what is material should be somewhat lower in amount for net favorable variances than for unfavorable ones.

When some adjustment to inventory must be made, a number of formulas can be used. The most common one is to add or subtract from ending inventory the amount of the variance found to be allocable to it after prorating the variance between the standard cost of the ending inventory and the standard cost of cost of sales in the period. In other words, add to or subtract from ending inventory at standard the amount arrived at by the following operation:

$$\text{Cumulative net variance for the year} \times \frac{\text{Value of ending inventory at standard}}{\text{Value of cost of sales at standard} + \text{Value of ending inventory at standard} - \text{Value of beginning inventory at standard}}$$

Here, raw materials and purchased parts not yet issued to production are part of the ending inventory at standard, whereas they are not in the somewhat similar allocation formulas of Chapter 6. This is because purchase price variances, at least in most companies, are recorded at the time materials are received. Thus this part of inventory already reflects standard values.

Revisions of standards can play a part in determining whether a variance is material or not. As noted in the previous chapter, a revision of standards at fiscal year end will almost always reduce the amount of the balance in the variance total just before closing the books. This reduction may bring the balance down to an immaterial amount. Even if it doesn't, it will still reduce the amount of the adjustment required.

Occasionally, a revision of standards for the coming year will produce standard costs above the actual costs of the year just concluded. This can occur because the new standards are set to reflect anticipated cost increases in the coming year. In such a case, the "lower of cost or market" accounting principle requires that an inventory reserve be set up on the balance sheet to bring the new standards reflected in the closing inventory down to actual costs. Typically, this reserve is not separately identified on published balance sheets but is merely used to reduce the inventory value shown.

Summary

The types of variance accounts used by companies on standard direct cost systems are reasonably uniform. Since variance accounts are most useful in the control of costs, the creation of special variance accounts to control cost problems unique to a company is to be encouraged. Certainly, a separate group of variance accounts should be kept for each production department or other area that is under the responsibility of a particular individual.

It is often necessary to allocate variance accounts to year-end inventory. The procedure is relatively simple, however, and the need to perform it should not cause any company to hesitate about adopting a standard cost system in view of its many advantages.

Variance accounting and analysis are virtually the same under direct costing as under absorption costing. The one important exception is that the fixed overhead volume variance does not exist in a direct cost system. Since overhead volume variances are a confusing factor in absorption cost systems, this is a real advantage of direct costing.

11

Direct Costs in Cost Control

WHEN accountants talk about cost control, they usually mean a system that compares actual cost with some other figure—costs of a prior period, standard costs, or budgeted costs—in order to determine whether current actual costs are out of line. The generation of a meaningful group of variances from standard has been found to be the most effective method of cost control. The generation of variances was discussed in the previous chapter. How the information developed by the variances should be used will be detailed in this chapter. The discussion will focus on variances from standard cost. However, almost all the procedures covered can also be applied (though not as well) to variances from a budget or, under actual cost systems, to cost differences compared with a prior period or a prior identical job lot.

The Place of Management Decisions in Cost Control

Costs can be controlled—that is, reduced—without comparing current costs against some measure of what the costs should be. Many of the management decisions discussed in Chapter 8 involved determining which of two courses of action would produce the lower cost. The data required for these decisions did not include any comparison of current costs with a standard or a past period. Yet, in many cases, a correct management decision may have a substantially greater impact on costs than weeks of follow-up on costs believed to be excessive in comparison with a standard.

Two types of management decisions deserve special mention because of their direct relationship to cost reduction. One is value analysis, a technique of looking at a product to determine what the customer is really interested in when he buys. Is it utility, appearance, durability, or certain special features? Once this has been determined, an analysis can be made to see if less costly materials or less costly operations can be used to produce the product while still meeting the customer's requirements. The advantage of direct costing or its close relative, relevant costing, in these studies is that any absorption of fixed overhead in calculating comparative production costs is ignored. Since fixed overhead will not change with a change in product design, it should not be part of the cost comparison.

The second type of management decision directly related to cost reduction is cost-benefit analysis. Here an attempt is made to compare the cost incurred with the benefit obtained from staff functions. For example, a company may believe that hiring plant guards will prevent neighborhood kids from stealing pieces of copper tubing stored outside the plant. How much tubing would have to be stolen per year to justify the salary and fringe benefits of a 24-hour guard detail, and is it likely that this much could or would be stolen? Similarly, suppose three industrial engineers can set direct labor quantity standards on the 20 percent of the production operations that account for 80 percent of the direct labor dollars. Does the difference in accuracy between engineered standards and estimated standards justify employing 12 more industrial engineers to set the standards on the remaining 80 percent of the operations that account for only 20 percent of the direct labor dollars?

Paperwork is a classic example of how cost-benefit analysis can pay off in cost reductions. One rather drastic method of reducing paperwork is to steal all copies of a weekly or monthly report before it is distributed. If the normal recipients of the report don't ask why they didn't receive it, the report is discontinued. A sounder approach is to ask each recipient whether he has taken any action recently as a result of the report or whether he reads it only to satisfy his curiosity. In the latter case, an effort should be made to discontinue the report.

Use of Variances in Cost Control

Most companies concentrate their cost control efforts on direct labor. However, in many companies today direct materials are a much larger proportion of total product costs than direct labor. The emphasis on direct labor goes back to the days when industry was less automated and when parts were rarely bought from outsiders. It is still true that in some companies the nature of purchased materials (for example, purchased parts) is such that waste is not a problem. In these instances, under the assumption that purchasing is obtaining the best prices available, there is no need to concentrate on controlling the cost of materials.

However, in industries where products are made from raw materials, control of direct materials can be very important. Indeed, it may be possible to reduce costs more by carefully controlling material usage than by controlling direct labor costs. Careful monitoring of scrap and spoilage can also be very fruitful. Other losses should be considered as well. For example, a product may require exactly two carriage bolts of a particular size. Spoilage of carriage bolts is nil. Still, if the bolts are requisitioned in kegs, some loss will be inevitable. Bolts needlessly find their way into outgoing trash, get permanently lost in other departments, and just seem to evaporate into thin air. This loss, too, deserves attention.

When variance data are used for cost control, the ideal procedure is to report the amount to the responsible supervisor; ask him to explain it in writing; ask him to suggest a corrective course of action in writing; ask him to report in writing on its implementation; and, finally, ask him to prepare a written report on the effectiveness of the corrective action. Two or more of these steps can be done simultaneously. Who is to receive the memos and whether copies go to others will depend on the way the company is organized. Of course, very few companies follow the formal procedure described above.

When explanations for variances are requested, a major educational effort is often required to get operating personnel to think constructively. A common (and useless) explanation of a variance created by the need to scrap 478 parts is that "the wrong gauge was issued and the error was not discovered until the run was almost over." A more constructive explanation adds the information that "the foreman has changed his procedure so he can make a personal check of gauge identification to the operation sheet within 15 minutes of the start of each new run." It is far from easy to get operating personnel to switch from the "alibi" type of explanation to the constructive type. However, analysis of a sample group of explanations, discussed with the plant superintendent from time to time, can be quite effective.

This leads to the question of who has the authority and responsibility to follow up on variances. Some companies limit the accounting department's role to preparation and distribution of the variance reports. Other companies expect the accounting department to analyze variances within the limitations of the data available in accounting records. Still other companies expect cost accounting personnel to find out the reasons for the variances and incorporate them in a cover letter or in footnotes to the report. Very few companies expect the accounting department to suggest corrective action or give it the authority to insist that suggestions be followed.

Accounting personnel frequently complain that little is done about the reports they prepare. It must be recognized, of course, that the operating people who receive the reports have major responsibility for getting production out on time, for maintaining good labor relations, and for monitoring product quality. The immediacy of these problems often overshadows cost control. However, if accounting personnel try to take a more active part in cost control, they will very likely be considered to be trespassing on the turf of line management.

One way to reduce this conflict is to place cost accounting directly under plant management, with only a "dotted line" relationship to the financial department. Another solution is to hold discussions between accounting personnel and the plant superintendent, with the superintendent carrying out the action decided upon. Still another approach is to have the foreman assist accounting personnel in preparing the cover letter for the report sent to the foreman's superior. The best approach for a particular company will depend on the personalities of both production and accounting personnel and on interpersonal relationships.

Whatever role accounting plays in variance follow-up, accounting personnel should spend enough time on the factory floor to become thoroughly familiar with the methods of operation, the peculiarities of materials and machines, and the morale of the labor force. This will reduce reporting errors and make contacts with operating personnel much more meaningful. Cost accountants should be familiar with every technical term used by operating management.

Exception Reporting

Every account in every department will probably show some variance, good or bad, in every period reported on. Minuscule variances neither receive nor deserve management's attention. Since each department has many accounts and since some executives receive reports from many departments, a technique that focuses attention on the important variances has considerable value. Exception reporting is such a technique. Under this approach, the performance report showing the variances includes only those accounts that have substantial variances (favorable or unfavorable) in the reporting period. Typically, department totals are also shown, whether or not they show variances.

In the few companies that used this technique before the days of computers, a lower-level clerk had to analyze the data and recopy the appropriate accounts—just to save a certain amount of executive time. Most companies found this was just not worth it. Today, computers have changed all that. The same EDP technology that makes it possible to produce voluminous detailed reports also makes it possible to condense these reports to show only the accounts that appear to require attention.

In most cases, the computer program instructs the computer to print only lines that show either a variance of *X* dollars or a variance of *Y* percent from the standard cost. When exception reporting is first adopted in a company, the *X* and *Y* amounts are frequently set quite low. Some manager points out that "$100 will buy a lot of chewing gum," so of course he is interested in any variance over $100; similarly, "10 percent is one out of ten," so of course he is interested in any variance over 10 percent. Unless the report covers only a one-day time span, these figures are much too low, and in many operations they would be too low even for such a report. A good way of determining appropriate *X* and *Y* values is to first decide on the largest number of variances a report recipient might have time to investigate before the next report is issued. The next step is to test various values of *X* and *Y* against past data until the predetermined number of variances results. When *X* and *Y* values are arbitrarily determined at low figures, a report may end up showing almost every account. This completely negates the benefits of exception reporting.

In a few computerized systems, different *X* and *Y* values are applied to the same data on reports going to different people. Ordinarily, the lowest-level supervisor sees more accounts for the one area under his control than the supervisor at the next higher level, who usually receives a report showing many departments individually. The highest *X* and *Y* values are used in reports to senior management.

The purpose of using both dollar and percentage criteria in exception reporting is to take advantage of two axioms in cost control:

1. It is easier to save $100 by finding a correctible cause for one-tenth of an unfavorable $1,000 variance than it is to save $100 by eliminating all of a $100 variance.
2. It is more difficult to eliminate a $100 variance on a $50,000 account than it is to eliminate a $100 variance on a $500 account.

In each case, the company gains $100, but the reporting of variances in both dollars and percentages helps the company's executives channel their time and energies into those areas with the greatest chances of success. Good variance reporting is the key to good cost control.

Timeliness is a very important element of effective variance reporting. If a foreman receives a daily variance report by midmorning of the next day, he may be able to correct conditions before much waste has occurred. In addition, since the conditions being reported on are still fresh in his memory, he can frequently determine the causes of the variance without having to dig back into records, either in his own department or in accounting. The importance of timely reporting in cost control cannot be overemphasized.

Responsibility Accounting

As noted earlier, the identification of the individual responsible for costs is an important part of cost control. The degree to which such responsibility accounting is carried out, however, varies widely from company to company.

In almost every cost system, separate performance reports are prepared for each productive department and separate expense reports for each service department. In addition, sales analyses are made for the marketing department and purchasing analyses for the purchasing department. Although this type of reporting partially recognizes areas of responsibility, it is only a somewhat accidental recognition and by no means the most effective one.

A somewhat more sophisticated approach is to segregate the cost accounts shown on the reports between those costs considered controllable and those noncontrollable. Many companies make this separation without fully realizing the implications of the two words and the likelihood that certain invalid assumptions may be drawn from them. In the first place, in production departments most variable costs are likely to be considered controllable and most fixed costs are likely to be listed as noncontrollable. It is important to realize, however, that the two classification schemes are not synonymous. An electric fractional horsepower motor being assembled into an end product is clearly a variable cost since its cost will increase in proportion to production, but it may not be controllable in any way by the department foreman. By contrast, the cost of the three assistant foremen may be a fixed cost that can be controlled to some degree by the foreman.

It must also be realized that the distinction between controllable and noncontrollable depends on the specific level of management involved. A cost may be noncontrollable at the foreman level but controllable at the plant superintendent level. An example is machinery depreciation in a company where all machinery purchases are decided at the plant superintendent level. Finally, the distinction between controllable and noncontrollable is usually based on the controllability of the cost on a daily, weekly, or monthly basis. Many accounts labeled noncontrollable *are* controllable when a longer-term view is considered. Again, machinery depreciation is an example. It is noncontrollable for machinery presently in place but becomes controllable when future acquisitions are being considered.

The term "responsibility accounting" usually refers to a much more complex program for assigning responsibility. The program is based on the principle that no cost appearing on the performance report sent to any manager should be outside his control *and* that every cost should be shown on someone's performance report. Advocates of this system point out, for example, that the foreman's salary should never appear (either as a separate item or buried in "supervisory salaries") in the departmental cost report going to the foreman. The foreman has no control over his salary, and it is unrealistic to expect him to try to hold his own salary to a minimum, as he is expected to do with other departmental costs. Since someone must be held responsible for every cost according to the basic principle of responsibility accounting, it becomes necessary to create a "superintendent's department" to cover the salaries of the various plant foremen. In addition, other costs that are authorized at the superintendent level will be charged to this department rather than spread to individual departments, as is the more usual practice. Examples include the costs of elevator operators, plant guards, and factory clericals as well as machinery depreciation and building maintenance. Certain costs including the superintendent's own salary go to a still higher level, and so on up the line. The result is that every line executive through the company president has a performance report that includes costs for which he has primary responsibility.

Consider a report going to a plant superintendent. If the plant has eight production departments, the traditional report will list the various accounts on the left and will have a column for each department and a total column. Under the responsibility accounting approach, a number of costs will be transferred from the individual department columns to a new column headed "superintendent's department." For some accounts, this new column will be blank and for some accounts it will be the only column showing an amount. For most accounts, only some of the dollars will appear in the new column. Also, for some accounts, the total column will show the same figure as the traditional report. In other accounts, the total will be lower, since some costs have been transferred to the cost report for the manufacturing vice president.

Conversion to full responsibility accounting will ordinarily require the addition of a number of new department designations to the company's chart of account. It will also require substantial changes in the coding of accounts payable and payroll cost entries. Often the numeric coding of accounts will also have to be revised, particularly when a report is prepared on a computer which selects the accounts going into each report according to a numbering system.

One of the major problems in attempting to prepare responsibility reports, even under traditional methods, is that cost variations are often attributable to the actions or decisions of two or more prople in different departments. If, for example, the president decides to add dental insurance to the fringe benefit package of all employees at midyear, any foreman who is criticized for above-standard fringe benefit costs in his department during the remainder of the year has a legitimate cause for complaint. On the other hand, if this cost is left in the president's report of his own area of primary responsibility, the foreman's efficiency variance on the fringe benefit account will not properly reflect the full cost of any excess direct labor within his department. The decision on where a cost should be shown is usually based on which individual is responsible for the day-to-day variations —in this case, the production department foreman.

There are numerous examples of dual responsibility. Two more may be mentioned. Purchasing may show an unfavorable price variance because production suddenly insists for quality control reasons that only a particular vendor be used as the source of certain materials. Production may show an unfavorable direct labor variance because sales accepted a number of rush orders requiring numerous setups for short runs and the operation of machines less efficient than those normally used for the products.

Responsibility accounting in its fullest sense is not widely used, although it is growing. Possibly this approach will have its greatest impact on costs in the general and administrative area. The many companies that report G.& A. costs as if the whole area were under the control of one person really have no cost control at all. For example, if "other salaries" are above the standard, is the variance attributable to salaries of a particular vice president's staff, or does it represent overtime incurred by the switchboard operators?

Management Reporting

The proper design of management reports is an extremely important aspect of cost control. Managers will inevitably take a greater interest in cost control if the reports they receive are pertinent to their area of responsibility, contain no irrelevant or confusing data, highlight the major items deserving attention, are as brief as circumstances allow, are timely, and are legible.

A fairly common and satisfactory practice is to prepare a report for the department supervisor and send the plant superintendent a summary report for all the departments under his charge, with copies of the departmental reports attached. With the power of modern computers, this approach can be improved by having the report for the plant superintendent prepared under the exception principle—that is, showing only the exceptions large enough to concern him. In addition, under full responsibility accounting the report will show some costs not included in the departmental reports.

Generally, each line of the report will show actual costs for the period compared with the standard (or with the prior year for companies using actual costs), as well as the variance and the percentage of the variance. Some companies using standard costing show both the standard and the prior year. This is not advisable. A report recipient is likely to compare the current actual cost with both figures and if one or the other figure is higher than the current actual cost, he goes on to the next item. Since the prior year may contain an abnormality, he should be guided only by the comparison with the standard. Usually, year-to-date information is also shown to enable the manager to determine at a glance if a condition is improving or worsening.

Every company should design its reports to reflect its chart of accounts, its departments, and its nomenclature and abbreviations. It is impossible to show a range of good reports for all industries in this book. Figures 11-1, 11-2, and 11-3 show a set of reports for a relatively small company using a simple direct cost system. In this com-

FIGURE 11-1. Monthly material usage report.

4 or 5 Weeks Ended __________

	MONTHLY				YEAR TO DATE			
Department	Std.	Actual	Var.	Var. %	Std.	Actual	Var.	Var. %
Molding								
Cleaning								
Stamping								
Assembly								
Packing								
TOTAL								

pany, the difficulty of measuring material used made it necessary to report material usage only on a monthly basis, following a month-end physical inventory. Labor and overhead were reported weekly to the departments. (Figures 11-2 and 11-3 show the monthly summaries sent to upper management.)

Some readers may question the classifications of indirect labor shown as fixed overhead in Figure 11-2. In the company illustrated, all rework was done by a salaried worker, and the company considered the cost fixed. Idle time, cleanup, and machine downtime represented time of direct labor not being used on production and were also considered fixed. Another company might well classify all four of these accounts as variable. This illustrates the need to examine company operations carefully before designing report forms.

Reports in hours, pounds, or numbers of people rather than in dollars are particularly effective for cost control. This is especially true in companies where production foremen have come up the ladder the hard way and are relatively uneducated and quite inexperienced in the finer points of accounting theory. A daily Flash Report similar to Figure 11-4 will often tell a foreman more quickly than dollar figures just exactly what he must do today to remedy the situation revealed in yesterday's report.

A particularly effective type of report for upper management is the Trend Report. The Trend Report shown in Figure 11-5 is a condensed monthly income statement for the entire company. A simi-

FIGURE 11-2. Monthly production departmental operating report.

Dept. Name ____________ Dept. No. __________ Week Ended __________

	WEEK				MONTH TO DATE			
	STD.	ACTUAL	VAR.	VAR. %	STD.	ACTUAL	VAR.	VAR. %
Direct labor								
Makeup pay allowance								
Overtime allowance								
Net direct labor								
Variable overhead								
Factory supplies								
Perishable tools								
General plant								
Total variable overhead								
Fixed overhead—indirect labor								
Rework								
Idle time								
Cleanup								
Materials handling								
Machine downtime								
Miscellaneous								
Indirect overtime								
Total indirect								
Total Department								

FIGURE 11-3. Monthly nonproduction departmental report.

Dept. Name _______________ Dept. No. _____ 4 or 5 Weeks Ended _______________

	Month				Cumulative			
	Budget	Actual	Variance (Unfavorable in Parentheses)		Budget	Actual	Variance (Unfavorable in Parentheses)	
			Amt.	%			Amt.	%
Salaries and wages								
Overtime								
Factory supplies								
Perishable tools								
Other								
Total								

FIGURE 11-4. Foreman's daily flash report.

Date 10/27 Dept. A

	Budget	Actual
Production in units	127,000	124,650
Employees on payroll		
Supervisors	2	2
Production workers	28	26
Indirect labor	9	9
Overtime hours	10	20
Pounds of steam used	120,000	147,400
Pieces scrapped	3,700	3,105

lar technique can be used to prepare income statements for any revenue-producing division or product line or for cost reports for any entity. The company in Figure 11-5 is on direct costing. The key figures in such a company are (1) sales, (2) marginal contribution, (3) fixed costs, (4) cost variances, and (5) earnings before taxes. In order to focus attention on the key figures, cost of sales has been omitted, and all variances (whether in production or S.G.& A., whether on variable costs or fixed costs) have been combined in one column. Cost of sales at standard direct costs is, of course, the difference between sales and marginal contribution at standard.

The most interesting feature of a trend report is that actual figures for past months and forecast figures for future months are reported in all columns except the fixed cost column, where only forecast figures are shown for all months and the variances are included in the expense variance column. The forecast for a past month can be determined by adding the favorable variance figure to the actual amount or by subtracting the unfavorable variance figure from the actual amount. However, knowledge of the forecast for a past month is rather meaningless when the variance is shown directly. The bottom line on the report, the current prediction for the whole year, can project a trend shown by the variances in past months (as was done in

FIGURE 11-5. Trend report format: Statement of earnings before taxes.

YEAR 1979	GROSS SALES		MARGINAL CONTRIBUTION AT STANDARD COST		FIXED COSTS	EXPENSE	EARNINGS BEFORE TAXES	
	ACTUAL OR PREDICTED*	VARIANCE	ACTUAL OR PREDICTED*	VARIANCE	PREDICTED	VARIANCE	ACTUAL OR PREDICTED*	VARIANCE
January	$ 7.182	$ (98)	$ 1.949	$ (22)	$ 1.516	$(120)	$ 313	$(142)
February	7.820	(300)	2.246	210	1.476	140	910	350
March	6.988	(262)	1.766	(198)	1.581	70	255	(128)
April	7.080*		1.917*		1.566		351*	
May	6.390*		1.730*		1.472		258*	
June	5.770*		1.563*		1.562		1*	
July	5.580*		1.511*		1.437		74*	
August	6.490*		1.757*		1.592		165*	
September	5.900*		1.598*		1.413		185*	
October	6.590*		1.785*		1.536		249*	
November	5.490*		1.487*		1.408		79*	
December	8.660*		2.345*		1.587		758*	
Year to date	$21.990	$(660)	$ 5.961	$ (10)	$4.573		$1.478	$ 80
Original prediction	$80.000		$21.664		$18.146	$ 90	$3.518	
Current prediction	$77.500		$21.654		$18.146	$ 90	$3.598	

ANALYSIS OF MARGINAL CONTRIBUTION VARIANCES

CURRENT MONTH

Forecast		$1,964
Price var.	$ 9	
Vol. var.	(102)	
Mix var.	(105)	(198)
Actual		$1,766

YEAR TO DATE

Forecast		$5,971
Price var.	$58	
Vol. var.	16	
Mix var.	(84)	(10)
Actual		$5,961

the case of sales in Figure 11-5) or merely reflect the variances to date when no pattern is indicated (as has been done on marginal contribution and earnings in the example).

The chief advantage of trend reports is that they show in very little space all the key data needed by top management to understand what is happening and what is likely to happen in the remainder of the year. Such a report can also aid management in revising plans for the rest of the year. An added advantage of the trend report is that it includes prior figures. Thus with each month's report, the previous month's report can be thrown away. When a senior executive is in the habit of taking reports home with him, has many reporting areas under his supervision, and needs to refer frequently to data for prior months, the advantage of having all the previous information on the current report is considerable. Filing time and space are also saved.

Charting

Charts are another effective way of presenting cost control data to management. Most people find it easier to grasp data in chart form than data in tabular form. Furthermore, small variances that are increasing gradually tend to escape management's attention when presented in tabular form, but they pretty well speak for themselves when charted. The two major types of charts are line charts and bar charts. Examples are shown in Figures 11-6 and 11-7 respectively. Pie charts and pictographs should be saved for the annual report to stockholders, since line and bar charts have generally been found adequate for management's needs. Color, of course, adds interest to any chart. A company that does not employ charts to emphasize current cost behavior to its executives is missing a very real cost control tool.

Direct Costing and Cost Control

Most managers find direct cost reports easier to understand than absorption cost reports. Since variable costs are expressed as so much per unit produced and fixed costs are fixed in direct costing, the relationship between costs and production is clear. The volume variance account which appears in standard absorption cost reports is not used in direct costing. Since the volume variance is difficult to understand, its omission clarifies the cost report.

Under direct costing, variances from standards developed separately for variable and fixed costs are also developed for S.G.& A. and marginal contribution. Although this can also be done under absorp-

FIGURE 11-6. Monthly and year-to-date expense variance chart; Everlast Shoe Corp.

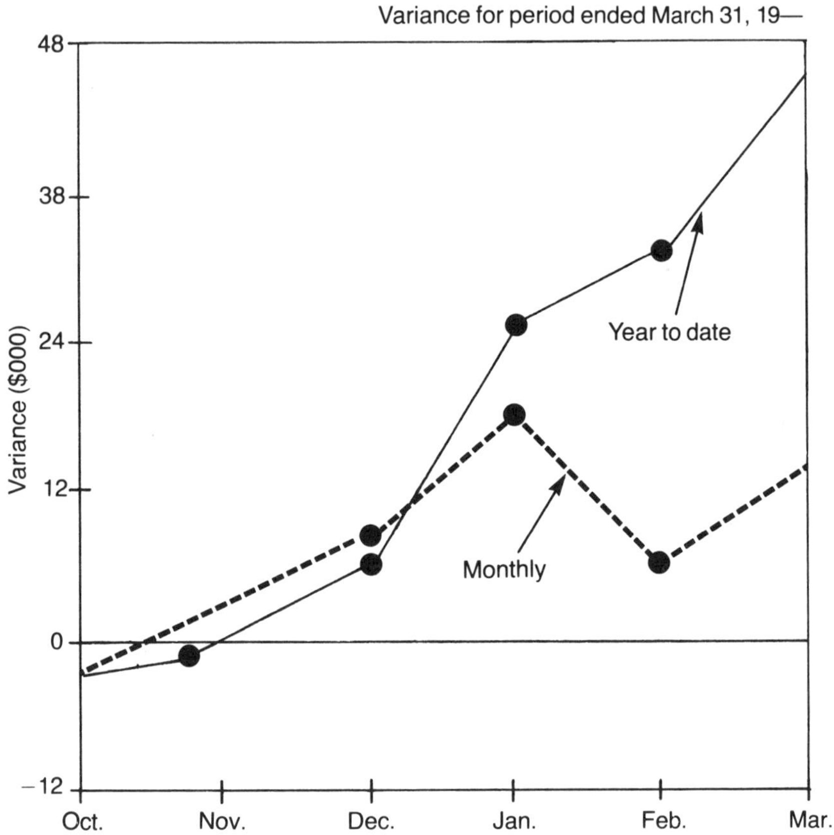

tion costing, it is not very common. The basic philosophy of direct costing requires that such variances be developed. Obviously, cost control is helped thereby.

Finally, direct costing requires somewhat less bookkeeping than absorption costing. Although the saving may not be great, it is not negligible. Under absorption costing, certain plantwide fixed costs must be allocated to departments on some basis and then absorbed by production on some basis. Neither the original calculation of the appropriate bases nor the monthly chore of allocating the fixed costs to them can be considered minor. This work is saved under direct costing, which does not allocate fixed costs to departments or to products.

FIGURE 11-7. Cost report—fixed costs for August 19—.

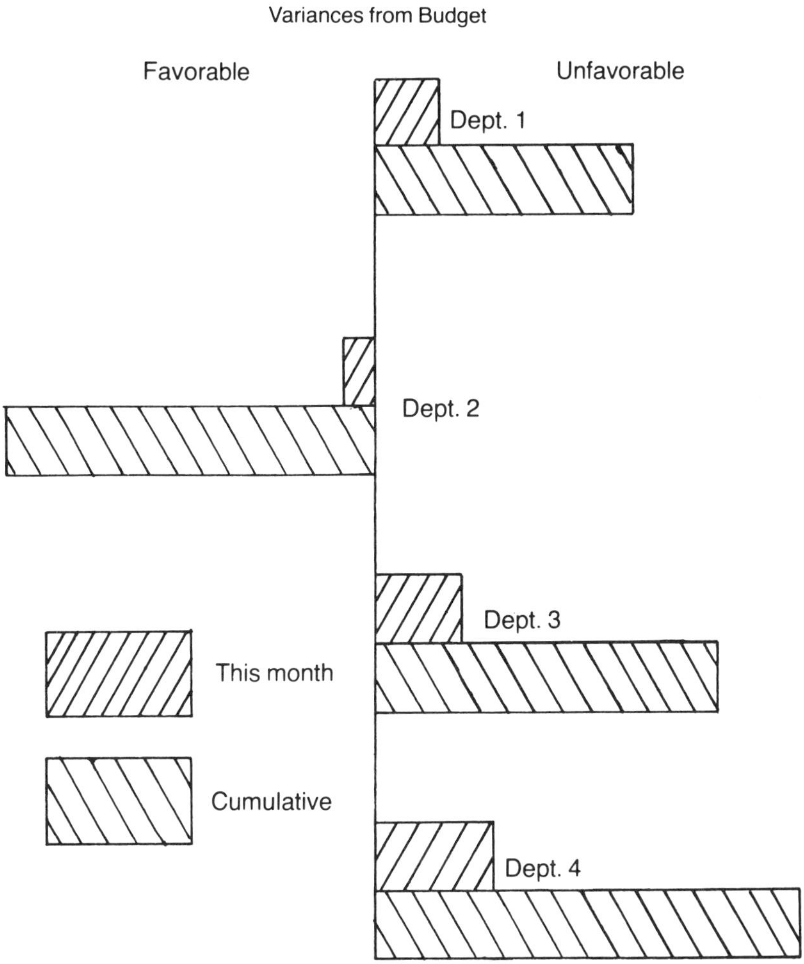

Summary

Cost control is the traditional purpose of cost accounting and remains a very important function. The major tool for cost control is the proper development, analysis, and application of variances in correcting cost overruns and in expanding the improved methods often revealed by favorable variances. Cost control is further helped by effective cost reports to management. Reports designed according to the principles of exception reporting and responsibility accounting have proved particularly valuable.

12

Analysis of Marginal Contribution Variance

AN important aspect of direct costing that is impossible to duplicate under absorption costing is the analysis of the marginal contribution variance. As already indicated, the marginal contribution is the difference between the net sales and the total variable, or direct, cost of sales. It cannot be emphasized too often that any change in the marginal contribution carries down at 100 cents on the dollar to net income before income taxes.

For many years, sales have been analyzed in almost every conceivable way. Summaries are prepared by product, by product group, by geographic area, by salesmen, by branch sales office, by distribution center, by sales tax area, by the industry of the customer, by method of sale (own salesmen vs. wholesalers vs. manufacturers' representatives vs. company-owned stores), by class of customer (wholesaler vs. department store vs. discount store vs. variety chain), and by size of customer. However, it is not sales that make the difference between a growing company and one headed for bankruptcy, although sales are certainly a major factor. It is the profits from sales that spell out the future of a company, and these profits show up directly in changes in marginal contribution.

Use of Standards in Marginal Contribution Analyses

Companies using standard costs invariably adopt the standard cost as the basis for determining the amount of the marginal contribution. This has the distinct advantage under direct costing of segregating the responsibilities of the marketing and sales department from those of the production department. It is the job of the marketing group to maximize the marginal contribution at standard cost, and it is the job of production to minimize any unfavorable variance between actual cost and standard cost. Of course, the marketing group is also responsible for variances in selling expenses, just as the administrative group is responsible for variances in G.& A. expenses, but the control of these expenses is handled through separate reports. Since variable S.G.& A. expenses are part of product costs under direct costing, only the spending variances need be considered on either variable or fixed S.G.& A. costs. These variances are relatively easy to understand even if they are not always easy to control. Thus it can be said that the marginal contribution at standard is the real measure of the effectiveness of marketing's effort (except in the limited area of controlling its own expenses).

Some companies under absorption costing analyze gross profit, again usually at standard, in much the same way that companies under direct costing analyze marginal contribution. However, gross profit analysis, though far superior to sales analysis, is not nearly as useful as marginal contribution analysis. This is so for three reasons:

1. If the sales forecast in physical units is higher this year than actual sales were last year, the standard costs will be lower this year than last year because the fixed manufacturing costs will be spread over more units, all other things being equal. This means that the year-to-year comparison of gross profit will reflect the change in production costs as well as the efforts of the marketing department. Although it might be said that the increased volume is also the result of the marketing effort, the figures are still confusing.
2. A customer class that shows a gross profit insufficient to cover the costs of selling to it may nevertheless be contributing to fixed manufacturing costs. This will appear as part of marginal contribution but not as part of gross profit.
3. A customer class may require high variable S.G.& A. costs—for example, freight out when absorbed by the company. These costs will

be deducted from marginal contribution, as they should be, but will not be deducted from gross profit.

The Three Marginal Contribution Variances

The total marginal contribution variance is a satisfactory measure of a company's progress and an equally satisfactory basis for determining if a particular product or customer group should receive more emphasis, receive less emphasis, or perhaps be abandoned altogether. However, it is not a satisfactory basis for determining the reasons for changes in marginal contribution from period to period or from the forecast. For this purpose, it is necessary to break the variance into three components: selling price variance, volume variance, and product mix variance.

Some very real problems exist in establishing the base from which the marginal contribution variance is measured. Any company that is forecasting an income statement has necessarily arrived at a total sales figure and, if it is on a direct cost system, a total figure for direct costs at standard, which of course gives the forecast marginal contribution. Furthermore, companies that are oriented toward sales analysis will very often forecast sales by product groups as an aid to production planning and by geographic area or by salesman as an aid to setting goals for regional sales managers or individual salesmen. Often, there are no forecasts for how much of each product will go into each territory; even less often are there forecasts of how much of each product will go to customers in each category when a classification other than geographic is used.

Although many companies have different expected prices for different geographic areas or different classes of customer, these prices are rarely reflected, except as averages, in the forecasts. In theory, the only way to obtain a completely accurate three-way division is to forecast sales in units of each product to each customer and, further, to forecast the average price at which each product will be bought by that customer after considering quantity discounts, promotional allowances, and any other factors that affect prices. This approach has proved to be impracticable for most companies, although it is used by some companies that supply parts to just a few other manufacturers.

The approach used by most companies is to analyze the prior year's sales according to the same classifications proposed for the variances—that is, by products, by one or more territorial breakdowns, and by one or more customer classes. The company then requests the sales forecasting group to estimate a price for each product and an overall increase or decrease in unit sales of each product.

The product prices are subject to review by top management. The estimate of unit sales must, of course, include any new products and their proposed selling prices. Both the price estimates and the unit volume estimates are converted to percentages of the prior year. This information can then be fed into a computer, which will quickly convert the prior year's data into a forecast in as much detail as required. Basically, the procedure involves cross-analyzing each territory and customer classification by product.

A company must be computerized if it proposes to use such a system fully. The analysis of the total company and a single subanalysis by products can be done manually, using sales statistics by product. However, a computer is needed to cross-analyze territory and customer class breakdowns by product, since every line item on every invoice must be costed out at standard and must also show the forecast selling price of the product. (Of course, neither figure is printed on the invoice copies going to the customer. In fact, in some systems these data are picked up in a computer memory record without being printed out at all.) The line-item data are needed not only to create the detailed forecast but also to calculate the current year's variances in marginal contribution. Because of this requirement, there is usually a one-year lag between the time the decision is made to create such variances and the beginning of the flow of useful data. The year is used to accumulate the standard cost and forecast selling price data by customer through the accumulation of line-item data.

Because of the great usefulness of marginal contribution variance analysis, companies inaugurating the system often decide to develop more customer classifications than they ever had before—for example, breakdowns by customer industry and customer size. Since the computer will compile the data according to customer code, the customer codes may have to be enlarged. This can be done at any time, but there will always be the one-year lag between the decision and the arrival of useful data.

Since the marginal contribution reports are generated monthly, seasonal variations must be reflected in the data. This, however, occurs automatically through the use of actual prior-year figures except for any adjustments necessary for new product introduction or product discontinuance.

Calculation of the Three Marginal Contribution Variances

Selling Price Variance

The selling price variance is the difference between the forecast price and the average actual price of each unit of each product sold to each customer extended by the number of units sold. The computer does not actually gather the data by individual customer; rather, it accumulates data by customer class for each analysis as it prints the invoice—unless a data base system is used. Under the data base concept, the data are stored from each invoice until needed for analysis.

Physical Volume Variance

In a few industries, executives think almost entirely in terms of units rather than dollars. If the president of a shoe manufacturer is asked "How's business?," he replies, "We are X pairs ahead (or behind) last year." These pairs of shoes may be of different styles and may sell at different prices, but that is how he thinks. Similarly, brewery executives think in terms of barrels produced. There are no doubt other industries with similar traditions. These industries will calculate their physical volume variance by the difference between the actual unit sales and the forecast unit sales of each category.

This approach will not usually work, however, for industries whose products have unit prices that vary widely—say, from the price of a 1-quarter-horsepower motor to that of a 500-horsepower motor, or from the price of a screwdriver to that of an industrial-type electric drill. In such industries standard cost is considered the measure of physical volume. Thus the physical volume variance is the difference between actual shipments to the customer at standard cost and forecast shipments to the customer at standard cost. These differences are again accumulated by product group, by territory, and by customer class.

Product Mix Variance

Virtually all companies expect to sell certain products at higher marginal contribution percentages than other products in the line. That is, the standard cost is a lower percentage of the forecast selling price on these products than on other products. If the proportion of these more profitable products actually sold is lower than forecast, there will be a drop in marginal contribution, even if the total of all products sold has a standard cost equal to the forecast and even if every product was sold at its forecast selling price. This drop is called an unfavorable product mix variance. If the proportion of the more profitable products sold rises compared with the forecast, the result is a favorable mix variance. A number of executives have difficulty with the concept of mix variances and find profit fluctuations difficult to explain when volume and prices are stable or even go in a direction opposite to profits.

It should be noted that it is impossible to have a product mix variance on a single product. However, when a number of products are combined into a product class or when a single product is sold in different sizes with different product standard costs for each size, a mix variance is entirely possible and will probably occur in one direction or the other.

The quick way to calculate the product mix for a customer or a class is to subtract the selling price variance and the physical volume variance as calculated above from the total marginal contribution variance of the product class, territory, or customer class. Of course, subtract in this sense means deduct unfavorable variances from a total unfavorable variance but add favorable variances to a total unfavorable variance. Similarly, a favorable selling price variance or physical volume variance would be subtracted from a favorable total marginal contribution variance but added to a total unfavorable marginal contribution variance.

The product mix variance can also be calculated directly rather than by subtraction. The formula is as follows:

> Actual shipments at standard cost *times* the marginal contribution per standard cost dollar, consisting of the actual marginal contribution per standard cost dollar *minus* the favorable selling price variance per standard cost dollar (or *plus* the unfavorable selling price variance per standard cost dollar) *minus* the forecast marginal contribution per standard cost dollar.

The formulas for arriving at the three marginal contribution variances are illustrated in Figure 12-1. In this example, the standard cost dollars are used as units, as is most generally done. The first three columns in the figure—those for the total company—were used to compute the selling price variance of $696, favorable. This figure was calculated by multiplying the $.098 difference between the forecast selling price per standard cost dollar, $1.983, and the actual selling price per standard cost dollar, $2.081, by the actual sales at standard cost, $7,100. The volume variance of ($190) was arrived at by multiplying the forecast marginal contribution per standard cost dollar, $.757, by the ($250) difference between forecast sales at standard cost, $7,350, and actual sales at standard cost, $7,100. The product mix variance of ($995) is the amount that reconciles these two to the ($489) total marginal contribution variance. It can be verified by the previously stated formula, which in this case is $7,100 × (.715 − .098 − .757).

FIGURE 12-1. Sales and marginal contribution report by products.

	Total Company			*Product Group A*			*Product Group B*		
	Forecast	*Actual*	*Variance*	*Forecast*	*Actual*	*Variance*	*Forecast*	*Actual*	*Variance*
Sales at Standard Cost Dollars	$7,350	$7,100	$(250)	$5,250	$4,800	$(450)	$2,100	$2,300	$200
Sales at Sales Dollars	14,574	14,776	202	10,176	10,176	159	4,557	4,600	43
Selling Price per Standard Cost Dollar	1.983	2.081	.098	1.908	2.120	.212	2.17	2.00	(.17)
Marginal Contribution above Standard Cost	5,565	5,076	(489)	4,200	3,903	(297)	1,365	1,173	(192)
Marginal Contribution per Standard Cost Dollar	.757	.715	(.042)	.800	.813	.013	.650	.510	(.140)
Selling Price Variance			$696			$1,018			$(391)
Volume Variance			(190)			(360)			130
Product Mix Variance			(995)			(955)			69
			$(489)			$(297)			$(192)

The variances in the two product group columns are calculated the same way. It should be noted that the forecast and actual amounts cross-add, as does the variance total. The individual variances do not. This is because of the change in mix between the product groups.

Uses of Marginal Contribution Variances

The total company variances in Figure 12-1 will suggest to marketing that in a successful effort to improve on selling prices it has apparently driven customers into its less profitable product lines to the point where the unfavorable product mix variance has become quite large, more than offsetting the favorable selling price variance. In addition, sales volume has suffered slightly. The fact that increased selling prices have hurt both product mix and volume is even more evident in the analysis of Product Group A. The favorable selling price variance is quite large, as are the unfavorable volume variances and product mix variances. Furthermore, there has been a shift in sales volume from the higher-profit Product Group A to the lower-profit Product Group B; this has further hurt the total company profits.

It should be emphasized again that the variances in marginal contribution are an exact measure of the effect of the selling price, volume, and product mix changes on the company's net profit before income taxes. This is always true under a direct cost system and never true under an absorption cost system. Thus the marginal contribution variances tell the marketing department in accurate amounts how effective its policies have been in contributing to company profits. A similar analysis of gross profit is quite inaccurate in this regard. The three-way analysis provides marketing with guidance on which of its policies are effective in terms of net profits and helps marketing managers revise these policies constructively.

Of course, not every suggestion arising from a review of marginal contribution variances should be followed. Often, factors unrelated to internal policies—increased competition, gain or loss of specific customers, quality problems with particular products, and the like—account for the variances. Nevertheless, marginal contribution variance analysis is a powerful tool in that it will reveal trends that are not obvious and that cannot be attributed to specific known factors.

As previously stated, marginal contribution analysis can be done by product class without using a computer or making a basic change in the company's recording system. Figure 12-1 shows only two product groups; the typical company would have between six and twelve and would get that much more useful information.

Figure 12-2 shows an analysis of marginal contribution variances by sales territories. Only the variances themselves are shown, since the derivation of the variances was illustrated in Figure 12-1. Note that the unfavorable selling price variance in Territory East was exactly offset by the favorable volume and product mix variances, indicating that the pricing policy in this territory was neither good nor bad in its impact on profits. On the other hand, the favorable selling price variance in Territory West appears to have caused larger unfavorable variances in both volume and product mix, suggesting that a review of this policy is in order. The total company figures show an unfavorable product mix variance, but an analysis by territory is required to show where this occurred and to suggest a reason for it.

It should be noted that the individual variances do not cross-add on Figure 12-2, again because of the product mix as between territories. Also, most companies will break down their territories into many more columns.

A variance analysis by territory or any other customer classification requires the recording of both the standard cost and the forecast selling price on every line item of customer invoices. This generally entails a revision of recordkeeping and requires a computer to be practicable. Marginal contribution analysis can also be done by industry of the customer, size of the customer, type of trade of the customer, or other classification. However, once the company's recording system is revised to make one of these analyses possible, much can be gained at little cost by doing all of them. Finally, marginal contribution analysis can serve as a guide to the profitability of individual customers and groups of customers and as a means of evaluating the justification for sales branch offices, number of salesmen, distribution

FIGURE 12-2. Marginal contribution variance analysis by territory.

	Total Company	*Territory East*	*Territory West*
Selling Price Variance	$ (32)	$(1,032)	$1,000
Volume Variance	100	220	(321)
Product Mix Variance	(468)	812	(1,079)
Total Variance	$(400)	-0-	$ (400)
Forecast Marginal Contribution	5,200	2,200	3,000
Actual Marginal Contribution	$4,800	$ 2,200	$2,600

warehouses, and advertising appropriations. These topics will be covered in the next chapter.

It should be mentioned that marginal contribution reports often show disturbing figures—disturbing in the sense that they indicate a substantial profit decrease from the forecast, with no apparent explanation. These figures can be cross-analyzed to obtain explanations. For example, it is possible to determine which salesman was responsible for the loss shown on Figure 12-2 in Territory West and, further, which products with low profits were above the forecast and which products with high profits were below the forecast in that territory.

Companies that do not wish to go through the forecasting procedure can still obtain valuable data by analyzing the marginal contribution variances from the prior year. This can be done by the three subvariances and by every classification of products, territories, and customer classes—just as in analyzing the variance from the forecast. Variances from the prior year are not quite as meaningful as variances from a forecast, since they include amounts which represent predictable changes. This obscures the unexpected changes which require some type of action. Nevertheless, variances from last year can be a valuable marketing tool. Comparisons with the prior year or several prior years show trends which can be quite informative.

Summary

A major management tool privided by direct costing is the analysis of marginal contribution by product group, territory, and customer class. In addition, it is possible to determine the marginal contribution variance from forecast, which reflects the variance from forecast of net profits before taxes. This can also be done by categories.

Marginal contribution analysis can be carried into separate variances for selling price, volume, and product mix to give marketing a picture of how it is doing as well as information on "why." This is the first step toward capitalizing on favorable trends and correcting unfavorable ones.

Considerable effort must be expended to obtain the data in most meaningful form. Some of the procedures cannot be performed without a computer. However, the reward is great. A company that fails to carry direct costing through to monthly marginal contribution accumulation and analysis—by at least all the categories traditionally used for analyzing sales—is not taking full advantage of the opportunities offered by direct costing.

13

Direct Costing in Marketing and Distribution

Of all the functions of industry, cost accounting has had its least impact on marketing and distribution. This is true of both profit-oriented management decisions and of cost control in these areas. In our view, cost accounting has the greatest potential for profit improvement in the future in those many companies that have largely ignored the application of cost data in the management of marketing and distribution. There are numerous examples of the usefulness of cost accounting in these functions. Some examples have already been given in the discussion of pricing policies in Chapter 5, in the uses of marginal contribution as a tool for profit planning in Chapter 7, and in the uses of marginal contribution analysis in Chapter 12.

A few companies, mostly consumer products manufacturers in the food field, have been using standard costing to control marketing and distribution costs for some years. The spread of this technique has apparently been slowed by absorption costing, which fails to relate variable costs to volume and fails to recognize that truly fixed costs are not affected by volume. A direct cost approach opens the door to a much wider use of cost accounting for the control of selling costs.

The Profit Derived from a Customer

As noted in the previous chapter, the costing of each line item on an invoice at direct standard cost will make it possible to analyze by groups of customers the changes from forecast in marginal contribution. The same costing of line items on invoices will make possible the summarization of direct standard costs and sales dollars for each customer for the year. Since direct standard product costs include all variable manufacturing costs as well as all variable S.G.& A. costs, the difference between net sales to the customer and the direct standard costs of the products shipped will indicate the contribution derived from that particular customer to the company's fixed costs.

A report of marginal contribution by customer frequently provides some very real surprises. It may show that some customers who are greatly valued because of their high volume are generating very little marginal contribution, perhaps because they are buying only low-margin products, are negotiating very favorable prices, or are confining purchases to promotional items. This is particularly true in the sale of consumer goods to retailers. Here the low-volume "mom and pop" store may account for a surprisingly large portion of the total marginal contribution dollars, whereas the high-volume discount department store chain accounts for a correspondingly low portion of the total marginal contribution dollars. Since the generation of marginal contribution dollars under a direct cost system is the key to profits, a report of marginal contribution dollars by customer is a much more valid guide to where the company should devote its selling effort than a sales analysis can be.

Territory Decisions

It is a rare marketing department that has not at some time considered abandoning a sales territory because of its low volume and high selling costs; that has not thought about expanding its geographic market; and that has not wondered whether the added costs of opening a sales office in some area now covered from a remote sales office would increase volume sufficiently to justify the added costs. Relevant costing, a concept based on the separation of variable from fixed costs, can supply considerable guidance on these questions.

Two examples of relevant costing in product abandonment decisions were given in Chapter 8. The application of this concept to territory abandonment decisions is more complex. In the first place, the current marginal contribution supplied by the territory may not be completely lost. It may be possible to replace salesmen operating out of a company sales office and supervised by a company regional sales manager by an arrangement with wholesalers or with manufacturers' representatives. Although such a switch usually results in a loss of sales volume, in some situations it can increase sales volume. In addition, the complete withdrawal of any real sales effort may still leave a few customers who order by mail or who can be called on economically from the home office.

When the plan is to use wholesalers or manufacturers' representatives, the estimated retained volume will, of course, show a lower per-dollar marginal contribution than when the company's own sales force is used. This fact must be weighed against the expense saving. Another problem to consider is whether any loss of volume expected to occur in the first year will become worse in later years. This problem may be particularly acute when some customers in the territory are branches of a chain that will continue to buy at the home office. As the time lengthens that the branch personnel have not seen company salesmen, their interest in the company's products decreases.

The decision in this case is easy to define, but it is quite difficult to arrive at volume figures, even approximate ones. After an educated guess has been made as to the likely volume loss, another educated guess must be made as to whether this loss will be at the average marginal contribution percentage or a higher or lower percentage. Typically, the lost volume will be at a higher than average marginal contribution percentage because the customers likely to be retained are the few large-volume, low-profit-percentage customers and those likely to be dropped are the many low-volume, high-profit-percentage ones.

The next step is to compare this loss of marginal contribution dollars with the saving in *fixed* selling expenses. Variable selling expenses are already reflected in product costs and are automatically considered to be saved as part of cost of sales. However, most companies reflect certain variable selling expenses in product costs on an average basis. An example is freight out when absorbed by the company. If the cost of freight to the territory being considered is substantially higher or lower than average, the difference can be estimated and added to or subtracted from the fixed costs saved.

The fixed costs referred to here are the relevant fixed costs—those that will be eliminated by abandonment of the territory. They include occupancy expense of the local sales office, salaries of personnel working in that office or out of it (with the exception of commission salesmen), and most of the expenses of maintaining that office. Depending on circumstances, a branch distribution warehouse might also be eliminated, along with its cost. Of course, any added costs of serving those customers that the company chose to retain in the territory would have to be netted against the cost savings.

When the cost savings so calculated are greater than the marginal contribution lost, it appears obvious that the territory is a loser. Unless a substantial turnaround can be reasonably expected in the not-too-distant future, the territory should be abandoned. However, if the potential cost savings are less than the current marginal contribution, the answer is not so clear. If the spread is substantial, the territory should be retained. If the spread is minimal, the company may well decide that the capital tied up in servicing the territory could be better employed elsewhere. In this sense, the capital employed includes not only the relevant fixed costs of the territory but also the direct standard costs of goods going into the territory divided by the annual turnover rate.

The same type of analysis can be used to determine whether a new territory should be opened up or whether a more concentrated (and more expensive) sales effort should be planned by splitting an existing sales territory into two. The only differences between these problems and the abandonment question is that the volume thus acquired will be more difficult to estimate and the marginal contribution of that volume will be more difficult to determine. In addition, such decisions are usually based on an expected net profit gain in two, three, or four years rather than on the estimate for the year ahead.

The Small Customer Problem

Let us assume that a company has a customer whose purchases are minimal and that the marginal contribution generated from this customer for the whole year is only \$50. It is hard to believe that a company does not incur more than \$50 in expense during a year in servicing such a customer. Yet when the expenses to be saved (other than the variable costs, which have already been deducted from the sales dollar in arriving at the marginal contribution) are listed, it turns out that there are virtually none. Most likely, because of the low volume of this account, the salesman calls on the customer only when he has some time left over after making a call on a larger customer in the same town. Keeping the customer's name in the accounts receivable ledger costs pennies, sending the customer copies of promotional literature may have an incremental cost of a dollar or two a year, and that is about all.

Based on this type of analysis, dropping the customer would probably have a negative effect on profits of between $40 and $45 per year. Not a very great loss, but a loss nevertheless. Here ROI need not be considered, since there is no reason to believe the percentage return on the investment for doing business with this customer is any different from that of any other. It thus appears that there is no reason to drop the customer, even ignoring the fact that the customer may grow in the future. After all, General Motors was once small too.

If the foregoing analysis is correct, why do companies frequently evaluate customers on the basis of their marginal contribution? Such an analysis, in which customers are sequenced by the size of the marginal contribution they generate, can lead to important policy changes. Generally, a report of this nature shows the customer generating the largest contribution at the top of the list and the one showing the smallest at the bottom. Cumulative percentages of the total marginal contribution are shown in the right-hand column. If the report shows, for example, that the top five customers on the list account for 60 percent of the company's total marginal contribution, the company is alerted to the devastating effect on profits that would occur if any one of the five were lost. This may suggest a renewed effort to attract a few other large customers or even a postponement of an expansion program until more customer diversification has been achieved.

A more common surprise is the finding that, say, the bottom 200 customers together account for only, say, 1 percent of the marginal contribution. Although, as has been shown, it is unlikely that dropping any one customer in this group will increase profits, the same cannot necessarily be said of dropping the whole 200. Such a move might make it possible to realign sales territories and thus reduce the number of salesmen, to drop an accounts receivable clerk, to reduce overtime in the traffic department, or to eliminate the printing of a special brochure designed for small customers. Here an analysis of relevant costs may be quite revealing.

It is quite unlikely that marginal contribution classification by customer industry or by customer type (department store vs. chain discount store vs. variety store vs. independent) will reveal any category that is a candidate for abandonment. What it will reveal is those industries or types of customers that are likely to reward extra marketing effort with the highest return in the way of profits.

Incurring Promotional Costs

As we saw in an example given in Chapter 7, a $25,000 increase in advertising that was estimated to increase sales by $100,000 seemed on its surface to be too high a cost for the results expected, but it turned out to be a very worthwhile move. Any increase in advertising, promotion, or other type of selling expense can be analyzed the same way. If the expected increase in marginal contribution exceeds the proposed expenditure, the program is justified. Conversely, any proposed decrease in advertising, promotion, or other selling expense that is expected to reduce marginal contribution by less than the expense reduction is also worthwhile. In both these decisions, long-range results as well as immediate results must be considered.

Cost Control

A number of companies have converted to direct costing from absorption costing primarily because of the guidance it provides (through the concept of marginal contribution) in making pricing policies and other management decisions and in carrying out business modeling. In order to arrive at the variable cost of sales, a company needs to know variable selling expenses on a product-by-product basis as well as variable manufacturing costs. If the company is on standard costs, it has naturally established standards for variable selling expenses. This not only accomplishes the purpose of establishing marginal contribution figures but also gives the company improved control over these costs.

As in manufacturing, variable costs in selling are expected to rise and fall in proportion to the rise and fall of the base against which they are being measured—in this case, sales dollars. Fixed selling expenses are also controlled by a standard, often referred to as a budget, but these are not expected to vary with sales. With this separation of variable from fixed costs, actual selling costs can be compared monthly with the costs that were predetermined to be reasonable for the sales level actually achieved. This measurement and control of selling expenses is almost an accidental by-product of a direct cost system, but it can be a very helpful one in reducing costs in a function in which costs have been traditionally hard to control.

Summary

Any company's marketing and sales division can enhance its ability to increase profits by focusing on the marginal contribution being derived from individual customers, from classes of customers, and from sales territories. The marginal contribution can be compared with the relevant costs (the costs required by a certain group of customers and only by that group) to determine whether any group is failing to contribute to net profits. Grouping by size of customer can be particularly informative in this type of analysis.

In addition, analyses of marginal contribution dollars and percentages to sales can reveal from which group of customers a sales increase will benefit the company most. In these analyses, it must be recognized that a cost that is relevant to one type of decision may not be relevant to another.

Finally, the segregation of variable selling expenses from fixed selling expenses under direct costing provides companies with a degree of control over selling costs that few companies under absorption costing achieve. It is particularly effective when companies on direct standard costing carry the standard cost concept into the selling cost accounts.

14

Direct Costing in Nonmanufacturing Companies

FROM a cost accounting viewpoint, nonmanufacturing companies fall into seven basic categories (each with many subdivisions): (1) service industries dealing with tangibles, (2) service industries dealing with intangibles, (3) construction, (4) transportation, (5) public utilities, (6) hospitals, and (7) distribution. Direct costing has a place in some of these categories but not in all.

Of course, any company can select some measure of volume and then determine which costs are likely to vary with this measure and which costs are basically fixed. It can then prepare a performance report very similar to one in a manufacturing company. However, if the costs reflected on the report are not directly related to the individual services whose sales support the company, the report is more apt to be called a variable budget and will not necessarily be part of the company's financial accounting system. For example, the research department in a brokerage firm may set a cost target per report issued on the prospects of some company whose stock is potentially of interest to the firm's customers. Although such research is supportive of both current and future sales, the number of reports cannot be related directly to income. It is possible to regard the separation of variable from fixed costs for cost control purposes of this type as an extension of the philosophy of direct costing. However, this chapter will discuss only genuine direct cost accounting systems.

Service Industries Dealing with Tangibles

Some service industries are manufacturers in every sense but one: They do not own the materials they are processing. Commercial laundries and photo-finishers are examples. This type of service industry can use a direct cost system exactly in the same way a manufacturer can and get virtually the same advantages from it. As in manufacturing, the advantages of direct costing are enhanced if the system is also a standard cost one.

There are a few differences in the use of direct costing in service industries versus manufacturing. For example, the make-or-buy decision (see Chapter 8) will not apply. The advantages of NIFO pricing as a guide to marketing (see Chapter 5) will almost certainly not apply, since fluctuations in material costs will not affect prices when a company is not paying for its materials.

A variation of a service industry is the manufacturer that sells products made from materials it owns but that also, on occasion, processes customer-owned materials. In the metal-working industry this is called "toll work." Here a real problem exists as to how the marginal contribution sought on goods produced from owned material should compare with the marginal contribution on customer-owned material requiring the same amount of direct labor and variable overhead. A calculation based on required working capital that reflects both the total direct costs of the two types of business and the respective working capital turnovers will give an appropriate answer. This answer, however, may have to be modified in light of the pricing policies of competitors in the industry. Also, if the company has a machine or process that represents a bottleneck—that is, if the company has more business than it can handle—the marginal contribution of the two types of business should be roughly proportional to the time required on the machine or in the process for each one. However, some consideration should be given to the lower investment in the toll work.

Repair services also fall into the category of service industries dealing with tangibles, even though they own and sell the parts required to make the repair and are paid for the labor and overhead. Most repair work is so diversified with so little time spent on each job that an actual job cost system meets the requirements. Absorption costing is generally preferable to direct costing in this type of situation.

Service Industries Dealing with Intangibles

Banks, savings and loan associations, stockbrokers, insurance brokers, and insurance companies (underwriters) are examples of service industries dealing with intangibles. These industries, particularly banks and insurance underwriters, have become increasingly interested in the management guidance and cost control available through cost accounting. Banks, for example, have worked out formulas for determining the profitability of a commercial loan customer over a period of time. The customer's profitability statement is credited with the gross interest collected and charged with a number of items. These items include the interest the bank pays to the Federal Reserve or to some other bank for some part of the loan after considering both the customer's average compensating balance and the percentage of the loan supplied by the bank's own equity capital. Charges also include an hourly rate, including overhead, for the loan officer's time and the costs of the checking account privileges that usually go with the loan.

In one situation, a bank that had not raised its fees for estate and trust management for some time wanted to know what the true cost of this service was in order to establish a current schedule of fees that would be fair to both it and its customers. Unfortunately, determining the profitability of a specific service in an operation such as a commercial bank involves many philosophical questions that have not yet been standardized. Almost every service offered not only produces revenue directly but is a feeder for other services that produce revenue. In addition, the usual way of allocating costs may be misleading in that certain operations may be absorbing costs for the benefit of other operations. For example, the square-foot rental costs of a bank operation that is not in contact with the public may be based on the going rate for a building in the most expensive area in the city. However, that location was selected to attract business for those parts of the bank that directly serve the public. Thus the operation not in contact with the public is absorbing costs for the benefit of some other department.

Under these circumstances, the merits of absorption costing versus direct costing will depend on the particular management decision being made. Thus the question of fair fees for the estate and trust department for existing business should be answered on an absorption cost basis. On the other hand, if the bank believed that a lower fee schedule would attract a certain number of new trust management accounts, the decision should be made on a direct cost basis. Certainly, if operation costs of individual operations, such as check processing and consumer installment loan accounting, are to be compared among the various branch offices of a bank, direct costing is the right approach because some of the different fixed costs of the branches are not a measure of the efficiency of the operations.

Construction

The construction industry includes general contractors and specialty contractors (electrical, plumbing, heating, ventilating and air conditioning, steelwork, and the like). It also includes highway contractors, bridge builders, and oilwell drillers. The industry is characterized by competitive bidding, in most cases on a job-by-job basis. In almost all other cases, work is done on a negotiated-price or a cost-plus basis. Because of these conditions, the industry prefers job costing on an actual cost basis.

Another distinguishing characteristic of the industry is its tradition of employing labor as needed, including some supervisory and clerical workers whose jobs would be considered fixed costs in most manufacturing industries. Thus as previously indicated, for general contractors certain types of overhead—including the costs of field superintendents, timekeepers, watchmen, hoist operators, and the rental of much equipment—vary with the duration of the job (although not with the amount of work done each day).

This variability of certain types of overhead has led to a number of interesting negotiations in the industry. Contractors have often asked for increases in firm contract prices when specification changes by the purchaser required different materials. These materials, which were placed on order long after the normal time for ordering materials, were delivered sufficiently late to delay completion of the job. Contractors have used the Program Evaluation and Review Technique (PERT) to determine the added overhead resulting from the delay. PERT is a variation of critical path scheduling (CPS), which, in addition to breaking the segments of a complex job into time requirements, assigns a cost to each segment. PERT can be used to control the costs of any job, even if no specification changes have been made.

The major purpose of cost accounting for construction companies is to sharpen the judgment of the estimators who determine the bid prices on the probable costs before negotiating a contract price. Typically, estimators divide the job into its various segments: excavation, foundation pouring, steel erection, brickwork, sashes, electrical, plumbing, flooring, painting, and the like. The final cost is arrived at by adding the estimated costs of these segments. However, many contractors' accounting departments ignore these distinctions and accumulate costs in terms of materials, labor, and overhead. Of course, if a number of the segments are performed by subcontractors on firm contracts, the loss of estimating accuracy is confined to that part of the contract performed by the general contractor with its own labor and materials.

Still, many contracting companies could improve their cost accumulation systems by setting up separate job numbers for each phase of the work. Those who do so find that it is possible to summarize not only the total actual cost of an individual job compared with the estimate but also the total actual cost of a particular segment (say, steelwork) on all jobs for a period compared with the total estimated costs for that segment on all jobs. Thus the company can determine whether the estimate on one particular segment is causing cost overruns on all jobs. The actual average costs can also be used to improve future estimating.

Because construction jobs tend to vary substantially in size, the segregation of variable from fixed costs becomes important. On one job, a field superintendent may be supervising 10 laborers and on the next he may be supervising 50. This can be reflected in the estimating process. In a very real sense, the estimate, when sufficiently broken down, can be used for cost control purposes much as a standard is used in manufacturing industries. However, to our knowledge, there is no accounting system based on standard costs in the construction industry.

The "field" fixed costs of a construction job are variable in the sense that they will not be incurred if the job is not done. Thus the marginal contribution is the difference between the contract price and the variable costs, including field fixed costs. This is the contribution that will be made to home office fixed costs and profit. Obviously, the difference between the costs arrived at under direct costing and those arrived at under absorption costing will be less in the construction industry than they will typically be in manufacturing. As a result, the advantages of direct costing for pricing purposes are also substantially less in construction than in manufacturing. Although construction firms do not use direct costing to a great extent, they often bid on jobs at prices that are not intended to cover all the home office costs which would ordinarily be assigned to the job. This is done because the company believes that a higher bid will not be acceptable, and the absorption of some home office overhead is better than no contract at all.

Transportation

Much of the transportation industry is under the jurisdiction of the Interstate Commerce Commission (ICC). Railroads and common carrier trucking companies are fully under ICC jurisdiction, and contract trucking companies are regulated to a somewhat lesser extent. The ICC has mandated that certain reports be prepared, with very specific rules set forth on cost accumulation. Also, prices are regulated. Under these circumstances, a company ceases to choose its cost system. Some observers believe that railroad passenger service would never have declined to its present sorry state had the ICC permitted incremental costing. Since it did not, many railroads abandoned their passenger service altogether. This not only inconvenienced the traveling public but necessitated an increase in freight rates as well. Ironically, it was for the purpose of preventing freight rate increases that the ICC refused to consider incremental costing.

Public Utilities

Public utilities are regulated by the Federal Power Commission (FPC) and the Federal Communications Commission (FCC) and by public utility commissions in the various states. Basically, public utilities rates are set to allow the utility a certain percentage profit (as defined) on its investment (as defined). Cost accounting then must follow the rules laid down. These rules are designed to produce the data needed for pricing. Only absorption costing can provide the required data.

Hospitals

Hospitals have a very high percentage of fixed costs, regardless of how these are defined. If fixed costs are thought of in terms of a single patient, essentially everything is a fixed cost except the raw food costs of his meals and a few medical supplies, possibly including X-ray film and laboratory reagents.

However, as the patient census in a hospital rises or drops by a substantial amount, certain employees must be added or can be dropped. A patient area (usually referred to as a nursing station) with 20 beds will require more nurses' aides if all 20 beds are filled than if only half have patients. If the census change affects several nursing stations, the hiring or laying off of kitchen personnel may be required. This is just an example.

A problem in cost control believed to be unique to hospitals is the difference in cost between a reduction of 10 patients in each of two 20-bed nursing stations and the reduction of 20 patients in one of them and none in the other. Typically, the second alternative would save the cost of the head nurse on each of three shifts and probably a ward clerk as well as the reduction in nurses' aides; the first procedure would not. Every hospital administrator is aware of this, but often the nature of a patient's illness makes consolidation of vacant beds impossible. For example, state laws for good reasons forbid the mixing of obstetrical patients with medical-surgical patients; Intensive Care Units, Coronary Care Units, and Recovery Rooms are all set up for only one type of patient; it is still considered improper to use a multibed room for patients of both sexes.

Most hospitals today receive a large proportion of their revenue on a cost reimbursement formula. Blue Cross, which pays the hospital bills of a large part of the population, adopted a cost reimbursement policy in some parts of the country in the late 1950s. Medicare, which reimburses hospitals for roughly one-third of their patients, has been on a cost reimbursement basis nationwide since its inception in mid-1966. As a result of subsequent rule changes, today Medicare will never pay more than costs, and it limits its reimbursement by certain other criteria when applicable. Medicaid, which became effective in 1967, has different rules in each state, but some states are on a cost reimbursement basis and some are on a cost reimbursement basis with a relatively low ceiling. The use of absorption costing for cost reimbursement purposes is entirely proper, as it is the only way to fairly apportion fixed costs to outside parties that have agreed to pay total costs.

The revenue received through cost reimbursement can be substantial, often amounting to over 90 percent of total revenue. The net effect is to make hospitals a regulated industry, although they are not ordinarily considered so. The Medicare Bureau of the federal government, the numerous state agencies handling Medicaid, and the various Blue Cross plans have set the rules on how costs are to be calculated. The rules for Medicare, Medicaid, and Blue Cross differ in certain details but are basically similar in all three. All require absorption costing and the use of the step-down method for allocating the costs of nonrevenue-producing departments to other nonrevenue-producing departments and to revenue-producing departments.

The step-down method of allocation is nearly obsolete in manufacturing. In the first quarter of the century it was quite common. The system recognizes the fact that many service departments provide service to other service departments. For example, the personnel department does the hiring not only for the production departments but also for the industrial engineering, quality assurance, and maintenance departments. The maintenance department will repair walls and floors not only in the production departments but also in the personnel, industrial engineering, and quality assurance departments. Advocates of the step-down system believe that costs are more fairly allocated to the various production departments if the costs of the service departments are first spread to one another. Step-down costing was abandoned in manufacturing when it was realized that the added accuracy it provided did not warrant the work required. Most manufacturing companies spread *total* service department costs to production departments on the basis of the service rendered to each production department as a proportion of the total services rendered to all production departments.

Hospitals, however, are required to allocate service department costs to service departments by one of several methods. A simple step-down procedure, and the one used by almost all hospitals, is to arrange the service departments in the order of number of departments served. Thus the maintenance department, which serves every department, is high on the list; the laundry, which provides minimal service to other service departments, is low on the list. Each department is spread to the departments further down on the sheet and then closed out. For example, the total costs of the maintenance department would be allocated to revenue-producing departments and all service departments lower down on the sheet, including the laundry. However, the total laundry costs (including the cost of laundry delivered to maintenance) would be allocated only to those departments below it on the sheet. The fact that the laundry might wash some overalls for the maintenance department would be ignored. Note that in hospital cost reimbursement, G.& A. is considered a service department and is stepped-down with the others.

A refinement of the simple step-down is the double step-down, in which all service departments are initially allocated to one another and departments are closed out only in the second round of allocations. The problem of service departments serving one another can also be handled through a computer technique called linear programming. Neither of these last two methods is in sufficient use, in either the hospital field or elsewhere, to warrant further discussion here.

To some extent, hospital cost accountants control costs by preparing budgets for comparison with actual and referring overruns to management. These budgets reflect the fluctuations in variable costs that are reasonably expected to occur with changes in the patient census while leaving fixed costs alone. The traditional measure of hospital volume is in-patient days, but some hospitals are becoming more sophisticated. They continue to measure certain variable costs in terms of in-patient days but measure other costs on the basis of out-patient visits, emergency room visits, X-ray procedures, laboratory tests performed, and the like. In fact, the government has performed some studies to determine if costs can be budgeted on the basis of the type of illness suffered by the patient. It is generally recognized that total cost per in-patient day will be affected by the average length of stay of the patient. This is because every new patient requires certain procedures such as laboratory tests which may not have to be repeated during the patient's stay. Surgical patients ordinarily require one use of the operating room, again unrelated to length of stay. Thus, the longer the patient's stay, the lower the average *per day* cost.

The hospital cost accountant must also make sure that the use of averages, inherent in every cost accounting system, does not penalize the hospital's reimbursement. For example, reimbursable cost percentages are usually higher in the in-patient area than the out-patient area. Since lighting costs are allocated on the basis of square feet, the out-patient area, which is open 8 hours a day, receives as great a charge per square foot as the in-patient area, which is in use 24 hours a day. Nothing can be done about this particular problem. The third-party reimbursers believe, quite possibly correctly, that such items are offset by other items that go the opposite way. However, the hospital's cost accountant must be alert to the problem and do everything possible within the rules to avoid a cost classification that works against the hospital's interest.

Despite the mandated use of absorption costing in the hospital field, direct cost concepts can be helpful in many management decisions. What, for example, will be the increase or decrease in costs per in-patient day of other patients if the hospital decides to close down the obstetrical service? Will it be worthwhile to incur a substantial nurse recruiting cost to avoid shutting down two nursing stations in the summer months? Both types of questions can be answered first in terms of how the decision will affect costs, but they must then be restudied to determine if the change in cost reimbursement will be greater than or less than the cost change.

Distribution

Retailers and wholesalers, particularly retailers, run the gamut from the most sophisticated to the least sophisticated in their use of accounting data in managing a business. It was in the department store field in the middle 1920s that controllers were first generally recognized as a major part of management, with a voice in merchandising policy and control over the size of inventories. In the middle 1930s, the National Retail Merchants Association, the major department store group, developed a system for measuring operating costs in the department store field that has many of the features of a standard cost system. Many retail specialty chains not only compare costs from store to store but also use standards in controlling costs in their central warehouse operations.

In addition, many department stores use the "retail system of inventory accounting" for controlling gross profit and for measuring employee thefts and customer shoplifting. The retail system is complex, but its basic rule is that inventories are recorded for certain purposes at selling price. Retail variety, grocery, and drug chains also use the retail system for holding store managers accountable for the merchandise delivered to their charge.

It must, of course, be realized that retailers and wholesalers, unlike manufacturers, think of the cost of the goods they sell as the amount shown on the incoming invoice. The costs of salespeople, stock pickers, and packers and the overhead that attaches to them are all to be covered by the gross profit—that is, the difference between the sales price and the invoice cost. Under this philosophy, the difference between absorption costing and direct costing becomes irrelevant.

However, in certain situations retailers do consider the variability of costs. If it takes a sales clerk no more time to sell a $10 widget that cost $6 than it takes him to sell a $20 whammit that cost $15, which is the more profitable sale? Obviously, the widget has a 40 percent gross profit, while the whammit has only a 25 percent gross profit. But the widget sale has generated only $4 toward store operating costs, while the whammit sale has generated $5. It is this philosophy which permits many stores to sell multiple units of an item at a lower per-unit price than single items. Even if the customer returned to the store after purchasing a single item to buy again, this would take the time required for two sales. In a very real sense, the salesperson's time in retailing is the bottleneck (see Chapter 5) that determines how the absorption of general operating costs should be assigned to products.

Summary

Direct cost concepts of separating variable from fixed costs have their place in cost control in all service industries. However, most service industries that have cost systems use absorption costing because the service is oriented to the customer's requirements rather than to the production of products. The concept of separating variable from fixed costs can also be useful in certain management decisions that come up frequently in service industries.

Generally, only those service industries that are manufacturers in every sense except one—the fact that they do not own the material they are processing—can benefit from a standard direct cost accounting system. Here the advantages of such a system are virtually the same as those described for manufacturerers.

15

Special Problems

CERTAIN cost accounting applications are of no concern to the majority of manufacturers. These include transfer pricing, by-product costing, joint product costing, the Cost Accounting Standards Board, segment reporting, replacement costing, casualty insurance on inventories, bidding on contracts, product mix decisions, material mix decisions, and warehouse stocking decisions. However, there are enough companies affected by each of these matters to make a discussion of the impact of direct costing on them a necessary part of this book.

Transfer Pricing

A transfer price is the price at which a company sells to itself, either to a division in the same corporation or to another corporation in the same ownership group. A transfer price must be established whenever two corporations that file separate tax returns are involved. This is true not only when one of the corporations is foreign but also in many cases when Western Hemisphere corporations and Domestic International Sales Corporations (DISCs) as defined in the tax laws are involved. Transfer prices may also be needed for internal purposes when subsidiary corporations (not filing separate tax returns) or divisions of a company are looked upon as profit centers. Often the selling function of a company is separately incorporated and buys products from the manufacturing corporation. Assuming there is a profit between the cost of manufacturing and the ultimate selling price to an outside customer, the transfer price determines how much of the profit will be reflected on the books of the transferor and how much on the books of the transferee. This can be important to the company in terms of income taxes and to individuals within the company in terms of their reputations for running their functions at a profit. In some companies, bonuses based on profits as well as reputations are at stake.

Transfer pricing applies only to revenue-producing entities. There is no need to establish a transfer price when a production department transfers materials, parts, or assemblies to another production department as part of the normal flow of work in process. Such departments are not normally considered profit centers and are responsible only for keeping costs down (and, of course, for maintaining product quality and getting the product out on time). They are not expected to operate as if they were selling the product.

There are three basic approaches to setting transfer prices, the first of which has several variations:

1. Cost
   - Standard or actual cost.
   - Standard cost plus an allowance for variances.
   - Standard or actual cost plus an agreed profit percentage on cost.
2. Market price
3. Negotiated price

Unfortunately, each one of these methods has serious disadvantages from a management standpoint.

Cost

The first two cost methods, standard or actual cost and standard cost with some allowance for unfavorable variances, deprive the transferor of any profit at all. The third cost method, standard cost plus a percentage of cost for profit, is arbitrary in that the profit percentage is predetermined and not within the control of the transferor. All three of the cost methods have the serious disadvantage of giving the transferor no incentive to reduce costs. In fact, in the "cost plus percentage of cost" method, the transferor has an incentive to increase costs. The Army found this out the hard way in World War I and shortly thereafter prohibited all contracts that provided for cost plus a percentage of cost. (Army cost contracts now call for cost plus a fixed fee.)

In addition to the transferor's lack of incentive to control costs, in certain instances the transferor's management may attempt to shift costs from products that are to be sold to others in a competitive climate to products being transferred within the company where costs are being reimbursed. There are any number of ingenious ways of shifting costs.

Transfer pricing at standard cost, with or without an allowance for unfavorable variances, means at standard absorption cost. To follow this formula on a direct cost basis would mean that no part of the transferor's fixed manufacturing overhead was being reflected in the price. This would obviously be unfair. A transfer at standard cost plus a profit percentage can be at either absorption or direct cost. However, if direct costing is used, the profit percentage will have to be sufficiently high to reflect the absorption of fixed manufacturing overhead as well as a profit.

When taxing authorities have an interest in transfer pricing—that is, when the transfer is between entities filing separate tax returns—a transfer at cost is not acceptable. Tax rules require that the total profit between the corporate group's incurred cost and the price to the eventual outside customer be reflected in part on each corporate tax return. Just how much goes on each is a matter of industry custom, judgment, and the tax effect of the allocation. Similarly, tax auditors may challenge the amount of the profit percentage in the "cost plus a profit percentage" formula.

Market Price

The first problem with the market price approach to transfer pricing is that there may be no market price. If the product is a specially designed part being produced by the transferor for assembly by the transferee into its product, no one else would want to buy it from the transferor—and no one else will have offered to sell it to the transferee. With this type of product, the market price approach to transfer pricing is just not feasible.

Even when a product has a market price, there are some disadvantages to this approach. To begin with, the market price information is often unreliable. An outside vendor quoting to a company which he has every reason to believe will never buy from him, because it makes its own product, may make his quote unrealistically high or unrealistically low. An outside customer who has other sources may offer to buy at a price well below what he is presently paying with the thought that only a much lower price would persuade him to change sources. It is difficult to obtain information on actual transactions occurring between two outsiders, and the quantities involved may be relatively small. Still, these considerations do not affect all types of products, and some can be priced at reliable and realistic market prices.

However, even in these cases, market prices are not a fair measure of what a transfer price should be. After all, the seller in a market situation has substantial selling costs, whereas the transferor in a transfer price situation has a captive customer and no selling expenses. This artificial situation can work either way. One manufacturing corporation incurred losses selling to its related sales corporation at market prices because the sales corporation—supported by the parent's president, who came out of sales—insisted on so many free samples that there was no profit left. In another case the parent's president, who came out of manufacturing, forced the selling corporation (a retail store chain) to accept at full price all the garment styles manufactured each season that outside retailers did not select. The transferee retailer found itself stuck with unwanted merchandise at full cost.

Thus the market price approach to transfer pricing is not always feasible and, even when it is, it is far from ideal. Generally, it is acceptable for tax purposes. The question of absorption costing versus direct costing is not relevant if this approach is used.

Negotiated Price

The third approach to transfer pricing is by negotiation between executives of the transferor and those of the transferee. This approach has two disadvantages. First, the executives involved may have very unequal negotiating abilities; this difference in skills will have a much greater impact than in a normal arm's-length negotiation, since neither party can walk away from the "sale." Second, and more important, the two negotiators tend to become personal enemies. This attitude can do much harm in other situations where they must work together for the company's well-being.

If the negotiated transfer price gives both the transferor and the transferee a reasonable share of the total profit, taxing authorities are not apt to question it. As in the case of transfer prices based on market prices, the question of absorption costing versus direct costing does not apply.

A Direct Cost Approach

Another approach, used by a very small group of companies, seems to avoid most of the disadvantages of the three approaches already discussed. It has not been listed above because it is not sufficiently well known to be considered by most companies. (An article by Roger Y. W. Tang, C. K. Walter, and Robert H. Raymond in the January 1979 issue of *Management Accounting* showed that only 2 of 232 companies surveyed used the approach.) This method uses direct costing and thus makes it easy for the transferee to think in terms of direct costs in pricing its finished product when that product incorporates parts acquired at transfer prices. Under any of the other three approaches, this can be done only through special analyses.

The approach involves setting transfer prices at the standard direct unit cost of the pieces to be delivered, plus an amount per time period to cover fixed manufacturing overhead for the anticipated number of pieces to be delivered, plus a profit for each period of time. Thus the transferor obtains the benefit of any favorable variances on standard direct costs, while the transferee obtains a benefit in the reduction of the per-unit application of fixed manufacturing overhead if it is able to increase the number of pieces it purchases. Each party gains the benefit of superior performance in the areas under its control.

One disadvantage of this approach is that taxing authorities may find the system difficult to understand (the group of companies using it filed consolidated tax returns, so this was not a problem). In addition, the anticipated volume over which the fixed manufacturing overhead is to be absorbed and the profit added must still be arrived at through negotiation. However, the process is much easier than the negotiation of a total price. For example, the volume selected could be the prior year's volume or the annual volume already projected in the company's budget, which takes into account economic conditions, the company's share of the market, and its marketing plans. This direct cost approach to transfer pricing appears to offer advantages over all the others.

By-Product Costing

One of the first decisions to be made in by-product costing is determining whether the product *is* a by-product or whether it is a joint product (discussed in the next section). The two are treated entirely differently under both absorption and direct costing. Generally, the distinction is made in terms of the relative value of the items. For example, frozen orange juice processors are able to sell the dried orange peel from the oranges used to make the juice as cattlefeed. The amount realized from the peel is a minute part of the value of the orange juice, so the peel is considered a by-product. On the other hand, oil refineries produce gasoline, kerosene, distillate, two grades of furnace oil, bunker oil, and asphalt from the crude oil they consume, and each of these products has considerable value. Therefore, they are all thought of as joint products of the crude oil and of the process.

There are no specific ratios that will tell a company if it should consider a product a by-product or a joint product. In most companies, however, the answer is obvious from the wide disparity of the values or from their relative closeness. In some cases, industry custom may be the determinant.

Once it has been decided that a certain item is a by-product, the cost accounting rules are clear. The main product is credited with the selling price of the by-product after deducting (1) the cost of any processing required by the by-product after it has been separated from the main product (including packaging, if necessary), and (2) any selling costs required to dispose of the by-product (including shipping costs).

Under absorption costing, the processing and selling costs deducted from the selling price are the absorption costs of these functions, which include an appropriate allocation of fixed costs. Under direct costing, the processing and selling cost deductions are only the variable costs of these functions. The direct cost approach is superior for setting prices on the main product. Under the absorption cost approach, the contribution of the main product to company profits is understated, though in most cases the amount of the understatement is not large.

Joint Product Costing

Once it has been determined that the lesser-valued product or products are to be handled as joint products rather than as by-products, there are three very different ways of accounting for the costs. The problem is, of course, to assign to each of the joint products an appropriate share of the raw materials that eventually become part of it, as well as an appropriate share of the cost of the processes that the material goes through before the products are separated.

One method that has many deficiencies but that is still in use in many companies is to allocate the material cost and the cost of the processes before separation on the basis of the weight of the respective joint products at the point of separation. It should be noted here that when more than two products are involved, there may be a point where, say, Product A is separated from Products B and C, but B and C go together through one or more additional processes before they are separated from each other. This presents no problem, since costs of material and processes up to the time Product A is separated out are allocated on the basis of the weight of Product A compared with the combined weight of Products B and C at this point. Subsequently those costs assigned to B and C are allocated between B and C on the basis of their respective weights at the point at which they are separated from each other.

The problem with this approach is that it will often give costs for the less desirable products that are above the selling prices which can be obtained for them. In such a case, the most desirable product will appear to have a fantastic profit. However, in most instances the proportion of each product produced is set by the nature of the raw material and is not within the control of the company. Thus this apparent diversity in profit percentages does not help management decide on what product to make, how to price the product for maximum profit, or how to determine sales promotion expenditures.

Some joint product industries do have limited control over the proportion of the joint products produced. For example, from the same grade and quantity of crude oil, oil refineries can exchange high gasoline yields and high bunker oil and asphalt yields with low yields of the medium-weight products for lower gasoline and heavy-weight product yields with higher yields of the medium-weight products. Similarly, meatpackers have some options in cutting up carcasses. In these industries, sophisticated computer linear programming techniques have been devised to relate costs and market prices on a day-to-day basis in order to help management plan the product mix for best profitability, within the limitations of the raw material.

A second method of allocating the cost of joint materials and joint processes is based on the selling prices of the finished products. This approach has the merit of recognizing that every quality of raw material does not have equal value even when the various qualities must be bought in a predetermined combination. The disadvantage of the method is that, in most cases, some of the joint products will require more expensive processing beyond the point of separation or more expensive packaging than other joint products. Because of this, the allocation of joint material costs and joint processing costs on the basis of selling price leaves out an important ingredient.

A third method tries to cure the defect of the selling price method by allocating joint costs on the basis of gross profit in an absorption cost system or marginal contribution in a direct cost system. It should be noted here that any allocation based on selling prices, gross profit, or marginal contribution must use some estimate of the selling prices that will obtain for each of the products for some future period (a year, for example). The nature of joint products virtually ensures that the selling prices of individual products will vary considerably from one another, often on a daily basis. This is because, with few exceptions, the demand for one product will create a supply of all the others. If the demand is less for the other products, the company will lower prices to prevent inventories from building up to unmanageable levels.

Chapter 8 warned against costing products backward from the selling prices obtainable in the competitive marketplace. Joint product costing is the exception. There is no other way to do it except by weight, which gives even less acceptable results. Figure 15-1 is a simplified version of joint product costing that involves two products and three operations. Operation 1 is performed on the material before separation of Product A from Product B. Operation 2 is performed on Product A only, and Operation 3 is performed on Product B only.

FIGURE 15-1. Joint product costing under direct costing.

	Combined Products	*Product A*	*Product B*
Forecast Selling Price per 100 pounds of raw materials		$83	$100
Variable Selling Costs		3	5
Net Selling Price		$80	$95
Material Cost	$50		
Operation 1, Labor and Variable Overhead	15		
Operation 2, Labor and Variable Overhead		$11	
Operation 3, Labor and Variable Overhead			$36
Marginal Contribution Before Combined Costs		$69	$59
Marginal Contribution (%)		54%	46%
Allocation of Combined Costs	$ (65)	35	30
Marginal Contribution after Allocation of Combined Costs		$34	$29

In the figure, variable selling expenses are deducted from the forecast invoice selling price to arrive at a "net" selling price. This deduction could also have been shown below the entry for Operation 3, but it is clearer when shown at the top. Only those manufacturing costs that apply to the products after separation are deducted from the net selling prices to arrive at the basis for allocating the joint costs to the products. In the illustration, the allocation of joint costs is heavier to Product A than to Product B ($35 compared with $30), even though both the forecast invoice selling price and the net selling price are higher for Product B than for Product A. This result arises because Operation 3, which is performed only on Product B, has a much higher cost than Operation 2, which is performed only on Product A.

The Cost Accounting Standards Board

The Cost Accounting Standards Board (CASB) was set up by Congress in the early 1970s largely at the urging of Admiral Hyman Rickover. He believed that suppliers of equipment to the armed forces on cost-plus-fixed-fee (CPFF) contracts and on negotiated-price contracts were taking advantage of the government by selecting whichever cost accounting rule was most beneficial to them. The use of Generally Accepted Accounting Principles (GAAP) in financial reporting was similarly criticized, but it may be confidently stated that whatever the flexibility of GAAP, it couldn't hold a candle to the wide variety of cost accounting practices. In fact, there was no single source for determining what cost accounting practices were generally acceptable. Each author of a book on cost accounting represented himself rather than a body of experts as had existed in the Accounting Principles Board, the final authority for GAAP at the time.

When Congress created the CASB, it anticipated that combining all the pertinent methods into one rigid set of standards would take only two years. This may not be the most off-base estimate Congress has ever made, but it ranks near the top. It is a fair guess that the CASB is here to stay. It is interesting to note that GAAP is largely nongovernmental, whereas the CASB standards are government promulgated and thus have the force of law in the areas to which they apply.

The CASB standards apply only to companies that do a substantial amount of business with the government on a cost-plus-fixed-fee or a negotiated-price basis. Originally, only Department of Defense contracts were covered, but the General Services Administration, which does the buying for most federal departments, has since adopted the standards for its own use. Because a company must do a very high annual dollar volume with the government before it comes under the CASB standards, the standards affect relatively few companies, but the dollar value of the contracts covered is huge.

The CASB standards follow the cost accounting methods commonly found in industry, with a few notable exceptions. (All CASB standards refer to methods and rules and should not be confused with standard cost standards, which are dollar amounts per unit of product for various costs.) Because of the exceptions, a number of companies have to keep a separate set of books for government contract costing. Since some of these companies already keep two sets of books—one for tax reporting (legitimately) and one for financial statement reporting—this may add a third set. Fortunately, most of the companies that come under CASB standards are large enough to have heavy computers to reduce what might otherwise be an unbearable amount of paperwork.

The CASB standards are all based on absorption cost principles. As indicated elsewhere in this book, any cost-finding process that involves charging outsiders for costs must be based on absorption costing. Accordingly, it seems that any company that comes under CASB standards cannot use direct costing for its basic accounting records. It can, of course, use direct cost principles in its management decisions, its profit planning, and its cost control through special analyses and subsidiary records.

Segment Reporting

Until the mid-1970s, relatively few publicly held companies published segment data. The majority of the companies that did limited the published information to an analysis of sales. Some also showed operating profits, but most gave no product line information. Investment analysts who believed different industries had different growth prospects found it difficult to forecast the future of diversified companies without these data. Since most major public companies are diversified, the problem was a major one.

In 1976, the Financial Accounting Standards Board promulgated standard FASB 14, which required all companies desiring certified financial statements to analyze their income statements by product line. Subsequently, nonpublic companies were exempted from the requirement. Just how product lines are to be determined and which ones can be combined is not pertinent here. However, two items are worth mentioning: (1) export sales, if material, represent a separate product line; and (2) transfer pricing is required when one segment sells to another, thus in effect reversing many of the elimination entries that go into the consolidation of an income statement.

There is no question that FASB 14 contemplates absorption costing, and any company preparing a segmented income statement on a direct cost basis would be in violation of it. This is perhaps unfortunate, since the principles of direct costing would place an investment analyst in a much better position to forecast the effect on profits of a growth or decline in one or more of a company's product lines than would absorption costing.

Nonetheless, under FASB rules, a company keeping its books on a direct cost basis must convert its cost of sales on a product line basis to an absorption cost basis. If the company is using Method 3 described in Chapter 6 for converting its financial statements, no problem arises. It simply costs out its unit shipments of each product line at the unit standard absorption cost of each. If, however, it is using either Method 1 or Method 2 for converting its financial statements, it must segregate its fixed manufacturing overhead. In some circumstances—for example, when a foreign plant is designated as a segment—the calculation is so easy that it virtually makes itself. In other circumstances—for example, when products made in the same department go to different industries and are therefore considered to be in different segments—the difficulties may be so great as to force the company to use Method 3.

Replacement Costing

Another problem in the consideration of financial statements from an investment point of view is whether traditional accounting methods provide an adequate guide to a company's future in a highly inflationary economy. The accounting profession, here and abroad, struggled unsuccessfully with this problem for a number of years. Then, early in 1974, the Securities and Exchange Commission (SEC) issued a ruling on this question. Under the ruling, the roughly 1,000 companies with inventories and fixed assets of over $100 million (with certain exceptions) must file estimates with the SEC on how fixed assets, depreciation on fixed assets, cost of sales, and ending inventory would be stated if they were valued on a replacement cost basis (as defined by the SEC).

Companies that come under this rule have generally found their most serious problem to be the revaluation of fixed assets, which is not a cost accounting problem at all. As to ending inventory, the revaluation of material content on the basis of most recent purchases at year end is apparently considered satisfactory. Cost of sales can be revalued as if the company were on LIFO, whether it uses LIFO for any other purpose or not. Therefore, a company on direct costing will have no more difficulty preparing the replacement cost data required by the SEC than a company on absorption costing.

Casualty Insurance on Inventories

Most manufacturers carry fire and theft insurance on finished-goods inventories, whether they are in the main plant, in a separate building in the vicinity of the plant, or in warehouses spread around the country. Assuming that production facilities are not producing to capacity, in a direct cost system the cost of replacing any finished goods that are stolen or destroyed by fire, flood, or other damage is only the variable cost of production.

It is common sense to carry enough insurance to cover losses, but to carry more than is needed to replace the lost goods is a gamble in which the odds are against the insured. An insurance carrier has to charge a premium sufficient to cover the average expected losses; in addition, the carrier must build into its premium its own quite considerable operating costs, including a sizable broker's commission. It would thus appear that any company that insured its finished-goods inventory only up to its direct cost value would come out ahead in the long run.

Any company that is considering limiting its casualty insurance coverage of finished-goods inventory to its direct cost value should be aware of two points. First, if the goods are stored very close to the production facilities, a casualty—say, a fire or flood—might put production out of commission so that customers couldn't be served at all. In this case, insurance based on direct costs is probably a poor policy. Second, most casualty insurance carries an 80 percent coinsurance clause. Thus it must be made clear to the insurance carrier that only the direct costs of the actual loss are being claimed and therefore the 80 percent must be related to the direct costs of the entire inventory.

Use of Direct Costs in Pricing Bids

Direct costing combined with probability theory can be used to help determine the price that should be quoted in a competitive bidding situation. The approach is useful when a company constantly makes bids on jobs that are individually quite small compared with the company's total business. Examples include job machine shops, commercial printers, and some electrical contractors. The approach cannot be used when a company makes bids on jobs that represent individually a high percentage of the company's annual sales. Even in companies where the approach can be used, some judgment will enter into the calculations.

Figure 15-2 illustrates the approach. It is based on an analysis of all bids submitted by the company for an extended past period. The analysis starts by calculating the marginal contribution percentage on each bid, whether the contract was won or lost. Then, for each marginal contribution percentage bracket, the contracts won are related to the number of bids submitted to develop "the chances of winning the bid" as a percentage. These figures are shown in column 5 of Figure 15-2. Column 1 of the figure shows possible prices for the new contract being bid upon; column 2 shows the direct cost of the contract; column 3 shows the marginal contribution by subtraction; column 4 shows the marginal contribution as a percentage of selling price; and column 6, calculated as column 3 times column 5, shows the average marginal contribution the company would receive after considering both the bids won and the bids lost if it bid all contracts on this basis. In the illustration, the company's marginal contribution will be maximum if it bids $175.

The figures in column 5 can be filled in from experience rather than from an analysis of past performance. However the figures are obtained, they may have to be adjusted by factors such as the season

FIGURE 15-2. Analysis of bid prices.

Possible Selling Price (1)	*Standard Direct Cost* (2)	*Marginal Contribution* (3)	*Marginal Contribution Percentage* (4)	*Chances of Winning the Bid* (5)	*Probable Marginal Contribution* (6)
$250	$100	$150	60%	5%	$ 7.50
225	100	125	56	10	12.50
200	100	100	50	25	25.00
175	100	75	43	40	30.00
150	100	50	33	55	27.50
130	100	30	23	80	24.00
120	100	20	17	98	19.60

of the year, economic conditions, and how hungry the company is for business at the time. For example, if losing the bid will mean unacceptable layoffs, the calling of a bank loan, or some other disaster, the company may do well to bid $130 or even $120. Despite these cautions, the approach will help many companies improve their profitability. A similar application of probability theory to gross profit in an absorption cost system will result in wrong answers.

Product Mix Decisions

Many manufacturing companies lose sales because they are unable to deliver a product by the date the customer wishes. Typically, this situation arises because other orders, also with required delivery dates, are taking up the company's production capacity at the time. Often the delay is caused not by a single bottleneck machine but rather by a series of machines any one of which can become a bottleneck depending on the product mix. In determining which orders to seek in such a situation, the company should be guided by the profitability of the product mix alternatives in light of the complex effect of the various bottlenecks on production.

Figure 15-3 shows a "trial and error" approach to a product mix decision involving only two products and two machines. In a typical company, the problem would probably involve more machines and would certainly involve more products. In such a case, a manual trial-and-error approach becomes impracticable; however, a linear programming approach (which is simply a computerized trial-and-error technique) can be used effectively. Because of the incredible calculating speeds of computers, optimum answers to complex trial-and-error situations can be obtained with a reasonable expenditure of time and money.

Both the manual technique and the computer technique can be understood from a study of Figure 15-3. It is assumed that both Product A and Product B must be processed through Machine X and then Machine Y. However, because of the nature of the products, Product B requires much more time per piece on Machine Y than does Product A. In the figure, the section on possible mixes shows how many days in a 20-working-day month each product could conceivably be assigned to each machine. Note that in the eighth column only 12¾ days of Machine X are assigned to Product B, although 14 days are available. This is correct, since the maximum amount of Product B that can be produced by Machine Y in the 17 days it can be assigned to Product B, in the alternative represented by the eighth

FIGURE 15-3. Product mix decision.

Production Capacity (pieces per day):

Machine X 20 pieces of Product A *or* 20 pieces ofProduct B
Machine Y 40 pieces of Product A *or* 15 pieces of Product B

	(1)	(2)	(3)	(4)	(5)	(6)	(7)	(8)	(9)	(10)	(11)
Possible Mixes											
Days of Machine X on Product A	20	18	16	14	12	10	8	6	4	2	0
Days of Machine X on Product B	0	2	4	6	8	10	12	12¾	13½	14¼	15
Total Days in use of Machine X	20	20	20	20	20	20	20	18¾	17½	16¼	15
Days of Machine Y on Product A	10	9	8	7	6	5	4	3	2	1	0
Days of Machine Y on Product B	0	2⅔	5⅓	8	10⅔	13	16	17	18	19	20
Total days in use of Machine Y	10	11⅔	13⅓	15	16⅔	18	20	20	20	20	20
Monthly Production											
Product A	400	360	320	280	240	200	160	120	80	40	0
Product B	0	40	80	120	160	200	240	255	270	290	300
Marginal Contribution											
If marginal contribution of Product A is $1.00 per piece and that of Product B is $1.30 per piece, monthly marginal contribution will be:											
Product A	$400	$360	$320	$280	$240	$200	$160	$120	$80	$40	$0
Product B	0	52	104	156	208	260	312	329	351	376	390
Total	$400	$412	$424	$436	$448	$460	$472	$449	$431	$416	$390
If marginal contribution of Product A is $1.30 per piece and that of Product B is $1.00 per piece, monthly marginal contribution will be:											
Product A	$520	$467	$416	$364	$312	$260	$208	$156	$104	$52	$0
Product B	0	40	80	120	160	200	240	255	270	290	300
Total	$520	$507	$496	$484	$472	$460	$448	$411	$374	$342	$300

column, can be processed by Machine X in 12¾ days. The subsequent columns show the same effect. Similarly, no Machine Y time is assigned to Product B in the first column because no time has been assigned to Product B on Machine X and therefore there is no Product B for Machine Y to work on.

The next section of Figure 15-3 shows the resulting monthly production in pieces of each of the products under the 11 different machine assignments.

The lower sections of the figure show the results under two different assumptions as to the marginal contribution per piece of the two products. In the first set of calculations, it is assumed that Product A has a marginal contribution of $1.00 per piece and Product B has a contribution of $1.30 per piece. The highest total marginal contribution is $472, found in the seventh column, and that is the alternative that would optimize profits under this assumption.

In the second set of calculations, it is assumed that the marginal contributions of the two products are the reverse of those in the previous calculations. In other words, Product A has a marginal contribution of $1.30 per piece and Product B has a contribution of $1.00 per piece. Here the highest total marginal contribution is $520, shown in the first column. Thus it appears that devoting all of Machine X's time to Product A will give the highest total marginal contribution even though Machine Y will be idle half the time.

The above calculations of marginal contribution are, of course, based on direct costing. Had gross profit under an absorption cost system been used, the resulting answers may or may not have led the company to the right decision.

Material Mix Decisions

A few industries produce finished products that must contain certain proportions of chemicals, but these proportions can be obtained by mixing various raw materials in different amounts. The fertilizer industry is one example; the cattlefeed industry is another. Manufacturers in these industries can obtain the desired properties of the finished product by using a variety of raw materials in different proportions. Another, very different example is a hospital kitchen, where the meals prepared must have a certain caloric content, a certain protein content, and certain vitamin contents, but can consist of a great variety of foods.

Typically, in these industries some or all of the raw materials fluctuate in cost. The problem then becomes one of determining the most profitable mix of raw materials to use to make an end product that will meet specifications, taking into account the particular purchase price of each raw material on a given day. The solution is either trial and error if two or three materials are involved or computerized linear programming if a large number of different materials are involved.

If all the raw materials are used in the mix in the form received, the cost accounting *system* is irrelevant, although considerable cost savings can result from a proper calculation. However, if one or more of the materials must be processed before entering the mix, the question arises as to whether preliminary labor and overhead costs should be assigned to the particular material at their direct costs or at their absorption costs. Since it may be assumed that fixed manufacturing overhead would not change in any way between the alternatives, the correct answer will be found through direct costing.

Warehouse Stocking

Companies that make the same product in several geographically distributed plants face complex problems of minimizing costs by determining the proper combination of production costs and shipping costs either to their distribution warehouses or directly to their customers. The problem is often complicated by capacity limitations on some products in some plants. For example, there may be a cost advantage to shipping to a warehouse in Richmond, Virginia, out of a plant in Atlanta, Georgia, as opposed to a plant in Paramus, New Jersey, but if the result is that the New Orleans warehouse has to be shipped out of the Seattle plant because of limited production capacity in Atlanta, the answer is almost certainly wrong. Richmond should be taken care of by the Paramus plant so that Atlanta can take care of New Orleans.

A second complicating factor is the saving that may result from combining shipments. Say that in the prior example Atlanta has the capacity to take care of both Richmond and New Orleans on those products it can make but it does not have the equipment to produce all the products in the company's line. The Paramus plant, on the other hand, produces all products. In this case, the apparent saving in shipping to Richmond out of Atlanta may be offset by the higher unit freight costs that apply when a shipment which would have been a carload lot out of Paramus becomes two smaller shipments, one out of

Atlanta and one out of Paramus, because of Atlanta's shorter product line.

This type of problem can be solved by linear programming on a computer. In fact, the warehouse stocking problem is the classic application of linear programming. From the cost accountant's viewpoint, the important point in warehouse stocking decisions is that the product cost that is to be added to the freight cost should be the direct cost. This can be illustrated by the following story, which occurred several years ago. (The events have been disguised slightly.)

The company manufactured a single product, packed in several sizes. The product was very cheap to produce and very heavy. The custom of the industry was to absorb freight out. The company had a plant in a fairly high tax area of New York City, in an old building with poor materials handling efficiency. It also had a plant just outside Chicago in a low tax area; the plant had been built to its specifications, and its materials flow was near perfection.

For a number of years the company had assigned customers located between the two plants according to which plant could ship the customer at the lowest freight rate. The result was a north–south dividing line that ran through Cleveland, Ohio. One day someone suggested that the freight rate was only part of the cost and that the unit cost of production in the respective plants should also be considered. This seemed to make sense and a policy change was made.

The company calculated its costs on an absorption basis and, because of the factors already mentioned, found that unit costs in New York were substantially higher than those in Chicago. Accordingly, under the new method of calculating which plant could supply a particular customer at lowest cost, the north–south dividing line was shifted eastward to Youngstown, Ohio.

Two months later, the unit costs of producing in the two plants were recalculated. Not surprisingly, the unit costs in Chicago had gone down because its fixed costs had been spread over the additional volume represented by the customers located between the north–south line through Cleveland and the north–south line through Youngstown. Conversely, the unit production costs in New York had gone up because of the loss of this same volume. Accordingly, customers were reassigned to the two plants on the basis of the new figures. The result was a north–south dividing line that again shifted eastward, this time through Altoona, Pennsylvania.

After several more bimonthly revisions, the north–south line was calculated as running through Hoboken, New Jersey, only five miles west of the New York City plant. At this point, the company became aware that only variable production costs should have been included in the calculations along with freight costs. Any other approach tends to increase total freight costs, with nothing saved on fixed costs at either end. Today the company still has its north–south dividing line, but under the second policy change, the one to a direct cost approach, the line is now at a point about halfway between Cleveland and Youngstown.

Summary

The problems covered in this chapter do not by any means apply to all companies. Even in companies where they are important, they do not represent daily worries. In some cases, the objective has been to show how a figure or statement that must be reported on an absorption cost basis can be derived from direct cost data. In other cases, the objective has been to show how direct costing is superior to absorption costing in providing management with data to guide it in handling special problems.

16

Maintaining the Accuracy of Dollar Book Inventories

THE story is making the rounds that the president of a medium-size manufacturer reported to the board of directors that "based on the results of the first 11 months of the year, our profits this year should set a new record." At the next board meeting, which took place after the year-end physical inventory had been calculated, a shamefaced president had to report that actual profits for the year had been negligible because book inventory was substantially higher than the actual physical inventory. In order to end the meeting on a more pleasant note, he assured the directors that he was taking steps to ensure that nothing like this would ever happen again. "In fact," he said, "I have already taken the first two of these steps." On inquiry, he indicated that the two steps involved were firing the controller and the chief cost accountant.

Whether or not this story is based on fact, it is certainly true that cost systems are criticized more often and more severely for coming up with erroneous book inventory dollars than for any other reason. Top management seems to be able to take in stride reports that don't really tell it what it wants to know, reports in formats that make it difficult to cull the pertinent information, late reports, and even product cost reports found to be inaccurate and reports of variances that are proved to contain errors. However, a totally unexpected difference between the dollar book inventory and the physical inventory which reveals that the book figure is overstated causes tempers to flare and sometimes heads to roll.

Of course, in such a situation, the accuracy of the physical inventory should be double-checked before the figures are released, since the error may be in the physical. (Usually, this possibility has been ruled out early in the procedure.) There is also the possibility that the shortage has been caused by theft. However, it is far more likely that the major shortage does, indeed, arise from flaws in the cost system or in the reporting that is part of the system.

The inventory shortage problem can arise under actual or standard cost systems, but it is somewhat more likely to escape notice under a standard cost system. Both direct cost and absorption cost systems have, on occasion, resulted in grossly overstated dollar book inventories, and the reasons for these errors and the suggested cures are the same under both systems. The only difference is that the overstatement in dollars as a result of certain types of errors will be less under direct costing than under absorption costing, since the book value of the work-in-process or finished-goods inventory is less under direct costing by the amount of fixed manufacturing overhead in the product. This is a very minor solace to advocates of direct costing, because an estimate of the fixed costs omitted from direct cost inventories is added back to the direct cost in preparing financial statements. This, in effect, puts the amount of the shortage at the same figure in both systems.

Inventory shortages are usually thought of in terms of their effect on the profits shown in financial statements. However, certain types of errors will also affect the accuracy of unit perpetual inventory records. Depending on whether raw materials, purchased parts, semi-finished parts and subassemblies, or finished goods is being controlled, errors in the balances of these records can create very serious problems in production scheduling and in service to customers. When the worker with the requisition for 1/4″ pipe finds that there is none in stock even though the recorded inventory balance indicates that there is, the production of a whole department can be delayed for a considerable period. Similarly, the salesman who tells a customer that a certain item "is in stock and will be shipped that day" when it isn't in stock faces a real problem of lost goodwill as well as a lost sale.

Although shortages in unit perpetual inventory records cause many more problems and much more serious problems than overages, the latter too can be costly. Assume a unit inventory record indicates that there are 100 widgets on hand when there are actually 250. All replenishment decisions made for the rest of the year will be based on the 100-piece balance. This is true whether the widget is a purchased part, a part in intermediate storage, or a finished product. In effect, the company has frozen the extra 150 pieces, so that they will be of no use until the error comes to light in the next physical inventory. In the meantime, the company has working capital and storage space tied up in a completely dead asset.

Controlling Inventories

The terms "inventory control" and "inventory management" have roughly the same meaning in ordinary English, but quite a few people in industry involved with inventories make a sharp distinction between the two. These people use "inventory control" to describe the ways of ensuring that total dollar book inventories are realistic and that unit perpetual inventories by item are accurate. By contrast, these people construe "inventory management" to mean having enough of everything on hand to ensure against production interruptions due to out-of-stock materials, parts, or subassemblies and to provide good customer service from finished-goods stocks without tieing up working capital unnecessarily in excess stocks of anything. In this book, we will adhere to the distinction between inventory control and inventory management while recognizing that it is not self-evident and may have to be explained by those using either term when the intended distinction is important.

Inventory control is generally not a separate function in a company. It encompasses the refinement of procedures being carried out for other purposes within the general accounting and cost accounting areas. Possibly, refining the procedures is less important than monitoring them to make sure they are being followed correctly. Another important aspect of inventory control is the monthly cross-check on various sources to determine the reasonableness of the total dollar inventory amount arrived at through the book entries. This aspect of inventory control will be covered toward the end of the chapter. Both the checking of input to the detail records and book entries and the cross-checks on reasonableness can be greatly facilitated if the cost accounting and inventory tracking functions are computerized.

Inventory management, on the other hand, is often a specialized function in a manufacturing company. It involves, at its best, relatively sophisticated techniques that are not part of any other system. A discussion of the many approaches to inventory management and how they can be combined effectively in a company is outside the scope of this book. However, it should be pointed out that inventory management cannot function properly unless inventory control supplies it with accurate data on the balance on hand of every item in the inventory together with information as to how much is on order and how much of the item is committed for by customer orders already in the house (in the case of finished goods) and by planned production schedules (in the case of materials and parts).

Coding Errors

Materials, parts, subassemblies, assemblies, finished products, and operations are ordinarily identified by numerical codes. It is very easy to record a wrong code number on a purchase invoice, a requisition, a time ticket, an inspection report, or a sales invoice. A 7 looks like a 1, a 5 looks like a 6, a 3 looks like an 8. A very common error is a transposition—for example, code number 863245 may be recorded as 836245 or as 832645. When invoices and other documents are used as the basic records for preparing the dollar inventory amounts and unit perpetual inventory records, the error can affect the dollar totals as well as the unit balances. This is because the code number is often used to extend the units by a unit cost value found either in some listing or in the computer memory. The error can occur in writing the original document, in copying it onto a summary list, in keypunching the data, or in selecting the card on which the entry is posted.

It is obvious that such an error will affect the unit inventory record of both the item that should have been charged or credited and the item that was erroneously charged or credited. The effect on dollar inventories sometimes appears to cancel out, but it doesn't. Suppose, for example, that part 863245 with a cost of $2 per piece is issued from stock into production but the requisition reads part 836245 with a cost of $1 per piece. Once the erroneous requisition is posted to the dollar book inventory records, the stockroom will have a dollar inventory with a cost value that is $1 higher times the number of units on the requisition than its actual cost. However, work in process will be $1 lower times the pieces on the requisition than it should be. When the company is on an actual cost system, the actual cost of the finished product will be the same dollar lower than it should be, giving a gross profit upon sale of $1 higher than the real situation. This extra dollar in gross profit flows through to net profit, yet it really represents the erroneous overvaluation of stockroom inventory and is not a profit at all. Under a standard cost system, completed products are credited to work in process at the standard cost of the finished product, which is, of course, not affected by the error. In this situation, the dollar will appear as a favorable variance between actual and standard. Since favorable variances increase the profit for the period, again a dollar has appeared in profit that represents an erroneous overvaluation of the stockroom inventory.

Under an actual cost system, an error of this type is unlikely to occur in the posting of an accounts payable invoice to the inventory records because the dollar value of the invoice is picked up directly. However, under a standard cost system, if part 836245 with a standard cost of $1 is received but entered as part 863245 with a standard cost of $2, the stockroom inventory will be overstated. Assuming that the part is requisitioned under its correct code number, the error will stand until the physical inventory is taken. Similarly, if finished product 647 with a cost value of $53 is shipped but the sales invoice is read as finished product 641 with a cost value of only $36, finished-goods inventory will appear to be $17 higher than it actually is until the error comes to light through the physical inventory.

Wrong operation numbers have no effect under an actual cost system, but wrong hourly rates do. Suppose an employee is charged to a machine or job on the cost records in error at $6 per hour; his real rate is $7 per hour and that is what the payroll department pays him. Work in process will reflect the extra dollar per hour in inventory long after the product on which the employee was working was transferred to finished goods and sold to customers. Here again, a false gross profit has been created by an overvaluation of work-in-process inventory.

Under a standard cost system, a wrong operation number will generate the charge to work-in-process inventory but the correct operation number is part of the product cost, which is credited to work-in-process inventory. If the wrong operation has a higher cost than the right one, the work-in-process inventory will be overvalued until the physical inventory comes along to correct the error.

Each of the foregoing examples results in an overvaluation of some part of the dollar book inventory. If the coding errors go the other way, a corresponding undervaluation will occur. When thousands of coded entries are made each month, it would seem reasonable to assume that enough errors will be made in each direction to produce a negligible net difference. There is no logical explanation for the fact that this does not happen. Indeed, experience shows that the more coding errors made, the larger the resulting net inventory overvaluation.

A number of techniques have been devised for minimizing coding errors. Under a manual system, an obvious approach is to spot-check the work of all those who make the original entries to the documents, those who prepare summary lists, and those who do the final posting. Another approach is to state all entries in dollar amounts. Then if a part costing $5 is being requisitioned for incorporation into an end product with a selling price of $2, it is likely to catch someone's eye. In fact, an eye check of all charges to a product can be quite productive if dollars are shown at every stage.

Some companies with computerized systems use check digits to detect errors. A check digit is a single digit added to a code number for the purpose of virtually guaranteeing its correctness. Earlier an example was given of a confusion between the numbers 863245 and 836245. Had these numbers been 8632452 and 8362458 with no other numbers in use starting with either of the first six digits of either number, the computer could be programmed to reject as invalid numbers 8632458 and 8362452, thus catching the error of writing either number as the other at its origin. The procedure involves either a calculation in which the end digit is arrived at by formula or a comparison of the number with a list of valid numbers. Under either system, errors will slip through only when two mistakes that exactly offset each other are made on the same code number. A transposition does not meet this requirement. Thus the odds against an error going through undetected become very high. Computers can also check validity of part numbers and operation numbers against a list of those appropriate to each end product. Another approach used with computer systems is to set a range of values for part numbers related to specific end products.

Cycle Counting

When wrong part or product coding fouls up unit inventory records, as it invariably will, cycle counting can be used to straighten them out. Under this approach, a physical count is made of a few items each day, week, or month until all items have been checked one or more times a year. Such counts are normally made during plant operating hours, but in certain industries it is easier to make them on Saturdays or, if the plant is operating on only one shift, in the evening. Cycle counts have become a way of life in many companies. Of course, cycle counting is possible only if a company keeps perpetual unit inventory records, but most sizable companies do this anyway.

Cycle counting requires that cutoff records be kept for both incoming materials and outgoing materials. In other words, the clerk posting the unit inventory record must know which of the documents coming through his hands represent items delivered to the area before the physical count and which represent items delivered after the count. The clerk must also know which documents represent items issued from the area before the count and which ones represent items issued afterward. Of course, only those documents coming through a few days before or after the count need be considered. Since only relatively few items are counted at a time, the clerical burden is not too great, but the problem is sufficiently important that the system *must* provide for it.

Many companies using cycle counts stratify the items in inventory in order to reduce the cycle-counting cost while improving control. Stratification means that fast-moving or high-cost items are counted more often than slower-moving or lower-cost items. For example, the 10 percent of the items that account for 60 percent of annual dollar usage could be counted every month, the 20 percent that account for 25 percent of the annual usage could be counted every second month, and the 70 percent that account for the remaining 15 percent of the dollar usage could be counted twice a year. (These percentages are realistic for many companies.) The result is less counting than if all items were counted four times a year and better data on total dollar discrepancies.

Some companies use cycle counting to aid in revising unit inventory records but never carry the findings through to the book dollar inventory totals. Such a policy makes no sense at all. Any shortages found should be used either to reduce the book inventory value directly or to create a reserve account against any inventory shrinkage that might be revealed by the next full physical inventory. In fact, a few companies extrapolate the shortage percentage found on the items counted by applying the same percentage against the entire dollar value of the inventory. The extrapolation policy involves some fairly tricky arithmetic, since the items are counted on various dates and, as the year progresses, certain items may be counted several more times.

Advocates of cycle counting believe that proper use of the system can eliminate the year-end inventory. Since many plants have to close down for several days for year-end inventory while paying many workers to help with the counting, this would indeed be a saving. Furthermore, advocates of the system believe that results are more accurate because all the people involved in cycle counts are selected for their inventory-taking abilities. Much of the counting in the annual physical inventory is done by machine hands and stock clerks. There is, however, a drawback. A dishonest management can shift known shortages into items that have just been counted in order to cover up shortages in items scheduled to be counted. This would require considerable collusion, but it could be done.

If cycle counting were used solely to uncover errors in material, parts, or product coding, it would hardly be worthwhile. However, it will also uncover many other types of errors. For example, it will obviously reveal simple wrong counting or wrong recording of a correct count of the number of pieces being transferred into or out of an area. Several other errors uncovered by cycle counting are discussed below.

Errors in Unit Designation

Errors caused by failing to designate the appropriate unit of quantity are amazingly frequent. Thus machine screws are ordinarily requisitioned by the package, but a worker may put down a 6 on a requisition when he needs six pieces without realizing this figure will be interpreted by someone else as six packages. Similarly, steel may be purchased in tons and requisitioned by the hundredweight, but again a worker who needs six pounds puts down a 6. One hospital pharmacy attempted to educate all requisitioners to order pills and capsules by the package rather than by number of pieces. After failing miserably in this attempt, the pharmacy reversed itself and requested that all quantities be specified in pieces. This effort was equally unsuccessful and, at last word, the pharmacy had an employee who spent most of his time correcting the quantities shown on the requisitions before they were sent to keypunching.

The techniques used to correct wrong unit designations are very similar to those used to mimimize wrong coding. Making a spot check is one; stating all documents in dollar amounts is another. In a computerized system, a range check on dollar amounts can be particularly useful. It must be kept in mind that a coding error may result in a large or a small dollar difference, depending on how far apart the unit costs of the two misinterpreted part numbers happen to be.

However, an error in unit designation is always a very large percentage. A ton is 20 times the cost of a hundredweight, which in turn is 100 times the cost of a pound. A yard costs 3 times as much as a foot.

Errors Affecting Raw Materials and Purchased Parts

Certain shortages may occur even before materials and parts enter production. On the incoming side, it is assumed that every company protects itself against duplicate payments by associating receiving reports with accounts payable invoices. However, other factors can be involved. One company weighed bulk materials being delivered by truck on their way to the receiving area and then weighed the outgoing truck to establish the tare weight to be subtracted. After some months of unexplained shortages, the company discovered that the driver sat in the truck during each of the deliveries but managed to step out to converse with the receiving clerk when the truck was weighed on the way out. The company was unknowingly reviving an old tradition of paying for a man's weight in some commodity—fortunately, not gold in this instance.

In another instance, a mill converted sheet steel from pounds to square measure on the basis of the standard weight of the particular gauge per square foot. However, the steel supplied by the mill weighed slightly over the standard weight. Under these circumstances, input by weight and outgo by square measure will always result in a shortage. Obviously, the corrective is to have any material bought by weight and used by linear or square measure checked from time to time for the incoming ratio of weight to measure.

Substitute materials can also lead to shortages. When a stockroom is short of a particular material or part that is badly needed for production purposes, a substitute material is often used. The substitute material is almost always more expensive, either because it is of unnecessarily high quality or because it generates a higher percentage of waste. (See the discussion of material quantity standards in Chapter 9.) Typically, the judgment of the individuals authorizing the more expensive material is never questionable. Under a standard cost system the result will be a dollar shortage, unless the difference is recorded as a material price variance. The corrective is to make sure that the system provides a form for reporting material substitutions, that all appropriate parties receive instructions on when and how to use the form, and that an effort is made to enforce these instructions.

Certain shortages can occur when materials bought for production are used for maintenance. Nuts, bolts, screws, wire (both electrical and plain), angle iron, grease, and paint are particularly vulnerable items. If an appropriate requisition is made out with a charge to the maintenance department, no shortage will result. The problem lies in enforcing this requirement. Locked stockrooms help, but this is not always practicable.

A related problem can arise when a requisition that calls for 100 parts is filled but the production worker subsequently returns to the stockroom for four more parts because of spoilage in production. Neither he nor the stockroom keeper wants to be bothered with a requisition for only four pieces, so they are handed out without paperwork and a shortage results. Again, locked stockrooms and enforcement procedures are the only answer.

Bulk materials pose special problems. Cling losses, overweighing, and hygroscopic materials (those that gain or lose weight depending on the humidity) were mentioned in connection with material standards in Chapter 9. Lot clearances are one solution. Lot clearance systems are used throughout the textile industry and occasionally in other industries to control liquids, powders, and other materials that are hard to measure. When a shipment is received, an extra digit or two is added to the material code to identify the particular lot. This identification number appears on the drums or on the shelf where the material is stored. The worker making out a requisition for the material does not enter the lot number, as he has no way of knowing it. However, when the stockroom keeper fills the requisition, he adds the lot number. At the end of a lot, the stockroom keeper may have to fill a requisition partly from that lot and partly from the next. In this case, he shows the weight filled from each lot. When accounting receives a requisition which indicates that a lot has been completely used up, all requisitions showing that lot number are added and compared with the incoming weight. If a shortage is found, both the unit inventory balances and the book dollar inventory balance are adjusted. If these shrinkages have been estimated and included in the standards in a standard cost system, the only problem is maintaining the accuracy of the standard. In an actual cost system, an account must be set up to allow for the estimated shrinkage.

As noted in Chapter 3, some companies average costs by taking the latest shipment and averaging it with all purchases of the year to date. When costs are rising, this will inevitably result in an overstatement of the remaining inventory. Assume, for example, that a company started the year with no inventory. The first shipment was 100 pieces at $1 each, or a total of $100. Before any other shipments were received, 50 pieces were used and the inventory account was credited with $50. A new shipment comes in with 100 pieces at $1.10 each. The average cost is now $1.05, consisting of the first shipment at $1.00 for 100 pieces and the next at $1.10 for 100 pieces. All 150 remaining pieces are issued at $1.05 and the inventory is credited with $157.50. Thus, from zero pieces in inventory to zero pieces in inventory, debits have been $210 and credits have been $207.50. The difference of $2.50 remains in the dollar book inventory but represents no value. The corrective for such a situation is not to use this system for costing materials.

Errors Affecting Work-in-Process Inventory

The dollar total value of the work-in-process inventory is subject to greater error than any other part of the inventory. In addition, it is very hard to find a way of cross-checking the figure without shutting down operations. The problem stems from the fact that actual costs are charged in but only costs that can be accounted for are credited out. A simple example will illustrate the point. Product X requires one piece of Part A. The stockroom issues to production a pallet load of Part A consisting of 10,000 pieces. In the course of the next few weeks 8,300 pieces of Product X are passed through to inspection. The presumption is that 1,700 pieces of Part A are still sitting in work in process. The fact may well be that only 1,147 pieces are still available, the other 553 representing unreported spoilage, parts used to repair customer returns, or parts used to repair the bicycle of the floor-sweeper's son.

As a matter of fact, unreported spoilage—common in just about every plant—is a major problem in keeping inventory totals correct. Workers do not like to report spoilage, even when they are not penalized or criticized for it. This was well illustrated in the glassware stockroom of a department store. The company recognized that a certain amount of smashed glassware was inevitable and did not try to reprimand those responsible. But it did wish to keep track of the style numbers involved for unit record purposes. Therefore, management put two barrels in a dark corner with a pad hanging over them and asked each stock clerk to record the number of broken pieces and the style numbers, without giving his name. Each morning, the barrels were emptied out and by evening they were both overflowing again. The pad would show one or two entries, accounting for perhaps 1 percent of what was in the barrels.

Another example was a small branch plant in the chemicals industry that had never submitted a spoilage report, as other branches did.

An investigation revealed that no one in the plant, up to and including the manager, knew that spoilage should be reported or had ever seen the form designed for that purpose.

Unfortunately, there is no airtight solution to this problem. Some help can be obtained by inspecting trash cans, reviewing sales of scrap, and making sure the proper forms are available and that everyone knows when and how to use them. Sometimes a comparison of scrap reporting among different departments or over different time periods in the same department will suggest that a particular foreman needs a reminder from his boss.

A close relative of unreported spoilage is rework that is reported as if it were new work. This type of error often arises because the employee doing the rework has no responsibility for the production problem that required the rework. Both he and his foreman believe he is entitled to have his personal records show his time spent in terms of pieces produced. This can still be done on a rework ticket. If it is done on a regular ticket, the operation will be debited to work in process twice but will be credited only once. Basically, the corrective is to make sure that the proper forms are available and that all employees know when and how to use them.

Just as stockrooms occasionally have to supply materials that are more expensive than the product specifications call for, production departments sometimes have to perform operations on the product that are more costly than those called for by the operation sheet used in the standard product cost. This may occur because an automatic machine is busy or broken down, necessitating the use of a semiautomatic or manual one, or because faulty material requires preliminary processing not called for in the operation sheet. In either case, the foreman's judgment that a change is needed is probably correct, but unless the change is properly reported it will create an overvaluation of the work-in-process inventory. Again, the corrective is to supply proper forms, with proper instructions on their use. In addition, a spot check should be made of the operation numbers related to the processing of a product against the operation numbers in the operation sheet. A computer can be programmed to do this.

Overcounting should not be overlooked. Its most common cause is the worker's acceptance of the number of pieces on the lot ticket as the amount he processed. Thus, if the lot ticket shows 5,000 pieces, a worker may report processing 5,000, without considering the fact that the previous operation lost 100 of the pieces through spoilage. Even if the spoilage report was made out correctly on the prior operation, the loss recorded would not include the cost of this subsequent operation.

Nor will work in process be relieved of this cost when finished-goods inspection credits work in process with only 4,900 completed products.

A less innocent example of overcounting occurred in a piece-work shop where the press of rush orders forced the breaking up of lots after they had been through one or two operations. The third operation, involving a lot of 4,000 pieces, was reported as being completed on 1,400 pieces one day, on 1,800 pieces on a day two weeks later, and on 2,400 pieces on a day a month later. Thus it appears that 5,600 pieces grew from the original 4,000.

Aside from good supervision, the corrective for such a situation is to establish a tie-in between cost accounting and production scheduling. This can improve the accuracy of both functions, since some types of errors will be more obvious in the cost accounting reports and some will be more obvious in the production scheduling reports. Also, computers can be programmed to flag "growth" situations.

The use of production materials for in-plant maintenance (and employee home repairs) was mentioned earlier in connection with stockroom inventories. This problem is much more likely to occur with materials already issued to production. Typically, these materials are lying around loose and are easily picked up. The only corrective, though not a very effective one, is to requisition against a variance account any unexplained deficiency in the materials needed to complete a lot of products when the full amount has presumably been issued.

Each of the foregoing problems can create substantial overstatements of work-in-process dollar inventory totals in certain industries under certain conditions. The correctives suggested have proved to be quite helpful but they cannot be expected to perform miracles.

Cycle counting is often not practicable for work-in-process validation. However, it is entirely practicable for checking intermediate storage—that is, parts and subassemblies that have been completed but are not immediately needed for the completion of finished products. These parts may be held in the raw material stockroom area or in separate stockrooms. Often, they are left in whatever area of the production department the last operation was performed. As long as there is a separate inventory record, they can be cycle-counted.

Intermediate storage is affected by the same types of errors that arise in any other storage area. Incoming and outgoing material may be miscounted, designated by wrong part numbers, or expressed in wrong units. Proper unit records are very important, since any shortage can delay finished-goods production and deliveries to customers.

Errors Affecting Finished Goods

The following discussion assumes that the controls provided by a company's general accounting system are such that no goods will be shipped to customers unless a sales invoice is recorded. These controls should, of course, cover not only shipments that go out with a bill of lading but also parcel post shipments and goods picked up by the customer's own truck.

Errors affecting finished-goods inventory include the use of wrong product codes and the designation of wrong unit quantities. In addition, products may be damaged through handling in this department. Accordingly, spoilage reporting forms should be available and should be well understood by stockroom and shipping department personnel.

One problem unique to this area is surreptitious product substitution. The customer orders style 42XA61. The company has none in stock and decides to substitute a very similar style 42XB49. Rather than write the customer a lengthy explanation of how similar the styles are, the salesman says, "Just bill it as style 42XA61; the customer will never know the difference." Unless some internal record is made of the substitution, two inventory records will be wrong—one over and one short—until the next physical count.

Finished goods are sometimes borrowed for displays, to provide a subject for the advertising agency's photographer or to impress visiting dignitaries. It is difficult for stockroom personnel to tell the marketing VP that he must keep the Senator waiting while he fills out the form required to remove the gadget from stock. Nevertheless, someone should fill out a form so that the inventory records are maintained correctly. Here again, a procedure should be clearly established and understood by all personnel concerned.

Repackaging can be a problem in some industries. One company sold a liquid product in both 5-gallon cans and 55-gallon drums. When one or the other was out of stock and an order came in for it, some repouring occurred in the finished-goods stockroom. No record was made. As a result, replenishment tended to be badly planned and the need for repouring was increased.

Finally, customer returns can sometimes create a problem that affects both unit records and dollar totals. What happens is this: The customer returns a product for any one of a number of reasons and is entitled to full credit. The entry is to credit accounts receivable and debit sales for the sales price and to credit cost of sales and debit finished-goods inventory for the cost value. Subsequently, possibly weeks later, the returned goods are examined, and some or all of them are found to be unsuitable for resale because of damage or obsolescence, or for some other reason. The goods are set aside or destroyed but no record is made. As a result, both the unit and dollar values remain in the finished-goods inventory records until a physical inventory is taken. Here again, proper procedures should be set up and enforced.

One company solved the return merchandise problem by debiting a suspense account at the time the return was first recorded rather than debiting finished-goods inventory. When the goods were inspected, the suspense account was credited and either finished-goods inventory or spoilage was debited as required. This system worked well.

Cross-Checking Dollar Totals for Reasonableness

In view of all the trouble that can arise when book inventory dollar totals prove to be substantially overstated, a company is well advised to check on their reasonableness and to establish appropriate reserves when necessary. A number of procedures have been devised for this purpose. The oldest known approach is to assume that this year's shrinkage figure will be approximately the same as last year's and to reserve one-twelfth of that figure each month. This method is not very satisfactory, however, since changes in operations and personnel can cause substantial variations in both the type and size of errors that occur from year to year.

An eye check of a company's total inventory value is almost entirely useless. No one is in a position to say just by looking at the inventory that a book value of $25 million is not off by half a million dollars. However, when that $25 million is broken down by raw materials, purchased parts, work in process, and finished goods, an eye check becomes a little more meaningful. If raw materials are further broken down into several types, if work in process is broken down by departments, and if finished goods is broken down by location, it becomes still more useful. The point can be illustrated by the discovery of a fraud in one store of a chain of supermarkets. The fraud was uncovered because the inventory value of meat when converted to cubic feet would not fit into the cubic space of the store's meat department.

If the work-in-process inventory is further broken down into its material, direct labor, and variable overhead components by department, a comparison of ratios from period to period can be a useful indicator of the need for further checking or even a special physical inventory.

In a computerized company, particularly one using standard costs, it is frequently possible to obtain an excellent check on raw materials, purchased parts, intermediate storage, and finished goods by extending the unit inventory balances by the unit costs. A small company with relatively few products of simple construction may find this approach worthwhile even under a manual system. Naturally, the cross-check will be much more reliable if the unit records have been validated from time to time by cycle counts.

In order to get a validation on work in process, a different and less effective approach must be used. The approach involves calculating the total value at standard cost of all production orders in process as if they had been completed. The ratio of the book work-in-process inventory to this figure is then determined and compared with similar ratios in past periods, including the physical inventory date. This procedure will provide a good feel for the reasonableness of the book work-in-process figure, particularly if it can be done by departments or, better yet, by departments in terms of material, direct labor, and variable overhead content. Generally, a computer is required for this approach.

It should be noted that the ratio of the value of work-in-process inventory to the full value of open production orders at the time of the physical inventory may be misleading. Many companies tend to "clean up the floor" before taking physical inventories. This can distort ratios substantially.

Summary

In view of the importance of accurate interim dollar book inventories for profit estimating and projection, every available tool should be used to improve their accuracy. From an operating point of view, the correctness of individual unit inventory balances is even more important.

Experience indicates that many errors can arise in the necessary recordkeeping, and some of these errors are very difficult to avoid. However, a number of techniques have been developed to improve the recording of input and output at each stage of inventory control. None of these methods can be considered 100 percent effective, but they help enormously.

In addition, there are a number of ways to check the dollar inventory totals for reasonableness. Between these cross-checks and the input control techniques, many companies believe that their interim figures are sufficiently accurate for the purposes for which they are used.

Except for the fact that direct costing and absorption costing use different manufacturing overhead figures in some calculations, the problems and their correctives are the same.

17

Converting to a Direct Cost System

OBVIOUSLY, the procedures involved in converting to a direct cost system will vary considerably depending on the company's preexisting cost system, if any. The procedures will also vary depending on whether the proposed system is to be a direct standard cost system or a direct actual cost system and on whether (and to what extent) the system will be computerized.

However, the major steps involved are very similar under all these circumstances. For clarity, the following discussion will assume a conversion from a manual standard absorption cost system to a manual direct standard cost system. (Chapter 19 deals with computerizing a cost system.) A few comments will be made on the differences required in other types of conversions, including the installation of a direct standard cost system in a company with no preexisting cost system.

Orientation

Whenever a company initiates a study of existing procedures, rumors begin to fly and anxieties rise. Clerical workers and executives fear that their jobs will be eliminated, that their value as employees intimately acquainted with the old procedures will be eroded, that new people with different skills will be brought in, and even that the study is preparatory to a takeover by another company or a move to another location.

Accordingly, it is worthwhile to hold a meeting with representatives of all departments and functions within the company to explain the project before the first piece of information is gathered or the first note written. In large companies, it may be necessary to restrict the kickoff meeting to 20 or 30 senior executives, with subsequent meetings held within departments for lower-echelon executives and senior clerical workers.

The kickoff meeting should cover the purposes of the change, why they are important to the company, the time the study is expected to take, the probable date of the conversion, the basics of the proposed system, and some indication of how various departments will be involved in the conversion. It should be frankly stated that the project will entail a lot of work and that this, on top of regular assignments, will require overtime by certain executives and other employees. If any saving in personnel is anticipated, it should be made clear that this will occur through normal attrition, not through layoffs. At both the kickoff meeting and subsequent orientation meetings, the meeting leader should open the floor to questions and in fact should encourage questions. Certainly, no questions should be brushed aside or answered in a way that embarrasses the questioner.

Organizing the Work

In the best conversion programs, a task force is selected to take charge of the project from beginning to end and to make all the necessary decisions. Typically, the task force consists of a representative from every functional department that will be deeply involved in the conversion process and/or in the use of the new system. These departments include marketing, sales (if it is a separate function from marketing), production, industrial engineering, purchasing, EDP, general accounting, and cost accounting. Many companies also include an outside consultant who has converted other companies to direct costing. This can save time and provide good insurance against mistakes which, even if corrected, could create a lack of confidence in the system for years. The executives selected for the task force should be high enough up in their respective departments to be thoroughly familiar with policies and problems but not so high up that their participation in the project will seriously affect the functioning of their departments. The second- or third-in-command is usually a good choice.

The task force is basically an advisory and decision-making group and operates through periodic meetings of one or two hours. Generally, its chairman comes from production or from the controller's group. The members of the task force have the additional assignment of introducing those doing the work to the people in their departments and making information in their departments easily available.

Often the system is designed and implemented by the cost accountant, who may have one or more assistants, depending on the size of the company. These people are, for the time being, employees of the task force. In most cases, their assignment will require all their time, so that arrangements must be made to relieve them of other work.

Some companies prefer to have the conversion work done by outside consultants, either because they do not have appropriate personnel within the company or because suitable personnel can't be spared from their regular work. Consultants can do the whole job, serve as advisers on an intermittent basis, or take the major responsibility for most of the work but use company personnel extensively for certain portions.

All the major accounting firms have knowledgeable consultants in cost accounting, but this is not to say that all their employees or even all their senior employees or partners have the necessary experience. All capable consultants will depend heavily on company personnel for information on the traditions and special problems of the company.

The Preliminary Study

The project leader, whether the chief cost accountant, an outside specialist, an internal management consultant, or someone else, should first familiarize himself with every aspect of the present system. He may feel he is already completely familiar with it, but a series of conversations with the people actually doing the work will reveal changes that have taken place since he last looked at the procedures. Many of these changes may not have been incorporated in the procedures manual. The changes may reflect special problems of which neither he nor the department head is aware. This preliminary information must be obtained at the grassroots level, since department heads quite often labor under some misconceptions about the details of what is going on. Certainly, inquiries should be made about any matters that make the work more difficult than it should be.

The next step is to hold a series of interviews with report recipients in order to determine how they use the reports they receive. Only after this question has been thoroughly explored and notes have been made should recipients be asked how they would like to see the reports improved. The project leader should be aware that people's responses are apt to be colored by their personalities. Many will say that a report is "OK as it is," meaning they haven't thought about it and don't really want to. Others will merely ask for greater accuracy and timeliness—which for all practical purposes means they haven't thought about it either. A few eager beavers will ask for the world with a ribbon tied around it. It is the project leader's job to suggest possible improvements to the first group and to cross-examine the eager beavers on what they really intend to use the requested data for. It may also be a good idea to question any of the project leader's suggestions that were accepted too readily by the others.

Designing the System

With this information in hand, the project leader is in a position to rough out a draft of the basic system that he feels would be appropriate. The draft should be submitted to the task force for suggestions, revisions, and eventual approval. The project leader should call a meeting of the task force to explain his proposal and leave copies of the draft with individual members for study. A second meeting should then be held for discussion and revision. Depending on the extent of the revisions suggested, a second draft and a third meeting may be required before approval. At this point, senior management should be shown the basic system and the management methods it will entail. Any questions raised should be resolved to the satisfaction of senior management.

The system design must include the contemplated method for converting the direct cost inventories to an absorption cost basis (see Chapter 6), since this will affect the way costs are to be accumulated and recorded. For example, if either Method 1 or 2 is to be used, the direct labor component of costs must be accumulated separately and may have to be accumulated on a departmental basis. If Method 3 is to be used, all standard product costs must show both direct costs and absorption costs. Whatever method is proposed at this point, the concurrence of the outside auditors should be obtained. A company just can't afford to install a system that its outside auditors reject at year end. It would then be much too late to accumulate the data the outside auditors want and a certificate might not be forthcoming.

After the system design has been accepted, the project leader should prepare a program of work to be done with an appropriate time schedule and an indication of assignments. The steps involved are described in the next section of this chapter; the order in which they are taken will depend on the availability of appropriate personnel. It may be worthwhile to prepare a Critical Path Schedule (discussed more fully later in the chapter) to determine which steps can be delayed and for how long without affecting the proposed installation date.

It will be obvious from the remainder of the chapter that converting a cost system in a company of any size cannot be done in days or weeks. A year is perhaps an average time, although some companies have been converted in less time and others have taken longer. A key factor on timing is the nature of the preexisting absorption cost system. One relatively small company that did not have a cost system but that had well-developed material and direct labor standards had a direct cost system installed in five months, but this is exceptionally fast. Installation was greatly aided by an EDP manager who met every request for analyses and reports with the response "no problem" and then proceeded to prove that, for a man of his ability at least, there indeed was no problem. All the data came out on time.

In setting the schedule, the project leader should keep two basics in mind. First, implementation should proceed one department or a few departments at a time, at about two-week intervals. This permits close supervision by the designer of the system. Second, some period of parallel operation with the old system is advisable, despite the added load on personnel and the extra cost involved.

The proposed system design need not contain all the features that have been mentioned throughout this book. However, certain features are essential; others are optional and may be omitted or deferred for implementation at a later date. The essential features include:

- Product cost sheets at standard direct cost.
- Performance reports that show by department by month (or a shorter period) a comparison of standard cost with actual and the variance by account.
- Dollar book inventory broken down into raw materials and purchased parts, work in process (preferably broken down further by departments), intermediate storage, and finished goods.

- Capability through a "where used" computer program or a manual cross-reference file to update all product cost standards for changes in the price standard of any material or changes in any labor rates.
- Capability of extending the unit inventory balances of raw materials and purchased parts, intermediate storage, and finished goods by the appropriate standard cost to verify the dollar book inventory amounts of each.
- The necessary data, depending on method used, to convert the direct cost inventories of work in process, intermediate storage, and finished goods from a direct cost basis to an absorption cost basis for financial statements.

Preparation of Hard Data

After all the preliminary data have been gathered and the system has been designed, it is time to begin collecting the actual facts and figures that will be needed to start the system off.

At this point, it is advisable to review any data from the old system that will be used in the new system to make sure they are not inaccurate or out of date. Attention should be paid particularly to bills of material, operation (or route) sheets, account definitions, and material and labor standards. Obviously, it is inadvisable to start off a new system with data that are no longer up to date. This may have been tolerated under the old system, but it is sure to cause criticism if it is carried over to the new one.

The next step is to determine which manufacturing overhead accounts are to be considered variable and which fixed. This distinction may have already been made under the old system, but in view of its added importance under direct costing the work should be reviewed. In addition, it must be determined which semivariable manufacturing overhead accounts should be split into two accounts. When this is not practicable, the fixed element of each must be calculated by one of the methods detailed in Chapter 4. Budgets (standards) must be determined for all fixed accounts and fixed components of semivariable accounts.

A determination must also be made as to whether variable overhead is to be absorbed on direct labor dollars or direct labor hours and whether each department is to have an individual variable overhead rate or a plantwide average variable overhead rate is to be used. In either case, the relationship of each variable overhead account of the base must be established—that is, a determination must be made of how many cents per direct labor dollar or direct labor hour the standard variable overhead will be in each overhead account.

The same calculations are required for all S.G.& A. expense accounts. This is likely to be a new area to which very little thought has been given. Here the base is always the sales dollar. Once again, budgets must be set for fixed costs and a ratio of cents to sales dollars must be established for each variable S.G.& A. account.

In all likelihood, semivariable accounts will be split into two in both manufacturing overhead and S.G.&A. This means the chart of accounts will be somewhat expanded. If it is contemplated to pick up more variances than before (see Chapter 10) even more accounts will be added. Thus now is a good time to consider renumbering both manufacturing overhead accounts and S.G.& A. accounts so that the numbers signal by a selected digit whether they are being treated as variable, fixed, or semivariable. This type of coding not only serves as a reminder to those preparing input and those using the reports but also makes the computer programming for report printing somewhat easier.

Product standard cost sheets may now be developed for each product. Based on the bills of materials (as reviewed), the operation sheets (as reviewed), and the standard variable overhead rates on standard direct labor dollars or hours, the necessary calculations are made and checked. If Method 3 described in Chapter 6 is to be used for converting direct cost inventories to absorption costs, a second set of standard cost sheets is prepared for each product on an absorption cost basis.

If the conversion is to be to a direct *actual* cost system, there will be no standards to review and no standard product cost sheets to prepare. However, some provision must be made for charging all costs as they are incurred to specific product numbers and for accumulating these costs by products. This is not ordinarily true in a standard cost system.

Next, it is necessary to design all input forms and reporting forms, or to refine the forms laid out as part of the basic system design. Much clerical time can be saved if input forms are easy to read and easy to fill out and if the order of the information called for follows the source document from which the form is made up and/or the document (say, a keypunch card) to which the data will be transferred.

The design of reporting forms is very important if the full advantages of direct costing are to be obtained. Decisions must be made on whether various levels of executives are to receive the same data in different formats suited to the particular uses they will make of the report. This could merely mean a difference in the extent to which data are summarized. Or it could mean entirely different analyses. For example, the plant superintendent may want a report showing actual, standard, and variance of material usage by production department. The purchasing agent may want to see actual, standard, and variance of material usage by type of material. Certainly, in a computerized system, a determination must be made on whether any of the reports should be in "exception" form.

Because of the importance of forms design, the final draft of all forms should be submitted to the task force for suggestions, modifications, and eventual approval.

Computerization

Chapter 19 describes the conversion of a manual direct cost system to a computerized direct cost system and also covers the conversion of a computerized absorption cost system to a computerized direct cost system. Here it is necessary to say only that, in both cases, the EDP manager will be able to estimate the time required for programming once the systems design phase is completed.

This time will govern the remainder of the scheduling for implementation of the new system. The data for the construction of the various computer look-up files can be gathered and keypunched while the programming is going on.

Implementation

As mentioned before, a dry run is advisable with any complex system installation. Ideally, a parallel operation should be carried on until the results of the new system are shown to be valid by comparison with the old for a whole period. When an absorption cost system is converted to a direct cost system, this check will have meaning only to a limited extent, since the figures under the two systems are *supposed* to be different. However, the new system can be checked against itself by determining whether the standard costs credited against the various departments match the standard costs of the products produced, with only a reasonable difference arising from changes in the amount of work in process. Another check involves determining whether the amounts of the variances generated under the new system look reasonable compared with the variances reported under the old system. In this particular check, volume variances under the old system should be excluded. An even more conservative approach is to maintain a parallel operation until the next physical inventory, but the cost is usually so great that justification may be questionable.

A number of methods for validating interim dollar book inventories were discussed toward the end of the previous chapter. Even if the company does not wish to use all these methods on a permanent basis, every effort should be made to use them until the next physical inventory demonstrates that the new system is operating well enough to abandon some of them. This is true even if the methods have to be applied on a manual basis.

There are, of course, a number of advantages to starting any new cost system as of the date of the beginning of the company's fiscal year. Quantities on hand can be based on the year-end physical inventory; standards will presumably have just been updated; and cumulative figures through the year will all be on the same basis. Many conversion programs are scheduled with this in mind. The schedule should, of course, plan on a dry run before the conversion date.

Whatever date is selected for beginning the new system, some planning will be required to make sure everything is ready on time. A technique called Critical Path Scheduling (CPS) can be used effectively here. CPS consists of diagramming a network in which a point representing the beginning of each part of the project is connected by a line to points representing the beginning of each part of the project that must be completed before undertaking the part being considered. The estimated time for completion of the prior job is entered on the line connecting the points. Figure 17-1 shows a simple network. Line A-C-D-E-G-I-J is the critical path, since it will require 20 days, whereas any other line will require less. Therefore, although all parts of the project from A to J must be done, a one- or two-day delay in part B, F, or H will not delay final conversion. This means that parts A, C, D, E, G, I, and J must be monitored closely.

FIGURE 17-1. Critical path scheduling network.

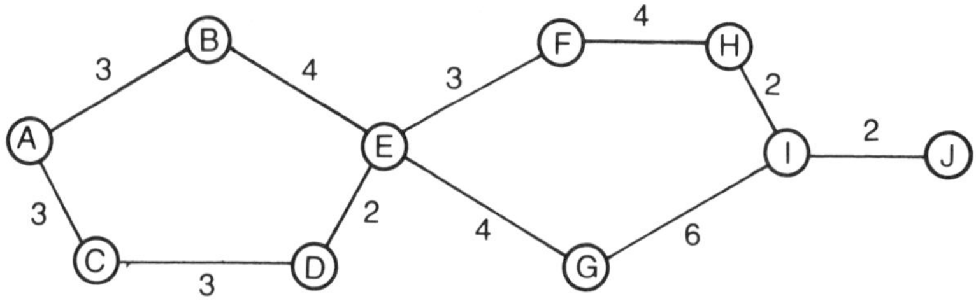

CPS is of considerable value not only in controlling time but also in determining at the outset whether the planned system installation date is realistic in light of all that has to be done and of the time sequence in which the parts must be done. CPS can also be useful in setting up closing schedules to ensure timely issuance of monthly reports. In this case, the times shown on the network lines are in hours rather than in days.

Computer programs are available to construct CPS networks, but these are generally used for complex construction or long-term manufacturing projects. For scheduling a cost system conversion, a manual approach is usually satisfactory. It should be noted that industries that use CPS in their operations frequently adopt a variation called the Program Evaluation and Review Technique (PERT) or (PERT-Cost), which combines scheduling with cost control. Since these industries do not generally use direct costing, the details of the technique will not be discussed here.

Although the beginning of the fiscal year is preferable for the conversion date, any other month end may be used, with certain disadvantages. Conversion in midmonth is not practicable. The extra work involved in conversion at an interim month end, depending on circumstances, may require a physical inventory. (One company that always had a midyear physical inventory converted at that time without problems.) If an interim month end is chosen and the absorption system is not continued to year end in parallel, the cumulative year-to-date figures on the monthly reports should show only the cumulative figures *since* the conversion date. Otherwise, apples and oranges will be added together.

During the dry run, personnel responsibilities for input should be closely supervised. The key people who will have to learn new procedures are those who code accounts payable invoices and those who analyze payroll into the various accounts. Obviously, it is helpful to prepare a procedures manual to guide the relevant clerks. It is also useful to design a "descriptive" chart of accounts—a book that lays out the content of each account in detail. Some highly successful systems people believe the procedures manual and the descriptive chart of accounts should be prepared only after the system has been in operation for a while and nearly all unusual transactions have come to light and their handling been determined.

A very important part of the implementation, and a step that is frequently overlooked, is the education of report recipients on how to interpret the new reports. A group meeting can be held to provide background information. Then the project leader should hand-deliver the first set of reports to each recipient, explaining the new formats and the differences in definition between the new cost figures and the old ones. Even more important, the project leader should explore how each recipient can use the new figures in the types of decisions that the executive is called upon to make. Thus marketing people should be given examples of the use of direct costs in pricing; advertising people can be told how direct costs relate to advertising appropriations; credit managers can be shown how direct costs can be used in credit-granting decisions; production people can be instructed in the real costs of breaking a production lot into two pieces, thus requiring duplicate setups; materials management people can be shown how direct costs revise EOQ formulas; and everyone can be shown the expense, on a direct cost basis, of incurring overtime. Since the major reason for converting to direct costs is to improve the profitability of management decisions, any effort devoted to this phase of the implementation is time well spent. If this step is skipped, the benefits of the new system will be realized *very* gradually.

The last step in the implementation process can be carried out over an extended period following the conversion. Basically, it consists of reinforcing the meaning of direct costing to report recipients. The project leader should visit with all recipients several weeks or months after the first reports are issued to determine if they have any questions about the new figures. The project leader should ask whether they find the reports useful, for what purposes the data are being used, and how they are being used. If a recipient does not mention a certain type of work he is involved in, the project leader should ask specifically about it. For some recipients a third or even a fourth visit, at perhaps longer intervals, may be needed.

Summary

Careful planning and scheduling are the key to successful conversion of any type of cost system, or no cost system at all, to a direct cost system. The conversion should involve in both an advisory capacity and a decision-making role at least one representative from each company function that supplies data to the cost system or makes use of its output. The conversion will take considerable time and will entail great effort on the part of people from several different departments. Since the project leader must coordinate the work, he will ordinarily have to be relieved of other duties.

The splitting of variable from fixed costs in both manufacturing overhead and S.G.& A. is likely to be the most time-consuming job, but it is not the most critical. The success of the system depends chiefly on the proper design of the reports produced by it. Similarly, although the training of clerks is time-consuming, it is not as important as providing report recipients with a full understanding of the reports and of how direct cost information can be used in their day-to-day operations.

18

Using Computers in Direct Cost Systems

Cost accounting was, of course, well established before computers were invented. So was standard costing. Direct costing was relatively new when computers first appeared, but there is no reason to believe its early growth was affected one way or the other by computers. Nonetheless, computers have added a whole new dimension to the way cost accounting data can be used.

Whenever companies replaced their manual systems by computerized ones, cost accounting was usually one of the last to be converted. Payroll, accounts receivable, general ledger, and unit inventory records seemed to be more logical candidates for conversion. These applications tended to be uniform from company to company, so programs were available from computer vendors and others for both large and small computers. Furthermore, in the early days of computers only the very large and costly machines had the storage capacity and the processing speed to handle a complex cost accounting system. Technological progress in computer hardware has changed all that.

The clerical savings produced by computerizing a cost system are hard to identify and are likely to be small. Indeed, until a number of companies had converted, the advantages of computerizing cost accounting were not obvious. Today, however, it is recognized that computerized cost accounting is a far better management tool than manual systems ever could be. This leads to two observations: (1) a company with or without a computer that now has a manual cost system should consider computerizing it; and (2) a company that is getting no more out of its computerized cost system than it could on a manual system is missing the boat.

Specific computer applications have been mentioned in other chapters but these and some other applications will be mentioned in this chapter in order to provide an overview of the place of computers in expanding the use of cost data in the management of manufacturing today.

This chapter will describe only those cost accounting applications which are so burdensome to perform manually that they are difficult or impossible to cost-justify in manual systems. Throughout the chapter, reference will be made to the low cost of accumulating certain types of information by a computerized system, as opposed to the unacceptable costs of accumulating the same information manually. However, it must be recognized that the systems analysis and the programming effort that precede each application are both time-consuming and costly. Nevertheless, the many companies that are today performing these functions have found the costs worthwhile.

The applications described will be grouped, not in accordance with how computer programs relate to one another but rather in accordance with how cost accounting objectives are logically related. Each section will refer to a previous chapter.

Actual and Standard Costs—Job and Process Costs

As noted in Chapter 3, only a few companies operate an actual cost system in parallel with a standard cost system. Most companies find it difficult to justify the added cost by the usefulness of the added information. In a computerized cost system the extra cost in the general accounting, cost accounting, and EDP departments is relatively small. Under a manual system, in marked contrast, these extra costs are relatively large. However, in either case, significantly greater paperwork is required on the shop floor. In order to accumulate actual costs, either timekeepers or the workers themselves must keep a record of how long each employee spends on each type of product.

Despite the extra costs on the shop floor, the small amount of other extra costs in a computerized cost system might persuade some companies to choose both actual and standard costs. As mentioned earlier, any company working on government contracts that bring it under CASB rules is permitted to use standard costs, but only with restrictions that are difficult to meet. Such a company might use actual costing for contract accounting but retain the cost control and management decision advantages of standard costing. Another type of company that might choose to operate a dual cost system is one that saw a real advantage to assigning variances to products or product groups. However, this type of information can be accumulated informally with sufficient accuracy to meet the needs of most companies.

In most of the discussions throughout this book it has been assumed that a process or operations cost system was in use. Under a standard cost process system in a company producing a group of products for the shelf, the standard product cost per the product cost sheet for the particular product times the number of pieces in the lot gives the standard cost of the production order. Thus, for companies producing standardized products, the data ordinarily obtained from a job cost system are available automatically. Even products made to varying customer specifications can be costed under a standard process cost system by accumulating the standards for the various parts and operations and then determining the standard cost of the job lot. However, under an actual cost system, job lot costing requires the identification of all cost input for both materials and labor and variable overhead by job number. If the cost control advantages of process costing are to be retained, a dual system is again required. The paperwork for a dual system is substantially reduced when a computer is used.

Separating Variable from Fixed Costs

The splitting of semivariable manufacturing overhead and semivariable S.G.& A. accounts into their variable and fixed components by the least-squares formula was described in Chapter 4. As illustrated in Figure 4-2, the calculation can be performed manually or with a calculator; indeed, a few companies were doing so before the advent of computers. Now, with the ease of computerized calculations, many more companies are using the least-squares approach, either as the basic tool for splitting semivariable accounts or as a check on the results of some other approach. It should be noted that most cost accounting computer applications virtually require an in-house computer because of the amount of data that must be stored and the timing requirements of reports. By contrast, least-squares calculations can be done on any computer, even if the company's cost accounting system is not computerized. If the least-squares calculations are few and far between, as they are likely to be, it may pay to use the services of a time-sharing computer company rather than to buy or develop a special program for company use in house.

In the least-squares calculation it is a good idea to prepare scatter charts to reveal aberrations and to eliminate them before feeding the data into a computer. Some computers can prepare the scatter chart as well as perform the calculation. This can save considerable time and will eliminate the plotting errors that commonly arise in hand charting.

Pricing

The problem of keeping pricing up to date when material costs fluctuate was discussed in Chapter 5. To reduce this problem, some companies revise standard product costs frequently—quarterly, for example (as discussed in Chapter 9). A preferable approach, used by most companies, is to supply marketing management with memos on updated product costs as often as necessary. This may be monthly, weekly, or even daily in the case of certain industries (such as cotton converters). The most meaningful product costs for this purpose are NIFO costs.

A computer can supply this information at little cost as often as needed. Since only the total product cost needs to be printed out for each product, the process is much faster than revising the entire standard product cost sheets for all products. It should not be overlooked that a change in some or all of the labor rates should also trigger a recalculation of standard product costs for the guidance of marketing.

Financial Statements on Absorption Costing Under a Direct Cost System

When the direct cost values of finished-goods and work-in-process inventories are converted to an absorption basis for financial statements, a computer can make all the difference in the accuracy of the figures obtained (that is, their nearness to the values that would have come out of an absorption system). In fact, companies that were initially reluctant to convert to direct costing because of this problem but that now have computerized their cost accounting need no longer fear the problem. In the early days of direct costing there was no SEC or AICPA requirement that financial statements be prepared on an absorption basis, so the problem did not arise. The computer's ability to aid the conversion has accelerated both the trend toward direct costing and the trend toward computerized cost accounting.

Under a manual system, a company that needs to convert its finished-goods and work-in-process inventories from a direct cost basis to an absorption cost basis is practically forced to select either Method 1 or Method 2 described in Chapter 6. In addition, it is virtually impossible to departmentalize either of these methods, and a certain amount of extra paperwork is required even to separate out the direct labor component of the product costs. Method 1 allocates total annual fixed manufacturing costs between cost of sales for the year and finished goods (and work in process) on the basis of the ratio of either the total direct costs of the two figures or the direct labor component of the costs of the two figures. A variation of Method 1 does the same thing on a departmental basis.

If the ratio of total direct costs is used in the calculation, the result is likely to be substantially different from the one that would have been obtained under a full-fledged absorption cost system. There is no way of telling whether the difference is greater or less, or how large it is. Many people believe that the allocation of fixed costs to products is meaningless and that some inaccuracy is therefore acceptable; however, it is far better to use a more complex and much more accurate method when it can be done so easily on a computer.

Much the same can be said for Method 2, in which fixed manufacturing overhead for that part of the year represented by direct costs still in inventory is allocated to the direct costs still in inventory. Here again, the total direct cost ratio may well be quite inaccurate, the direct labor ratio is hard to accumulate on a manual system, and the departmental direct labor approach involves mountains of paperwork.

Method 3, which involves preparing product standard cost sheets on both a direct cost basis and an absorption cost basis, is used by most computerized companies. Since the total cost of each product on both bases is stored in the computer memory (core, disk, or tape), the company need only feed in the unit inventory balances at the time of the physical inventory to obtain a dollar value under each of the two costing principles. The same calculation can be made at year end under a manual system with some additional work. However, when a company wishes to make the double calculation at every month end from the unit perpetual inventory balances, the advantages of computerization become quite marked.

A general ledger computer system can also be used to prepare monthly income statements on both cost bases. Some companies prefer to prepare an absorption cost statement in the format that will be used for reporting to the public rather than just adjusting the direct cost operating profit shown at the bottom of the direct cost income statement by "change in fixed manufacturing costs in inventory" to arrive at the absorption cost operating profit.

Profit Planning and Business Modeling

The computer is practically a must for the type of profit planning (business modeling or simulation) described in Chapter 7. Only companies with very short product lines and relatively few operations—for example, companies whose sole manufacturing function is the assembly of a few models of a product from parts fabricated by others—can hope to perform profit planning manually.

Computers are a necessity if a company wishes to use sensitivity analysis, which shows the effect on profits of possible variations of actual from several of the assumptions, or probability theory, which arrives at a most likely result through assigning probabilities to the major assumption. Some companies perform both sensitivity analysis and probability calculations manually in capital project evaluations. In these cases, however, a single project or at most three or four projects are being subjected to the techniques. In profit planning, dozens of possible policy changes are usually being considered at one time. Computers can also simplify the conversion of one or more operating profit plans into forecast balance sheets at several future dates, into source and application of funds statements, and into cash forecasts.

The relative ease and low cost of preparing interim comparisons of actual monthly and year-to-date costs to standards and to prior-year figures has encouraged many companies to expand the scope and frequency of such reports. Some companies have added balance sheet data by profit centers. Other companies have provided more detail on an account-by-account basis.

Management Decisions

As noted in Chapter 8, direct costing modifies the figures that should be applied in the Economic Order Quantity (EOQ) and Economic Lot Size (ELS) formulas used in inventory management. These formulas not only require square-root calculations (which are available today even on pocket calculators) but often involve so many digits that they exceed the capacity of most calculators. Since hundreds of EOQs and ELSs may be required each day, the computer can be of considerable help. Again, this is a special-purpose computer application that can be performed whether or not a company's entire cost accounting system is computerized.

The replacement of worn-out machines is another example of a management decision that can be aided by a computer. Frequently, in noncomputerized companies, a machine is replaced because a foreman *believes* the recent repair history indicates that a new machine will be less costly than continuing to maintain the old one. Under computerized cost accounting, it is possible to accumulate material, labor, and variable overhead repair costs by machine number. Thus the replacement decision need no longer be based on a "belief." This type of cost accumulation is a way of life for many auto and truck fleet operators—whether the fleets are owned by a manufacturing company, a common carrier, or a truck leasing company. These fleet operators keep separate statistics on chassis, tires, motors, and even individual components of motors such as batteries, generators, and water pumps. The results help not only in replacement timing but in vendor selection.

Setting Standards

As mentioned earlier, standards for the variable component of a semivariable account can be determined by the least-squares formula, aided by scatter charts. Both of these techniques can be performed most easily on a computer. Obviously, the fixed component of the account as determined in the calculation becomes the standard for the fixed cost under the same account name.

This is not the only assistance the computer can provide in setting standards. As indicated in Chapter 9, both manufacturing overhead standards (variable and fixed) and S.G.& A. standards (variable and fixed) are based primarily on historical costs. These standards must be set initially and then revised at least once each year. In both cases, the computer can supply the historical cost data faster and more accurately than a manual system. It can also rank the weekly payroll costs in each overhead and S.G.& A. labor account so that eye checks can be made for aberrations that should be omitted from the average. This can be done simply by inspection; or the decision can be made after the reason for the aberration has been investigated. Variable costs are ranked in terms of cents per direct labor dollar or cents per direct labor hour in the case of variable overhead costs and cents per sales dollar in the case of S.G.& A. variable costs.

The same computer capabilities through the "where used" program that makes it easier to supply updated costs on a memo basis to the marketing department as material unit costs and labor rates fluctuate, also permits the year-end or interim revision of standards for use in the cost accounting system to be performed faster and more accurately. Decisions on which material unit cost and which labor rate to incorporate in the standard will take as much time under a computerized system as under a manual one. However, once these decisions are made, the computer can update the standard product costs as fast as it can print. Under a manual system, the same job is very time-consuming and can result in many errors. This may influence the decision on how often standards should be revised.

Variance Analysis

Chapter 10 described an approach to reporting in which every change in method or product design is immediately incorporated into the standards being used for performance reports. These changes in standard are omitted from the accounting records used to prepare the income statement pending the next regularly scheduled standards revision date. This is done through the creation of a change-in-standards variance account.

It is virtually impossible to carry out this improvement in performance reporting for cost control purposes under a manual system. There are too many changes to keep track of, involving too many operations that affect too many products. The difficulty is compounded when changes are made to earlier changes. However, a computer, again through a "where used" program, can update the standards quite easily and can also accumulate all the differences so that the transfer of production to finished goods can credit work in process at the new standard, debit finished goods at the old standard, and debit or credit the difference to the change-in-standards variance account. With the look-up tables in computer storage (core, disk, or tape), all this can be done automatically by merely keying in the nature of the transaction, the product code number, and the number of pieces transferred.

The computer's greatest contribution to variance analysis is the fact that it enables a company to expand the number of variance accounts without unduly increasing paperwork costs in either data accumulation or report preparation. Purchase price variances are a good example. An accounts payable invoice may include several items that are sufficiently different in type to warrant separate control of the purchase price variances. Under manual systems including those using bookkeeping machines, each item has to be posted separately. Under a computerized system, a code number on the item will identify the proper grouping, and the computer can do the rest. Actually, the computer is posting the invoice to several accounts, just as in a manual system, but the time-consuming part of the manual work is performed at computer speeds.

Companies with computerized cost accounting usually break down their variances into much more detail than noncomputerized companies. In such a case, tracing the reasons for the variances and correcting the causes of unfavorable ones are substantially easier and therefore much more likely to be done.

Cost Control

Good reporting is the key to good cost control. As mentioned in Chapter 11, good reporting involves tailoring each report to the needs of the recipient, reporting on a responsibility basis (at least in part), and using exception reports. Under a computerized system, every account—including the actual amount, the standard amount, and the variance—can be coded for inclusion in certain reports but not in others. An account can also be coded to appear as a detailed analysis in some reports and as one unidentified component of a larger analysis identified by a group label in other reports. A similar approach under a manual system is generally too costly but the marked improvement that it provides has relatively little cost in a computerized system.

The same may be said of responsibility accounting. Typically, under a manual system, all costs of manufacturing are spread to the production departments, so that a totaling of the costs of the individual production departments will give the plant costs. Little attention is paid to whether the foremen in the various departments have control over any of these costs and therefore whether they should have any interest in them. Under a computerized system, it is relatively easy to maintain the distinction between costs that are controllable at the foreman's level and costs that are not by omitting the noncontrollable costs from the departmental foreman's report. Those costs omitted in the foreman's report are then picked up in a separate column in the plantwide report.

As noted in Chapter 11, the computer can print exception reports on the basis of predetermined dollar and predetermined percentage criteria. The standard deviation of the particular cost can also be used for exception reporting. The normal range of the cost, both above and below the average, can be determined from past history. The standard deviation can then be calculated easily on a computer from historical data on disks or tape files. Only those costs found to be outside the normal range for the period are printed as exceptions. This approach gives a different dollar or percentage definition of an exception in each account. The definition depends on the range of past fluctuations in the account.

Charting is of course one way to dramatize the changes in performance that are occurring for a whole department, for a specific account within a department, or for any other area where cost control can be applied. Some computers can prepare charts directly. In most cases, the basic data to be charted are already in computer-readable form; thus charting involves relatively little cost and can have a much more significant impact than the mere tabulation of figures. Many engineering (analog) computers can draw lines, but even business (digital) computers can prepare fairly clear charts by printing *x*'s and *o*'s at the appropriate heights and distances. Some computers can even perform these operations in several colors on CRT terminals to highlight the various trends being shown.

Analysis of Marginal Contribution

The great value to management, particularly marketing and sales management, of knowing the marginal contribution by customer group was fully explored in Chapter 12. There is no great difficulty in determining the marginal contribution by product or product group under a manual system if unit sales are known by product, as they almost always are. However, to obtain these data by customer groupings virtually requires a computerized system, since every line item on sales invoices must be costed out. The computer's look-up table in core or disk storage provides the unit standard cost applicable to the product as identified by the product code which ordinarily shows on the sales invoice anyway. The computer then makes the extensions by the number of units shipped.

As the computer totals the sales value of the invoice, it also totals the standard cost. Both amounts are then entered in the records of the several customer categories to which the particular customer belongs—state, sales region, salesman, type of industry, type of customer (for example, discount entitlement), size of city, and size of customer based on the business done with the customer last year. When these figures are totaled for a quarter or a year, much valuable information is provided for the guidance of future sales effort, future industrial magazine advertising, future local advertising, and the assignment of research time to products of interest to certain industries or certain sections of the country. An enormous clerical effort would be required to obtain the same data on a manual basis. The costing-out of the invoices alone would be very time-consuming, and the posting of both the sales value and the cost value to half a dozen customer categories would be extremely expensive. Of course, some companies do a similar job on sales through tabulating equipment or the McBee Keysort. But the analysis is usually limited in scope and, of course, entails less than half the work required by an analysis of both sales and costs. In the latter case, each invoice must be totaled in a way required for no other purpose.

If the analysis is carried to the point of determining the variance of the marginal contribution from the forecast, with a further breakdown of this variance into its selling price, volume, and product mix components, the work on a manual system becomes astronomical for any sizable company. To begin with, a standard selling price must be added to each line on the invoice and must be extended by the number of units sold and then totaled to arrive at the standard or forecast sales value. This figure is then compared with the actual selling price to arrive at the selling price variance. Next, the standard cost of the actual units shipped to the customer or the customer category must be accumulated and compared with the forecast shipments at standard cost. The difference is then multiplied by the average forecast marginal contribution per standard cost dollar to obtain the volume variance. (This is done by individual customer under a data base approach and by customer category under any other approach.) Finally, the difference between the total marginal contribution and the two variances already calculated is figured and is designated as the product mix variance. The analysis involves far too many calculations and postings for a manual system or even a tabulating system. Even on a computer, considerable time and storage capacity (though not necessarily core storage) are required. However, the value of the information for spotting sales trends and guiding marketing management on their probable causes makes it all worthwhile.

Special Problems

Chapter 15 examined a number of problems for which computers are either essential or useful. In joint product costing, computers can be useful in accumulating the joint costs before separation for all products and the subsequent costs for each product after separation.

Computerization is particularly valuable when the products derived from the basic material input are not all separated at the same point in the process. Since selling prices of the various products fluctuate, the calculation may have to be made several times a year. This is quite burdensome under a manual system.

Linear programming is useful for product mix decisions in production when several potential bottleneck operations or processes make it impossible to accept all available orders. Linear programming can also be of value in the selection of materials to use to produce certain end-product specifications when the choice depends on the relation of the current costs of the various materials. Linear programming is almost wholly confined to computers. It can, in theory, be done manually, but the procedure is just too time-consuming. To solve either of the above problems by linear programming does not require that the company's cost accounting system be computerized.

Companies subject to the special rules and regulations of the Cost Accounting Standards Board may have to do their cost accounting in two ways in order to conform to these rules and at the same time stay within GAAP. Even though the differences are minor, they may affect the cost of every product, every department, and every contract. Some companies may find it practical to keep the records one way and then adjust them at year end. Obviously, keeping two entire sets of cost records is a considerable burden no matter how it is done, but it is less of a burden if the system is computerized and if the transactions which must be treated differently are appropriately coded. Similarly, in segment accounting the computer can save much manual analysis time if all costs are coded by segment in the original input to the computer.

Finally, probability theory can be useful in pricing bids and in quoting prices. If several dozen bids or other quotes must be made each week, the computer is a real time-saver and also reduces arithmetic errors. This application can be performed on any computer, whether or not the cost accounting system is computerized.

Inventory Control

Computers have taken over the maintenance of perpetual unit inventory records in most computerized companies. In addition, they are used extensively for material requirements planning and production scheduling, two functions whose input is often used for cost accounting. However their unique feature for inventory control lies in two main areas: (1) providing certain checks not otherwise available on the accuracy of input to the cost system; and (2) making it easier to divide dollar inventory totals into subaccounts so their reasonableness can be verified.

Chapter 16 examined some of the input checks, including the use of check digits for verifying material codes, part codes, operation codes, and product codes. Check digits originated with some of the later models of keypunches in the days of tabulating (sometimes referred to as Electric Accounting Machines, or EAM, to distinguish them from EDP, which stands for Electronic Data Processing), but they have no counterpart under manual systems or in bookkeeping machines. Checks on valid code number, valid code number as related to a particular product, and valid dollar range are available only on a computer, although some errors in these items would be caught under a manual system by alert and knowledgeable clerks who process the documents at some later stage.

As to the accuracy of piece counts, the computer can tie in the cost accounting input with production scheduling input, using the same document to update both reports. Thus, if any error is found in the course of using either report, both reports can be corrected. Some systems can be set up to track production order quantities through the sequence of operations and reject any input that calls for more pieces to be processed on an operation than were processed on the preceding operation.

Another computer function in the inventory control area—a function related to both input correction and the verification of dollar book inventories—is the explosion of unit perpetual inventory records of raw materials, parts, intermediate storage, and finished goods by the standard cost of each item. This is a long and tedious job on a manual system. It can be done quite easily on a computer, particularly if only the grand total of the category is required rather than a printout of the quantity and cost of each item. Assigning lot numbers to bulk raw materials in a lot clearance system and tracking the use of each lot separately are also much easier on a computer.

The computer's usefulness in establishing the validity of dollar inventory totals by category lies in its ability to handle a number of subaccounts at negligible extra cost compared with handling only the one account total. Thus it can subdivide the total dollar book inventory into raw materials, purchased parts, work in process, intermediate storage, and finished goods. It can also subdivide some of these categories—for example, materials by type, work in process by department, and finished goods by location. The results make it possible for knowledgeable people to determine the reasonableness of the figures. All these subdivisions are occasionally found in manual systems, but the added cost is quite high.

It is rare to find a further subdivision of work in process or finished goods into the material component, direct labor component, and variable overhead component in manual systems. However, the ease of obtaining these figures in a computerized unit perpetual inventory system, particularly under a standard cost system, makes the subdivision worthwhile in view of its usefulness in checking reasonableness through a ratio calculation.

Finally, the computer can retrieve from its memory storage (core, disk, or tape) all the production orders on which materials have been issued but which have not yet been completed. These can be extended at their value "as if completed" to see if the work-in-process cost value bears the same relation to the as-if-completed cost value of in-process production orders that it did in past periods.

Summary

Computers can be applied to almost every aspect of cost accounting. In a few cases, a computerized system reduces the cost of operations that would otherwise be done manually, but this is a relatively minor advantage. The real impact of computerization is the extent to which it makes possible reports and other data which would be so costly to prepare under a manual system that they are just not done.

The vast majority of the applications reviewed in this chapter depend on the cost system being run on the computer. With a few applications any computer can be used because they are unrelated to the cost data being run through the computer or in its storage.

Accuracy of input is always basically the problem of supervision at the source. A flood of grossly inaccurate source documents will cause any system, manual or computerized, to break down. However, a computer can detect certain types of input errors. This can be very helpful if the source documents are reasonably error-free.

A computer can be just as helpful in improving reporting under a direct cost system as under an absorption cost system. It has two additional advantages if used in a direct cost system: (1) the computer makes the conversion of ending inventories to an absorption basis easier and more accurate; and (2) the combination of direct costing and the computer makes possible an extremely valuable analysis of marginal contribution and marginal contribution variances. This management tool, whose full value depends on computerization, has no exact counterpart in an absorption cost system.

19

Computerizing a Direct Cost System

DESPITE all the advantages of a computerized cost system, there are times when a company would be well advised not to put its cost system on a computer. Because of the rigidity of computerized systems, it is best to defer computerization if the cost system will undergo considerable changes in the fiture. Conversion should not take place until management is satisfied, under the manual system, that it has what it wants.

For this reason, it is inadvisable to put a company's first cost system on a computer at the outset; the system can be converted after a year or two of satisfactory experience on a manual basis. Similarly, if a company is moving from a manual absorption cost system to a direct cost system, computerization should be deferred until experience on the manual direct cost system has accumulated. Very small companies may find it impossible to cost-justify a computerized cost accounting system, primarily because some of the advantages a computerized cost system has over a manual one require a relatively large computer.

Even so, a company with a computerized absorption cost system that wishes to convert to direct costing is virtually forced to go directly to a computer. This has been done many times with no more headaches than can be expected in any major system change.

Why Companies Computerize

Companies often decide to computerize their cost accounting system for the wrong reason. In such a case, the system is apt to be designed without incorporating the features that make computerization worthwhile. The poor reasons include:

To reduce clerical costs. A clerical cost saving may or may not occur. In any case, it is doubtful that the saving will pay for the tangible and intangible cost of converting the system. The cost saving, if any, is likely to be greater in converting an absorption system to a computer than in converting a direct cost system to one. This is because of the computer's ability to perform the allocation of fixed costs to departments and cost centers—a burdensome task on a manual basis.

To reduce errors. A properly programmed computer can catch certain types of errors (see Chapter 16). However, if a company has a large number of errors in its cost system to begin with, so many errors will be fed into the computer that the system won't operate at all or will get out reports too late to be useful. When this problem is prevalent, errors must be attacked at their source.

To take advantage of unused computer capacity. This is the worst reason of all to computerize. The odds are that the existing system will be computerized by EDP people without any real involvement of the report users. A small clerical cost saving may result, but the design and programming costs will be almost as great as those involved in installing a better system.

There is one and only one good reason to computerize a cost system: to obtain better cost control and greater information for management decisions. Most of the improvements in these areas could not be implemented at acceptable costs in a manual system. As noted earlier, many of the added reports are more useful on a direct cost basis than on an absorption one. Product cost revisions for pricing purposes and marginal contribution variances for purposes of revising pricing policies are examples. Thus it may be said that the gains from computerizing a direct cost system are generally greater than those from converting a manual absorption cost system to a computer.

Basics of Computerizing a System

A general discussion of computerization is beyond the scope of this book. Detailed descriptions of how to computerize any system—be it payroll, general ledger, invoicing, or cost accounting—can be found in many books and articles. (See the bibliography at the end of this book.) However, certain points in the system design and implementation are particularly important in computerizing a cost accounting system. A number of these points apply specifically to direct cost systems and are described below.

Putting such systems as payroll and accounts receivable on a computer requires very little involvement of executives outside the financial area. The reverse is true of cost accounting. Since the purpose of computerizing the cost accounting system is to provide management with more and better information, executives in production and marketing must be heavily involved from the beginning. The task force approach suggested in Chapter 17 is excellent. It is usually not practical to put all the applications described in this book into the system when it is first computerized. However, the data input forms, coding structures, record lengths, and the programs themselves should be designed to permit later expansion along these lines.

Initial Steps in the System Design

As in any system design, the first step is to define the problem and the restrictions, possibly unvoiced, of management. This can be done by obtaining the answers to three questions:

1. What does management want?
2. What expense is management willing to incur to get it?
3. When must the system be operational?

The first two of these questions should be broken down into "now" and "later."

The next step is to make sure that the design is not so future oriented that the system when first operational lacks some of the features of the present manual system. This is not to say that a report which is found to be useless must be continued. Still, great care must be taken to make sure that no report is abandoned through carelessness or through an incomplete analysis of its worth.

It is almost certain that the manual cost system being replaced produces reasonably accurate product costs and reasonably accurate and timely departmental performance reports, that it helps to ensure the accuracy of interim dollar book inventories, and that it is useful in preparing budgets. The manual system may also be generating variances for investigation and follow-up and be providing data for certain types of management decisions. The proposed system should be able to do at least as well at its inception as the system being replaced.

Since this is a direct cost system, the direct cost value of finished-goods and work-in-process inventories will have to be converted to an absorption cost value for external reporting; the system must also provide the data (see Chapter 6) for making this conversion. The company's independent auditor should approve the method to be used for conversion early in the system design.

One feature of a computerized cost system not available on manual systems is sufficiently valuable to justify its inclusion at the system's inception. This feature is the ability of the computer to update all standard product costs for a change in the price of any material or a change in the pay rate of any labor category. This is done through a "where used" computer program. The program can be used for the annual or quarterly revision of standards but is even more useful for providing marketing with memos on current product costs at frequent intervals. For this purpose, NIFO is often used.

It should be noted that certain types of errors in a manual system are frequently caught by the individuals processing transactions at various steps. In a computerized system, fewer people process the transactions and they are often lower-level employees. The computerized system should be designed with computer checks to make up for the potential for error detection by eye check that has been lost. One further warning: The speed of the computer may cause management to believe that computer-generated reports will be at least as timely as manually prepared ones. Experience has shown that this will not occur automatically. The timing of reports must be carefully planned, possibly through the CPS approach discussed in Chapter 16, not only to leave room for edit runs and proofing of totals but also to make allowances for other systems (such as payroll) that require the use of the computer at critical times.

Additional Steps in the System Design

As already stated, the conversion date is usually a poor time to expand the system. However, the design must leave room for the improvements that will make the computerized cost accounting function of much greater value to the company than a manual system could ever be. After all, that is the reason companies computerize their cost accounting.

Each company will have its own ideas of what new capabilities it is seeking; a review of the material in Chapter 18 may provide some further suggestions. However, each company has certain data that are critical to its management, and providing these data should have first consideration. Possibilities for general consideration include:

- Expanding the different types of variance accounts, with a further breakdown by subdepartments.
- Moving toward responsibility accounting by identifying the level at which costs are considered to be controllable.
- Preparing reports with the same data summarized to an increasingly greater degree for higher levels of management.
- Exception reporting.
- Costing line items on invoices, possibly including forecast selling prices.
- Coding customers to make accumulation of marginal contribution data by customer classes easier. For this purpose, customers are classified in several different ways.

Final Steps in the System Design

It should be recognized that cost accounting interfaces with many other systems in the company. It obtains data from the payroll system, the accounts payable system, the accounts receivable system, the unit perpetual inventory system, the plant ledger system, and the general ledger system. Cost accounting may also be related to the production scheduling system and the material requirements system and the budget system. Since it is likely that some or all of these systems are already computerized, the new system design should plan on making use of any input to these systems which can also be useful to the cost system.

All other computerized systems in the company should be studied to take full advantage of input that can serve a dual or triple purpose. Nothing makes a system designer look more foolish than collecting on a new form data that are already being collected on some other form for another system. It is generally recognized that much of the cost of any system is the collection of data for input. To the extent that this cost can be spread over multiple uses, it is much more efficient and may even make the difference between a system that is cost-justified and one that is not. Because the cost system has so many interfaces, this aspect of system design is particularly important.

Full advantage should also be taken of the possibility of computerized direct transfer of the output of other systems into the cost system. For example, the purchase price variances developed and summarized by the accounts payable system could be listed on the monthly income statement without having to be printed on a report and then reentered into the computer for income statement purposes.

Mechanics of the System Design

The system design begins with a survey to ascertain, in considerable detail, the needs of management. The makeup of the survey team will vary from company to company, but a formula found to be successful is a senior-level cost accountant accompanied by an EDP systems analyst. Generally, the cost accountant is the team leader. The team will interview present recipients of cost reports, potential recipients of cost reports (particularly in the marketing area), and employees at all levels who are responsible for preparing input to the system.

As indicated in Chapter 17, care must be taken to determine the real needs of those being interviewed. Some people may initially ask for too much or too little. The cost accountant and the systems analyst can discuss the requests with each interviewee to determine what real needs exist and which ones can be met within acceptable cost limits. Often a second interview will be required after a study has been made of the expense of programming and computer time involved in meeting a request.

This is also a good time to prevent new "defensive" reports from being introduced and to eliminate existing "defensive" reports. A defensive report is one whose sole purpose is to demonstrate that some individual is not responsible for a foul-up. The nature of defensive reports can be illustrated by the following story. One day five years ago a shipping room foreman was severely criticized for failing to get a shipment out on the previous afternoon. He believed that he had not received the goods from production before the actual (and scheduled) departure of the truck, but he couldn't prove it. Ever since that time, the foreman has kept a meticulous record of the time of day each shipment is received from production. The record has never been used to expedite the receipt of goods, but *if ever* the shipping foreman is again blamed for a late shipment he will have a good defense. Happily, the record requires only a couple of man-hours per day and two file drawers.

The results of the interviews should be summarized in a "Detailed Function Statement," similar to Figure 19-1. The statement is self-explanatory except for the lines "Trigger" and "Restrictions." A trig-

FIGURE 19-1. Computer systems analysis and design: Detailed function statement.

FUNCTION ______

TRIGGER ______

RESTRICTIONS ______

OUTPUTS ______

INPUTS ______

PROCESSING STEPS ______

VOLUMES ______

FREQUENCY ______

ger is an event that sets in motion the preparation of a report or the entry of data into the computer. Examples of triggers include "end of the month," "completion of payroll analysis," "notification of change in price of a major material," and "request from plant superintendent."

A restriction is some requirement that must be met. Examples include "cannot be prepared until payroll analysis has been reconciled," "must be available by the fifth working day of the month," and "must be approved by the controller prior to distribution." Limitations on the project should also be stated—such as "no change in the Chart of Accounts is to be made" or "no additional hardware is to be allowed."

Of course, at some time a schedule must be prepared leading to a conversion date. This problem is fully discussed in Chapter 17.

Additional Decisions to Be Made

In any computerized system there is a real advantage to entering data where they originate through some type of terminal. This improves accuracy, reduces the time lag of reports, and eliminates various processing steps. The terminals may be in the accounting department, in which case CRT (cathode ray tube) terminals are preferable. Or the terminals may be out on the shop floor; here plastic personnel cards and prepunched tabulating cards for each production order can reduce the operator's keyed-type input to a simple record of the operation number and the quantity. Remote entry is particularly advantageous in a cost system, because so much of the detail originates on the shop floor. Although terminals add to the cost of the hardware needed in the system including the cost of the central computer and telecommunications equipment required to accept terminal input, current hardware prices make the use of terminals much more attractive.

Storage requirements should also be reviewed. Most cost systems require a good deal of core storage and a surprising amount of online disk storage. If either core or disk storage must be added to the existing computer, the additional costs must be justified as part of the system study. If they cannot be cost-justified, some other approach must be used. This problem is a difficult one because, in a cost system, the justification for an expense lies not in its potential for reducing clerical costs but rather in its potential for reducing production costs and marketing costs and for helping management make profit-oriented decisions in virtually every facet of the operation. This benefit is very difficult to quantify in dollars.

At some point, a decision must be made on whether the company will purchase one of the many available packaged programs or whether it will design and program the system completely in house. The two major advantages of purchasing packaged software are that it shortens, sometimes substantially, the time required to develop and implement the system and that it invariably costs less than in-house programming. However, these advantages must be considered in the light of certain problems with packaged programs. In fact, in some cases, it may prove to be impossible for the company to go the packaged program route, because of the many other systems with which the cost system must interface. If these systems are already operating on software developed within the company or by some other software vendor, the difficulty of making the package compatible with other systems or vice versa may be insuperable.

This same problem may bind the company to the software vendor that supplies the cost system package for future systems development outside the cost area. Some companies may not find this restriction acceptable. Certainly, the company should make sure that the software vendor will provide it with the source program as well as the object program so that potential program revisions and enhancements can be made in house.

Of course, no package will meet all a company's needs without modification. This means that the time required to install the packaged system is by no means negligible, though it is much less than that required to design and program a system completely in house. The same applies to the in-house programming costs for the necessary modifications.

The next decision to be made, and it is an important one, is whether the system is to be on-line or batch process. Although most systems using remote entry terminals are on-line, terminals used exclusively for cost input generally do not need to be on-line with the computer. Since cost data are rarely needed on a minute-to-minute basis, the allocation of computer time for massive on-line data entry, given the slow speed of the terminal input, is inefficient and rarely useful. A terminal can feed a tape or disk within the terminal or at a remote location, and the stored data can later be fed to the computer at magnetic tape or magnetic disk data transfer speeds. There may, however, be reasons why terminals should be on-line—for example, if the cost data are also being used for other systems such as production scheduling. The next decision relates to whether data are to be accumulated in individual disk or tape files or through a data base management system. Because of the many systems with which the cost system interfaces, the data base concept has certain advantages, and the trend is toward data base management in larger companies. However, the storage required is greater, as is the technical complexity, so that many companies have decided in favor of individual data files for the cost accounting system.

Any system that affects the company's financial statements, as the cost system definitely does, must be auditable. Computerized systems, particularly on-line ones, inevitably present certain auditing problems. Accordingly, it is advisable to submit the system design to the company's auditors so they can determine whether the audit trails designed into the system are satisfactory or whether the design must be modified to provide further audit trails.

Because of the number of departments and number of accounts required in performance reporting of production departments in a cost system, it may well develop that certain reports being prepared manually on columnar paper will have a horizontal spread beyond the widths permitted by computer printers. A decision must be made on whether the manually typed report is to be continued in its present format, using data generated by the computer, or whether a computer report is to be designed in a different format. The latter is ordinarily preferable and can be done through a summary report with the detail contained in several attached subsidiary reports.

Another matter to be considered is how often transactions occur that do not fit exactly within the system. Examples include the substitution of materials or operations, the use of a special learner's direct labor standard, and the tracking of the direct material and direct labor related to a specific purchase of materials. If these transactions are sufficiently infrequent, they can be handled best through adjusting entries to the computer data manually. However, if transactions of this type are quite frequent, the system should be designed to allow for their routine entry.

Generally, programming time will be saved if no detailed programming work is begun until the content and form of every report to be generated by the system has been approved by all contemplated users. This may not always be practicable, but certainly approval should be obtained before work is started on programming the parts of the system leading into a particular report. In larger organizations approval should be in writing.

Computerizing a cost system requires so much extra work on the part of all concerned that it is a poor time to attempt to clean up the data in the files from the old system which will also be used in the new system. However, it is also the *only* time that this can be done. Any errors in bills of material, route sheets, material pricing, labor rates, classification of overhead accounts between variable and fixed, variable overhead rates, and coding of departments, part numbers, operations, and customers are much more likely to cause trouble in a computerized system than in a manual one. Furthermore, the misleading reports that result from such errors may destroy management's confidence in the system. Therefore, however burdensome it may be, all basic data to be used by the new system should be reviewed before the system is allowed to become operational.

Summary

The computerization of a cost accounting system, like that of any other system, requires certain steps in a certain sequence. These steps include:

Problem definition.
System conceptual design.
System detailed design.
Report design.
Management approval of the four steps above.
Programming.
Program testing and debugging.
Entering the data into appropriate computer look-up tables and files.
Training personnel.
Documentation.
Preparation of procedures manuals.
Providing security against accidental loss of data.
Arranging for refresher training and training of any new personnel.

In view of the great benefits a company can gain from a computerized system, only the smallest companies should hesitate to embark on the project. However, everyone concerned should recognize that the project is a major one, that it will take months and even years to accomplish, and that the costs will be high. If these facts are publicized at the outset, no one will push the panic button when there is nothing to show for the costs that begin to appear in the financial statements after a number of months go by. If management is patient, the company will soon obtain benefits from its computerization that can usher in a new and better level of management effectiveness.

20

A Perspective on Direct Costing

EACH year more and more companies make the move from absorption cost systems to direct cost systems. And each year a larger proportion of companies installing their first cost system decide that they want a direct cost system. Discussions with representatives of auditing and consulting companies confirm these statements. Furthermore, the trend is accelerating and is expected to continue.

Additional evidence of this trend is the growth of enrollment in courses on direct costing. Also, registrants in general courses in the cost accounting field are showing greater interest in direct costing. Those attending the direct costing courses are about equally divided among cost accountants in training at companies already on direct costing, financial executives of companies on absorption costing that are about to convert to direct costing, financial executives of companies on absorption costing that are considering a conversion to direct costing, and senior executives of small companies that are about to install their first cost system and are wondering whether direct or absorption costing will serve them best. Many of the companies represented in the first two groups are leaders in their fields, both in size and in reputation for good management.

Why Direct Costing Is Growing

The growth of direct costing can be attributed to the fact that for many companies its advantages, both in theory and in practice, exceed its disadvantages. These advantages and disadvantages have been detailed elsewhere in this book but are summarized below.

Advantages of Direct Costing

1. Product costs under direct costing are a superior aid in pricing and setting marketing policies.
   - □ Direct cost product costs are the costs of making and selling one more.
   - □ Direct costing recognizes in product costs the variable elements in S.G.& A. expenses.
2. Direct costing is a great aid in many types of management decisions.
   - □ It simplifies planning of all types, including profit planning and business modeling.
   - □ Changes in marginal contribution, both those incurred and those planned, flow through dollar for dollar to net profit before taxes.
3. Direct costs are superior to absorption costs for cost control.
   - □ Direct costing forces a segregation of variable costs from fixed costs in both manufacturing overhead accounts and S.G.& A. expenses.
   - □ The volume variance account, sometimes called under- and over-absorbed overhead, is eliminated under direct costing. As a result, line production personnel are less confused about the meaning of these accounts and the extent to which they are responsible for the amounts shown.
4. Direct costing aids marketing in nonpricing policies as well as in pricing.
   - □ It provides a valid measure of the profitability of individual customers and groups or categories of customers.
   - □ It permits marketing policies to be revised through the information provided by splitting the variance between actual and planned marginal contribution into its three components—selling price variance, physical volume variance, and product mix variance.

5. Direct costing reduces the burden of the cost system on the accounting department.

- ◻ It is unnecessary under direct costing to establish a so-called normal capacity figure, which is, at best, open to both misinterpretation and dispute.
- ◻ Direct costing avoids the need to set up and measure multiple allocation bases for the various types of fixed costs.
- ◻ Direct costing avoids the monthly work of allocating fixed costs on the allocation bases chosen.

6. Interim financial reports prepared under direct costing are a better guide to management on the company's progress than reports prepared under absorption costing.

- ◻ The interim statements will generally be available earlier than they would be under absorption costing because of the reduction in accounting work.
- ◻ The interim statements are not distorted by reflecting profits that arise purely from increases in finished-goods inventories or by reflecting losses that arise purely from reductions in finished-goods inventories.

It should be noted that a few of these advantages will be available only in computerized cost accounting systems, although most are available under manual systems as well. However, with the growth of computerization in general and the advent of minicomputers in particular, almost any company that chooses to adopt direct costing can now obtain all the advantages listed.

Disadvantages of Direct Costing

1. Direct costing can encourage price cutting to unrealistically low levels. The added volume resulting from a price cut often increases the dollar marginal contribution and therefore, under a direct cost philosophy, should be profitable. However, it may not work out this way because of one or more factors:

- ◻ Volume may not increase if competitors meet or exceed the company's price cut.
- ◻ If the price cut is intended to apply only to certain customers, other customers may learn of it and insist on equal treatment.
- ◻ The extent that added volume increases working capital requirements and the resultant effect on ROI may have been overlooked.
- ◻ If the volume increase is expected to be permanent, the tendency of fixed costs to rise with permanent volume increases may have been overlooked.

2. The requirement to convert the value of work-in-process and finished-goods inventories to an absorption cost basis for external reporting is burdensome. In addition, the different profits shown on the internal versus external statements may be confusing.

3. Direct costing is not practicable in any company that has cost-plus or similar cost-related contracts or cost-related pricing arrangements with customers. In addition, construction contractors have so few fixed costs, other than those which vary with the duration of the job, that direct costing is more likely to be misleading than helpful to them.

On balance, most companies that try direct costing will find that the advantages far outweigh the disadvantages. This has been the experience of the many companies that have used direct costing, some for more than 30 years.

Impact of Direct Costing on Financial Management

As indicated earlier, the use of direct cost data in many types of management decisions tends to add more and more financial analysis to decisions formerly based largely on judgment and on past results of similar decisions. This in turn requires the participation of financial executives in many major decisions in which the potential contribution of accounting personnel was traditionally not recognized.

Today more and more major companies are selecting their chief executive officers (CEOs) from the financial end of the business. A recent survey by Main, Jackson & Garfield, Inc. of New York shows that among the 800 companies listed by *Forbes* magazine the proportion of CEOs from the financial area increased from 23.9 percent of the total in 1971 to 29.1 percent in 1977. These percentages exceeded those from any other single function. Furthermore, 37.6 percent of the 106 newly appointed CEOs in 1977 came from the financial area. It seems reasonable to assume that this trend is related in part to the impact of direct costing. However, it illustrates even more the value to a business of sound financial thinking. As indicated throughout this book, direct costing cannot fail to contribute to sound thinking and thus have a beneficial effect on profits.

Bibliography

Cost Accounting

Anthony, Robert N. "A Case for Historical Costs," *Harvard Business Review*, November-December 1976.

Anthony, Robert N. "The Rebirth of Cost Accounting," *Management Accounting*, October 1975.

Anton, Hector R., and Peter A. Firmin (eds.). *Contemporary Issues in Cost Accounting.* Boston: Houghton Mifflin, 1977.

Beyer, Robert, and Donald J. Trawicki. *Profitability Accounting for Planning and Control.* Cincinnati, Ohio: The Ronald Press Company, 1972.

Bierman, Harold, Jr., and Thomas R. Dyckman. *Managerial Cost Accounting.* New York: Macmillan, 1976.

Boone, William R. "Standard Costing: A Management Tool for Future Profits," *The Magazine of Bank Administration*, May 1972.

Conroy, C. A. "Implementing the Standard Cost System," *CPA Journal*, September 1976.

Crowningshield, Gerald R., and Kenneth A. Gorman. *Cost Accounting: Principles and Managerial Applications.* Boston: Houghton Mifflin, 1974.

Dopuch, N., and J. G. Birnberg. *Cost Accounting: Accounting Data for Management Decisions.* New York: Harcourt, Brace & World, 1974.

Fekrat, M. A. "Conceptual Foundations of Absorption Costing," *Accounting Review*, April 1972.

Franke, Reimund. "Costing with Matrix Analysis," *Management Accounting,* April 1976.

Godin, William N. "A Framework for Cost Accounting Information," *Managerial Planning,* January-February 1974.

Goold, G. R., and B. L. Feldman. "Introduction to Cost Systems." *CPA Journal,* December 1975.

Henrici, Stanley B. *Standard Costs for Manufacturers.* New York: McGraw-Hill, 1960.

Jones, Reginald L., and H. George Trentin. *Budgeting: Key to Planning and Control.* New York: American Management Associations, 1971.

Kelly, Warren H. "Cost Accounting and Control of Routine Operations," *Management Accounting,* November 1975.

Matz, Adolph, et al. *Cost Accounting: Planning and Control.* Cincinnati, Ohio: South-Western Publishing Company, 1972.

Mayer, Harry O. "Cost Accounting Standards," *Management Accounting,* October 1975.

Neiman, J. "Cost Accounting and Management Decision Making," *CPA Journal,* March 1976.

Neuner, John J., and Edward B. Deakin. *Cost Accounting: Principles and Practices.* Homewood, Ill.: Richard D. Irwin, 1977.

Schomer, A. J. "Implementation of Cost Accounting Systems," *CPA Journal,* May 1976.

Shillinglaw, Gordon. *Managerial Cost Accounting: Analysis and Control.* Homewood, Ill.: Richard D. Irwin, 1977.

Simini, Joseph P. *Accounting Made Simple.* New York: Doubleday, 1967.

Simini, Joseph P. *Cost Accounting Concepts for Nonfinancial Executives.* New York: AMACOM, 1976.

Snellgrove, William F. "A Cost Accounting System for Service Companies," *Management Accounting,* February 1971.

Thomas, William E., Jr. (ed.). *Readings in Cost Accounting, Budgeting, and Control.* Cincinnati, Ohio: South-Western Publishing Company, 1973.

Wells, M. C. "Costing for Activities," *Management Accounting,* May 1976.

Direct Costing

Bennett, Earl D. *Cost Administration: Cases and Notes.* Englewood Cliffs, N.J.: Prentice-Hall, 1960.

Boer, Germain B. *Direct Cost and Contribution Accounting: An Integrated Management Accounting System.* New York: Wiley-Interscience, 1974.

Current Application of Direct Costing. Research Study 37, National Association of Accountants, 1961.

Direct Costing: Key to Dollar Decisions, PRIME 100. New York: American Management Associations, 1968.

Dudick, Thomas S. *Cost Controls for Industry.* Englewood Cliffs, N.J.: Prentice-Hall, 1976.

Flock, Henry H. "The Change to Direct Costing in a Multiproduct Company," *Management Accounting,* August 1976.

Gillespie, Cecil. *Standard and Direct Costing.* Englewood Cliffs, N.J.: Prentice-Hall, 1962.

Grinnell, D. J. "Product Mix Decisions: Direct Costing Versus Absorption Costing," *Management Accounting,* August 1976.

Horngren, Charles T. *Cost Accounting: A Managerial Emphasis.* Englewood Cliffs, N.J.: Prentice-Hall, 1977.

Keller, I. Wayne, and William L. Ferrara. *Management Accounting for Profit Control.* New York: McGraw-Hill, 1966.

Marple, Raymond P. (ed.). *National Association of Accountants on Direct Costing: Selected Papers.* Cincinnati, Ohio: The Ronald Press Company, 1965.

Schulte, R. Gregg. "One More Time: Direct Costing Versus Absorption Costing," *Management Accounting,* November 1975.

Swalley, R. W. "Benefits of Direct Costing," *Management Accounting,* September 1974.

Taggart, Herbert F. "Cost Justification." Ann Arbor, Mich.: University of Michigan, Bureau of Business Research, 1959.

Williams, B. R. "Measuring Costs: Full Absorption Cost or Direct Cost?" *Management Accounting,* January 1976.

Wright, H. N., Jr. "Comparison of Absorption and Direct Costing Methods," *Management World,* August 1976.

Wright, Wilmer. *Direct Standard Costs.* New York: McGraw-Hill, 1962.

Wycoff, David W. "Direct and Idle-Time Cost Accounting," *Management Accounting,* December 1974.

Computerized Cost Accounting

Condon, Robert J. *Data Processing Systems Analysis and Design.* Englewood Cliffs, N.J.: Prentice-Hall, 1974.

Cushing, Barry E. *Accounting Information Systems and Business Organizations.* Reading, Mass.: Addison Wesley, 1974.

Ijiri, Yuji. "An Application of Input-Output Analysis to Some Problems in Cost Accounting," *NAA Management Accounting,* April 1968.

Jones, R. D. "Development and Application of Cost Control Systems," *Cost and Management,* December 1967.

Livingstone, J. L. "Input-Output Analysis for Cost Accounting, Planning, and Control," *Accounting Review,* January 1969.

Lynch, Gerard P., and John W. Merrill. "Third Generation Processing—A Cost Accounting Proposal," *The Magazine of Bank Administration,* March 1968.

McCosh, A. M. "Computerized Cost Classification System," *Management Accounting,* April 1972.

McDonald, Howard E., and T. L. Stromberger. "Cost Control for the Professional Service Firm," *Harvard Business Review,* January-February 1969.

Mason, Paul. "EDP Systems for Functional Cost Analysis," *The Magazine of Bank Administration,* July 1968.

Tyran, Michael R. *Computerized Accounting Methods and Controls.* Englewood Cliffs, N.J.: Prentice-Hall, 1972.

Related Publications by the Authors

"Direct Costing—Today and Tomorrow," *CPA Journal,* May 1975.

"What Didn't We Earn Last Month?" *Management Review.* October 1973.

"Relating Pricing to Costs," *Financial Executive,* December 1971.

"Making Business Odds Work for You," *Management Services,* November-December, 1970.

"Price Changes and Profitability," *Management Accounting,* May 1970.

"More Meaningful Earnings Statements for Top Management," *Financial Executive,* October 1968.

"Management Services by Accounting Firms," Cincinnati, Oho: The Ronald Press Company, 1967.

"The Fundamentals of Profit Planning," *The New York Certified Public Accountant,* May 1962.

"Cost Accounting in Sound Business Decisions," *NACA Bulletin,* June 1952.

"What Budgeting and Financial Forecasting Will Do for a New Company," *NACA Bulletin,* December 1948.

"Inefficiency Engineering," *Modern Management,* August 1946.

"Maximizing Accounting and Marketing Efforts—Partners in Profits and Sales," Dartnell Publications, 1968.

With Ray W. Cheesman:

"Providing Help for a Company in Trouble," *Management Adviser,* September-October 1973.

With Edgar A. Mack:

"A Seasonally Adjusted Costing System," *Journal of Accountancy,* June 1966.

"A New Approach to the Breakeven Chart," *Management Services,* March-April 1964.

Index

absenteeism, 98–99
absorption costing, 3–6
  allocation of fixed costs in, 84
  analysis of gross profits in, 161
  book inventory accuracy under, 208
  bookkeeping in, 158
  by-product costing in, 193
  computers for, 251
  converting to direct costing from, 224–234
  in Cost Accounting Standards Board standards, 197
  in dual reporting systems, 65–71
  in FASB standard 14,198
  financial statements on, under direct costing systems, 239–241
  fixed overhead standard costs in, 127
  in hospitals, 183–184
  inventory control under, 60, 62–64
  in joint product costing, 195
  in management decision making case studies, 93–95, 100–101, 104–106, 108–109
  in marketing and distribution, 170–171
  product pricing and, 45
  in public utilities, 182
  in transfer pricing, 190
  in variable budgets, 78
  variable and fixed costs under, 29
  variable overhead standard costs in, 124
  variance accounts in, 133–134, 141
account analysis, 32–33
accounting
  cost control reports and, 147
  cost and management, 13–15
  history of, 10–11

accounting (cont'd)
  management versus financial, 11–12
  of responsibility, 149–152
  of revisions in standard costs, 131
Accounting Principles Board, 64
activity analysis, 32
actual costing, 22–25
  book inventory accuracy under, 208, 211
  computers for, 237–238
  in converting to direct costing, 230
  standard costing compared with, 27–28, 130
  in transfer pricing, 189–190
  variance accounts for, 141
administrative costs, 3–6
  see also selling, general, and administrative expenses
advertising costs, 30, 175
  in business modeling, 86–90
  cooperative, 126
American Institute of Certified Public Accountants (AICPA), 5, 6, 63–65
analog computers, 245
analysis of marginal contribution variances, 160–169
annual budgets, 73
Armstrong Cork Co., 6
Army, U.S., *see* Defense, U.S. Department of
assets
  budgeting of, 77
  in replacement costing, 198–199
  in returns on investment, 48
attainable standard costs, 113–115
auditing
  of computerized systems, 259
  conversion to direct costing and, 227–228
  variances in, 142
average costs, 23

Babylonians, 10
backward costing, 58–59
bad debts, 103
banks, 179–180
base period standard costs, 113–114
bidding, direct costs in pricing for, 199–201
billing, 41
Blue Cross, 183–184
book inventories, 207–223
  computers for, 248–249
bookkeeping
  in absorption costing, 158
  for Cost Accounting Standards Board, 197
books of account, reconciling cost accounting records with, 8–9
borrowing
  in cash budgets, 76
  profitability in (for banks), 179
bottleneck analysis
  case study of, 97–98
  pricing and, 56–57
breakeven charts, 82–85
  in new product line case study, 101–102
  in personal investment decisions, 110
breakeven points, 82–83
budgeting, 72–85
  in hospitals, 185
business modeling, 85–90
  computers for, 241
by-product costing, 192–193

capacity
  pricing by, 57
  utilization of, 49–50
capital
  in pricing decisions, 57–58
  tied to sales territories, 173
capital asset acquisition budgets, 77
CASB, *see* Cost Accounting Standards Board
cash budgets (cash forecasts), 75–77
  cost accounting and, 80
casualty insurance on inventories, 199

Caterpiller Tractor Co., 6
change-of-standard variance, 139–140, 243
charting
  computers for, 245
  for cost control, 157
check digits, 212, 248
coding errors, 210–212
commissions, standard costs for, 126
competitive bidding, 180–182
computers
  business modeling on, 88–89
  in conversion to direct costing, 229–231, 233
  in direct costing, 236–249, 250–260
  exception reporting by, 148
  inventory accuracy and, 212
  linear programming on, 201, 215
  marginal contribution analysis by, 163, 168
construction industry, 180–182
consultants, 225, 226
contracts
  actual costing for, 24
  in construction industry, 180–181
  cost-plus and negotiated-price, 12
  job costing for, 19
  product pricing and, 51–52
contribution margin, 4
controllable costs, 149–150
controllers, 111
conversions
  to computers, 250–260
  to direct costing, 224–235
cooperative advertising, 126
cost accounting
  backward costing in, 59
  budgeting and, 80–81
  computers in, 236–237, 250–252
  in construction industry, 180–181
  in hospitals, 185
  in marketing and distribution, 170
  in public utilities, 182
  reconciling books of account with, 8–9
  in service industries dealing with intangibles, 179
  systems for, 10–16
Cost Accounting Standards Board (CASB), 8, 24, 196–197, 247
  on machinery depreciation, 37
  standard costing allowed by, 238
cost-benefit analysis, 145
cost budgets, 74
cost control
  budgets in, 81–82
  computers for, 244–245
  direct costs in, 144–159
  in marketing and distribution, 175
  process and operations costing for, 21–22
  standard costing in, 26–27
  variances used in, 133
costing systems, 17–28
cost overruns, variance accounts for, 27
cost-plus contracts, 12
  actual costing for, 24
  in construction industry, 180
  Cost Accounting Standards Board and, 196
  job costing for, 19
  product pricing and, 51–52
  cost reimbursement systems (in hospitals), 183–185
costs
  in breakeven charts, 82, 83
  fixed and variable, 29–42
  in inventory management decisions, 109
  product, updating, 55–56
  setting standards for, 113–131
  in transfer pricing, 189–190
  volume as variable in, 14
CPS (Critical Path Scheduling), 180, 228, 232–233, 253
credit policy, case study in, 102–104
Critical Path Schedules (CPS), 180, 228, 232–233, 253
CRT (cathode ray tube) terminals, 257

customers
  in analysis of marginal contribution, 160–162, 245, 246
  direct costing analysis of profit from, 171
  returns by, inventory errors and, 220–221
  small, 173–174
cycle counting, 212–214, 219

decision making
  in computerizing costing systems, 257–260
  computers for, 241–242
  in conversions to direct costing, 226
  cost control in, 144–145
  direct costing in, 92–112
  on marketing territories, 171–173
  on materials mix, 203–204
  on product mix, 201–203
defective materials, 117
Defense, U.S. Department of
  Cost Accounting Standards Board and, 196
  cost-plus-fixed-fee contracts of, 51
  transfer pricing in contracts of, 190
Defense Contract Audit Agency, 19
  on double counting, 42
departments
  in conversion to direct costing, 225–226, 228
  transfer pricing and, 189
  variance accounting according to, 137
department stores, 186–187
depreciation, as variable cost, 37
Detailed Function Statements, 255–257
direct costing
  analysis of marginal contribution variances in, 160–169
  book inventory accuracy under, 208
  in budgeting, 72–85
  in business modeling, 85–90
  by-product costing in, 193
  computerizing, 250–260
  computers in, 236–249
  conversion to, 224–235
  in cost control, 144–159
  definition of, 8
  growth of, 6–7, 261–264
  history of, 11
  in insuring inventories, 199
  inventory control under, 60–71
  in joint product costing, 195
  in management decision making, 92–112
  in marketing and distribution, 170–176
  in nonmanufacturing companies, 177–187
  not used for segment reporting, 198
  other costing systems and, 17–28
  in pricing bids, 199–201
  prime costing and, 2–3
  product pricing and, 43–59
  setting standard costs for, 113–131
  in transfer pricing, 192
  variable and fixed costs under, 29
  variable selling and administrative costs under, 3–6
  variance accounts in, 133, 134
direct labor costs
  actual costs, of, 22, 23
  in cost control, 146
  in dual reporting systems, 67–71
  in financial statements on absorption costing, 240
  in job costing, 18
  in prime costing, 2
  quantity standards for, 121–123
  rate standards for, 120–121, 128
  as variable cost, 38
  variances to revise standards for, 140
direct labor cost variances, 135, 140
direct material costs
  actual costs of, 22

in job costing, 18
in prime costing, 2
distress materials, 116–117
distribution, direct costing in, 170–176
distribution industry, 186–187
Domestic International Sales Corporations (DISCs), 188
double counting, 41–42
double-step down allocation method, 184–185

economic lot size (ELS), 80, 109, 241–242
economic order quantity (EOQ), 81, 109, 241–242
economies of scale, under Robinson-Patmat Act, 50–51
EDP, *see* computers
Egyptians, ancient, 10
electricity, 37
Electronic Accounting Machines (EAM), 248
Electronic Data Processing (EDP), *see* computers
encumbrance budgets, 75
engineered standard costs, 115, 140
engineering (analog) computers, 245
estimation, of standard costs, 115–116
exception reporting, 147–149, 152
computers for, 244–245
in conversion to direct costing, 231

favorable product mix variances, 164
Federal Communications Commission (FCC), 182
Federal Power Commission (FPC), 182
FIFO (first in, first out) costing, 22
financial accounting, management accounting versus, 11–12
Financial Accounting Standards Board (FASB)
creation of, 11
on shifting of profits, 64
standard 14 of, 197–198
financial statements
on absorption costing, under direct costing systems, 239–241
direct costing prohibited for, 5–6, 63–65
in dual reporting systems, 65–71
finished goods, errors affecting inventories of, 220–221
fixed budgets, 77–78
variable costs in, 80
fixed costs
in breakeven charts, 82–84
in construction industry, 181
in hospitals, 182–183
in product costs, 2
product line targets for absorption of, 56–57
of selling, 172
selling, general, and administrative expenses, standard costs for, 127–128
separating variable costs from, 238–239
service departments as, 125–126
variable costs distinguished from, 29–42
variances in, 141
fixed overhead standard costs, 126–127, 129
flash reports, 153
flexible budgets, 78–79
forecasting
cash budgets for, 75–77
in fixed budgets, 77–78
marginal contribution analysis and, 169
of sales, 162–163
forms, in conversion to direct costing, 230–231
formula of least squares, 34–36, 84, 238–239, 242
freight costs, 126, 172
in railroad industry, 182
fringe benefits, 96–97

fringe benefits (cont'd)
in direct labor rate standard costs, 120
in variable overhead standard costs, 123
fuel, 37

general expenses, *see* selling, general, and administrative expenses
Generally Accepted Accounting Principles (GAAP), 196
General Services Administration, U.S., 196–197
government
actual costing for, 24
Cost Accounting Standards Board and, 196–197
cost-plus contracts with, 12
job costing for, 19
restrictive budgets in, 74–75
Robinson-Patman Act and, 50–51
gross margin, 4
gross profit at standard (line in cost systems), 4
gross profits, 161
in absorption costing, 4
gross sales, 4

Harris, Jonathan, 1, 6
Harrison, G. Charter, 1
Health, Education, and Welfare, U.S. Department of, 8
Hernandez, William H., 12
historical standard costs, 115, 140, 141
hospitals, 182–186

ideal standard costs, 113–114
Imhoff, Eugene A., Jr., 7
implementation, of direct costing systems, 231–234
income, net, marginal contributions in, 160
income statements
based on orders received, 110
inventory valuation and, 64
standard costing for, 27
incremental costing, 3
indirect labor, 7–8
as semivariable cost, 37–38
inflation
base period standard costs and, 114
changing standard costs for, 129, 131
insurance on inventories, 199
Internal Revenue Service, U.S. (IRS), 6
on depreciation, 37
direct costing prohibited by, 64
on prime costing, 2–3
variances and, 142
Interstate Commerce Commission, U.S. (ICC), 182
inventories
book, maintaining accuracy of, 207–223
casualty insurance on, 199
in changing standard costs, 129
in cost accounting, 80–81
during conversion to direct costing, 232, 233
management decision making on, 109
variances in, 141–143
in warehouse stocking, 204–206
inventory control, 209–210
computers for, 247–249
inventory management, 209, 210
inventory valuation, 60–71
direct costing and absorption costing for, 12
FIFO, 22
LIFO, 23, 26
maintaining accuracy of, 207–223
NIFO, 55–56
prime costing for, 2–3
retail system of, 186
inverse variables, 36–41
investments
capital, pricing decisions, 57–58

personal, decision making on, 109–110
returns on, 48–49
invoicing, costs of, 126

job costing, 18–20
actual costing in, 24
computers for, 237–238
joint product costing, 193–196
computers for, 246–247

labor, *see* direct labor costs; indirect labor
learning standard direct labor costs, 123
least squares formula, 34–36, 84, 238–239, 242
leveling factors (in time studies), 122
LIFO (last in, first out) costing, 23, 26, 199
linear programming, 185, 201, 205, 247
line-by-line budgets (restrictive budgets), 74–75
long-range budgets, 74
losses (material), in cost control, 146–147
lot clearance systems, 216
low-price orders 47–48, 85

McBee Keysort, 246
machinery
computers in decisions on replacement of, 242
depreciation on, 37
variable overhead costs associated with, 125
Main, Jackson & Garfield, Inc., 264
maintenance departments, 136
charging requisitions to, 215–216
make-or-buy case study, 93–94
makeup pay, 121
management
computers in decision making by, 241–242
cost control in, 144–145
direct costing in decision making by, 92–112
importance of book and physical inventories to, 207–208
of inventories, 209, 210
needs for cost accounting systems of, 15–16
management accounting
cost accounting and, 13–15
financial accounting versus, 11–12
management reporting, 152–157
manufacturers' representatives, 172
marginal contributions
analysis of, by computer, 245–246
analysis of variances in, 160–169
by customer, 171, 174
product pricing and, 44–45
marginal costing, 3
margin contribution at standard (line in cost systems), 4
marketing
direct costing in, 170–176
policy decisions and product pricing, 44
market prices, 190–191
materials
case study in substitution of, 108–109
in construction industry, 180
in cost control, 146–147
decisions on mix of, 203–204
inventory errors affecting, 215–217
in joint product pricing, 193–194
price standards for, 116–117, 128
quantity standards for, 117–120
variable overhead costs associated with, 125
Mathieson Alkali, 1
Medicaid, 183–184
Medicare, 183–184
modeling, 85–90
computers for, 241
monthly budgets, 73
MTM (Method-Time-Measurement) system, 122

National Retail Merchants Association, 186
negotiated-price contracts, 12
  actual costing for, 24
  in construction industry, 180
  Cost Accounting Standards Board and, 196
  product pricing and, 51–52
negotiated prices, in transfer pricing, 191–192
net income, marginal contributions in, 160
net profits, variances in marginal contribution as measure of, 167
NIFO (next in, first out) costing, 55–56, 239, 253
nomenclature, 7–8
noncontrollable costs, 149–150
nonprofit organizations, restrictive budgets in, 74–75

occupancy costs, in fixed overhead standard costs, 127
oil industry, 193, 194
Olin Industries, 1
operating budgets, 75
operating profits, in absorption costing and direct costing, 5
operations costing, 21–22
orders received, income statements based on, 110
overhead, 8
  actual costing of, 23–24
  computers for setting standard costs for, 242
  dividing into variable and fixed, 229–230, 238–239
  in dual reporting systems, 66–71
  fixed, standard costs for, 126–127
  fixed, in transfer pricing, 190
  in flexible budgets, 78–79
  removing fringe benefits from, in costing, 120
  as variable, fixed, and semifixed costs, 38–41
  variable, standard costs for, 123–126, 128–129
  variances in, 141
  see also fixed costs
overruns, cost, variance accounts for, 27
overtime costs
  case study of, 95–97
  in direct labor rate standard costs, 120
  as supervariable, 36

performance, variances for revisions of standards for, 140–141
performance budgets, 74
performance reports, 148, 149, 177
period costs, *see* fixed costs
perpetual unit inventory records, 208–209, 213
  computers for, 247, 248
personnel costs, as step costs, 36
PERT (Program Evaluation and Review Technique), 180, 233
physical inventories, 207–209
physical volume variances, 162, 164
piece rates for labor, 121
power, in variable overhead, standard costs of, 124
preliminary profit plans, 86
price cutting, 52–55
prices
  of materials, standard costs for, 116–117
  selling, variances in, 162–164
  transfer, 188–192
pricing
  computers for, 239
  product, 43–59
  transfer, 188–192
prime costing, 2–3
probability theory, 89
  in case study, 98–99
  computers for, 241
process costing, 18, 20–22
  computers for, 237–238

productivity, case study of
 bottlenecks in, 97–98
product lines
 abandonment of, case studies of, 104–108
 assigning fixed costs to, 56–57
 case study of profitability in, 94–95
 new, case study of, 99–102
 in segment reporting, 197–198
product mix, 201–203
product mix variances, 162, 164–165, 168
product pricing, 43–59
 for by-products, 192–193
 for joint products, 193–196
profitability
 for banks, 179
 case study in, 94–95
 product pricing and, 45–46
 standard costing in determination of, 27
profit planning (business modeling), 85–90
 computers for, 241
profits
 in breakeven charts, 83, 85
 in cash budgeting, 75–76
 credit policy and, 103
 by customer, direct costing analysis of, 171
 inventory shortages and, 208
 inventory valuation and, 62–64
 marginal contributions to, 160–161
 product mix variances and, 164
 in transfer pricing, 190
 variances in marginal contribution as measure of, 167
Program Evaluation and Review Technique (PERT), 180, 233
programmed costs, 30
programs (computer), 258, 259
project budgets, 73
promotional costs, 175
public utilities, 182
purchase price variances, 134–135

quantity standard costs
 direct labor, 121–123
 material, 117–120
quarterly budgets, 73

railroads, 182
ratio delay (work sampling) system, 122
Raymond, Robert H., 192
records, inventory, maintaining accuracy of, 207–223
relevant costing, 106, 108–109
 marketing territory decisions and, 171–172
 in value analysis, 145
repackaging, inventory errors and, 220
repair services, 178–179
replacement costing, 198–199
reporting
 computerization of, 255–257, 259
 in conversion to direct costing, 227, 230–231, 233–234
 in cost accounting systems, 15–16
 for cost control, 244–245
 dual systems for, 65–71
 of exceptions, 147–149
 financial, direct costing prohibited for, 5–6, 63–64
 management, 152–157
 by segments, 197–198
responsibility accounting, 149–152, 244
restrictions, in Detailed Function Statements, 257
restrictive budgets, 74–75
retailers, 186–187
retail system of inventory accounting, 186
returns on investments, 48–49
revenue and cost budgets, 74
rework, misreporting of, 218
Rickover, Hyman, 196

Robinson-Patman Act (U.S., 1937), 50–51
rolling budgets, 73
royalties, 126

sales
 analysis of margin contribution and, 160, 161, 168
 breakeven point for, 82–83
 in business modeling, 86
 forecasting of, 162–163
 marketing and distribution in, 170–176
 variable costs in proportion with, 29–30
 variances tied to, 134
salespeople
 replacement of, 172
 underpricing by, 52–53
Sangamo Electric Co., 6
scatter charts, 33–34, 36, 84, 239, 242
Securities and Exchange Commission (SEC), 5, 6, 63–65
 on replacement costing, 198, 199
segment reporting, 12, 197–198
selling, general, and administrative expenses (S.G. & A.), 3–6
 budgeting of, 81
 computers for setting standard costs for, 242
 dividing into variable and fixed, 230, 238–239
 fixed, standard costs for, 127–128
 as fixed and variable costs, 41
 in inventory valuation systems, 62, 63
 variable, 29
 variable, standard costs for, 126
selling prices, in joint product costing, 195–196
selling price variances, 162–164
semifixed costs, 32–36
semivariable costs, 32–36
 overhead, 229
sensitivity analysis, 89–90, 241
service departments
 as fixed cost, 125–126
 in hospitals, 184
 variances and, 136
service industries
 dealing with intangibles, 179–180
 dealing with tangibles, 178–179
S.G. & A., *see* selling, general, and administrative expenses
shrinkage
 inventory accuracy and, 216
 in material quantity standards, 119
simulation (business modeling), 85–90
software, 258
spoilage
 inventory accuracy and, 217–218
 in material quantity standards, 119
 variance accounting of, 139
standard costing, 25–28
 actual costing superseded by, 24
 book inventory accuracy under, 208, 211
 computers for, 237–238
 computers in setting standards for, 242–243
 in conversion to direct costing, 230
 in dual reporting systems, 70–71
 history of, 11
 in marginal contribution analysis, 161–162
 setting standards for, 113–131
 in transfer pricing, 189–190
 variances in, 132
 variances for revisions in, 140–141
standard data systems, 122
standard deviations, 244–245
standby workers, in case study, 98–99
step costs, 36
step-down method of allocation, 184
storage (computer), 257
stratification of inventory, 213
supervariable costs, 36–41

Tang, Roger Y. W., 192

task forces, for conversions, 225–227, 231
taxes
  inventory valuation and, 64
  marginal contribution and, 160
  prime costing and, 2–3
  transfer pricing for, 188, 190, 192
terminals (computer), 257, 258
territories (marketing), 171–173
time studies, 121–122
transfer pricing, 188–192
transportation industry, 182
trend reports, 153
triggers, 255–257
trucking industry, 182
turnover, in returns on investment, 49

underpricing, 52–55
unfavorable product mix variances, 164
unions, piece rates and, 121
unit costs
  cost accounting of, 80
  in inventory management decisions, 109
  volume and, 43
unit designations, errors in, 214–215
updating product costs, 55–56
utilities, public, 182
utilization of capacity, 49–50

value analysis, 145
variable budgets, 78, 177
variable costs
  in construction industry, 181
  cost accounting of, 80
  fixed costs distinguished from, 29–42
  in hospitals, 185
  in product costs, 2
  separating fixed costs from, 238–239
variable overhead, in overtime costs, 97
variable overhead efficiency variances, 135–136
variable overhead spending variances, 135–136
variable overhead standard costs, 123–126, 128–129
variable selling and administrative costs, 3–6
variable selling, general, and administrative expense standard costs, 126
variance accounts, 26, 27
  basic, 133–137
  special, 138–139
variances
  in absorption costing and direct costing, 5
  in actual and standard cost comparisons, 130
  analysis of, 243–244
  in attainable standard costs, 114–115
  budgeting of, 81
  in cost control, 144, 146–147
  developing, 132–143
  exception reporting of, 147–149
  of marginal contributions, analysis of, 160–169
  in material price standards, 116–117
variances, labor
  in direct labor quantity standard costs, 122–123
  in direct labor rate standard costs, 120
volume
  in breakeven charts, 82, 83
  in marketing decisions, 172
  product pricing and, 45–46
  as variable in costing, 14
  variable and fixed costs and, 31
  unit costs and, 43
volume variances, 162, 164

Walker, C.K., 192

warehouse stocking, 204–206
waste
  in material quantity standards, 117–119
  see also spoilage
"where used" computer programs, 243, 253
wholesalers, 172, 186–187
WOFAC (Work Factor) system, 122
Woolworth's, 43
working capital, in pricing decisions, 57–58
work-in-process inventories, 217–219
work sampling, 122